For Christina, my life's companion, whose unfailing support
for all my schemes and dreams underlies every page of this book.

Also by Thomas A. Williams

Mallarmé and the Language of Mysticism
Eliphas Lévi: Master of Occultism
The Bicentennial Book
We Choose America
Tales of the Tobacco Country
How to Publish Your Poetry
Poet Power: The Complete Guide to Getting Your Poetry Published
How to Publish Weekly Newspapers and Free Circulation Shoppers
How to Publish City and Regional Magazines
The Query Letter That Never Fails
The Self-Publisher's Handbook of Contacts and Sources
How to Make $100,000 a Year in Desktop Publishing

Publish Your Own Magazine, Guidebook, or Weekly Newspaper

How to Start, Manage and Profit from Your Own Homebased Publishing Company

Thomas A. Williams, Ph.D.

SENTIENT PUBLICATIONS, LLC

First Sentient Publications edition

Cover design by Kim Johansen, Black Dog Design
Book design by Thomas A. Williams

Notice and Disclaimer

The author and publisher of this book have described the publishing projects contained herein based on the personal experience of the author. We make no guarantee of the success or failure of others in duplicating these projects. Whether the reader will succeed with his own projects depends on current market conditions, the individual skill and energy of the entrepreneur, and many other factors beyond the control of the author. Furthermore, the author is not an attorney, and any discussion of legal matters, contracts, copyright law or similar matters are presented as discussion only. The reader should consult an attorney before making any decisions on legal matters.

Library of Congress Cataloging-in-Publication Data

Williams, Thomas A. (Thomas Andrew), 1931-
    Publish your own magazine, guidebook, or weekly newspaper
  : how to start, manage, and profit from a homebased publishing
  company / Thomas A. Williams.
      p.cm.
    Includes index.
    ISBN 1-59181-003-5
    1. Desktop publishing industry-United States-Management.
  2. Home-based businesses-United States-Management.
  3. Periodicals-Publishing-United States. 4. Newspaper publishing-
  United States. I. Title.
  Z244.645.U6W55 2002
  338.4'768622544-dc21

                                                                    2002010934

Parts of this book were originally published as *Kitchen Table Publisher: The Master Manual.*

Printed in the United States of America

10 9 8 7 6 5 4

SENTIENT PUBLICATIONS, LLC
A Limited Liability Company
1113 Spruce Street
Boulder, CO 80302
www.sentientpublications.com

Table of Contents

How To Use This Book

The opening chapters of this book contain general information that you will need to know, no matter which publishing project you decide to undertake first. The following chapters get into the specifics of particular projects. They include hard, how-to information that I have gleaned from years of experience.

Although most of the following chapters deal with one particular kind of publication, all contain sales tips, marketing tips, design tips and management tips that will be applicable to all of them. There is a great deal of cross-referencing and cross-fertilization. It was neither possible nor desirable to repeat all of this information each time I moved on to a new project. The best plan, therefore, is to read through the entire book, then come back to the projects that interest you most. This manual is, I hope, open-ended. The principles and techniques described in these pages will work for the many other publishing opportunities that you will surely encounter, whether I have covered them specifically or not.

Throughout you will read about such things as rate cards, media kits, sales reports, ad approval forms, and many similar items. What do these things look like and where do you get them? Throughout the book I have reproduced samples of the forms that I have found to be serviceable. They work, and they are included for you to modify and use as you see fit.

What It Takes to Succeed

Each of the publishing scenarios described in this book is a possible one. The one you choose will depend on your temperament more than anything else—and your mastery of the success principles and trade secrets of the business.

Can I guarantee your success? No, I cannot. I do not know your capacity for work, the amount of time you have available, or the quality of your attention to detail. I do not know your willingness and ability to learn from the experience of others. Nor can I judge your skill in managing the work of others, always a key element.

What I can guarantee, though, is that the ideas and techniques presented in this book have worked for me; that they have worked for others; and that they can work for you, too, to the degree that you study them carefully and put them into practice with skill and energy.

Introduction

I started a new publishing business some years ago with a Mac Plus, a LaserWriter I, and two used desks. Just four years later my company was grossing nearly $800,000 annually. I had no special qualifications beyond a burning desire to succeed in the field of publishing. To do this I learned to appreciate and harness for my own purposes the enormous potential of the computer hardware and software required for what I have dubbed *Entrepreneurial Publishing*.

I learned by trial and error. At that time there was no other way. I asked a lot of questions and came up with a lot of ideas. If an idea worked, I added it to my repertoire and repeated it as often as possible. If it didn't, I scrapped it and tried something else.

The effort paid off. I went on to publish *NCEast*, a regional magazine; *Tar Heel*, a magazine with statewide circulation; the *North Carolina Travel and Tourism Guide*; *Welcome to Wilmington*, a full color, slick paper newcomer's guide to this major metropolitan area; *Homebuyer's Handbook*, a real estate buyer's guide; *Washington and Beaufort County Magazine*, a city magazine; and *Renter's Helper Apartment Directories* in nine cities. I published both hardcover and softcover books and weekly newspapers and shoppers. At present I am undertaking a major expansion of my book publishing company, Venture Press.

Anyone Can Do It

Who can succeed in home-based publishing? Anyone can. I am convinced that I could take my Macintosh, a few business cards and a change of clothes and generate a sizable income for myself in any town in America. Among the successful independent publishers I know are some who have backgrounds in sales; others come from the ranks of graphic designers; some are free-lance writers who, tired of sending articles to other people's magazines, decided to create a publication of their own. Some are simply management types with an idea they believe in and the willingness to give it a try.

Publishing Is Profitable

Independent, home-based publishing is a business in which you can eventually earn *almost as much money as you desire to earn*—so long as you are willing to learn the business and work for it.

How much money one desires to earn varies greatly from person to person. Some of us love the laid-back life, want to live simply and modestly, and find the publishing life a delightful way to do it. Others are satisfied to clear sixty or seventy thousand dollars a year.

Some ambitious souls shoot for the biggest prizes of all. They want to develop strong publications, duplicate them in every imaginable market, franchise them, go public and become millionaires.

What You Will Learn When You Read this Book

To begin with, you will need a thorough grounding in the trade secrets of the business. Such valuable information, the stock-in-trade of every business enterprise, is rarely shared. Trade secrets are usually closely guarded and hard to come by. Yet, it is precisely these secrets that I share with you in the pages of this book. What will you learn when you read these pages?

- What you can profitably publish and what you cannot. You will learn how to evaluate the publishing potential of an idea or undertaking and what the chances of success in a certain project really are. You will learn how to estimate costs and potential revenues so that, when the dust clears, a surplus of the latter will be nestled securely in your bank account.
- How to analyze sales and profit probabilities for any books you may wish to publish.
- How to sell advertising for your newspaper, tabloid or magazine.
- How to obtain the services of others who have time and expertise that you yourself may be lacking; moreover, you will learn how to get these people to work for you in such a way that you can pay them after the money begins to come in.
- How to design and print your published product.
- How to price your product profitably and competitively in any given marketplace.
- How to structure any publication for success through effective market analysis and product positioning.
- The three success secrets and how to use them.
- How to recognize market needs and how to satisfy them profitably.
- How to size up and win out over the competition, capitalizing on their weaknesses and topping their strengths.
- How to position your publication in the market for success over the long haul.
- How to implement each and every one of the very wide range of publishing opportunities open to you. There are more of these than you ever thought possible.

- How to combine primary and secondary profit centers to create a financially stable, long-lived business.
- How to create and manage your own publishing business, day-by-day — and on an ongoing basis.

The Nuts and Bolts of Publishing

There is nothing theoretical in these pages. Every fact, every practical success tip included here was drawn from hard-earned experience, my own personal experience.

I have successfully carried out every project I describe in this book. I have personally wrestled with and mastered the challenges of publication start-up, pricing, cost control, design, production, circulation and sales management. And I have done all these things without the benefit of any significant capital whatsoever.

Do you want to be in business for yourself? Do you want to be a publisher? With this manual as a guide you have all the information you need to build a lucrative publishing business operating from your own home. The sky—and your imagination and energy—will be your only limits.

1

Entrepreneurial Publishing:
An Overview

This book contains detailed, step-by-step instructions. The person who studies and follows them can make money, sometimes considerable amounts of money, in the field of periodical and specialty book publishing. All that is required is the ambition, the know-how, and the latest desktop publishing equipment.

You have the ambition, or you would not be reading this book. You can purchase or lease the desktop publishing equipment you need for less money than it would take to buy a good used car. I have the know-how, and that's precisely what I intend to reveal to you in this book. I can personally vouch for the workability and profitability of these publishing projects because I have carried each of them out myself. Each was easily manageable, even those undertaken while I was working full-time as a college professor. Each made real money. And each was begun with little or no up-front cash investment.

Clearly, when you put down this book there will still be a great deal more that you can learn—there always is. But these pages constitute a treasure map of the unknown territories of independent desktop publishing, a map you can rely on and chart your course by. When you have read the book you will know far more than I did when I proudly printed "Thomas A. Williams, Publisher" on the masthead of the first magazine my brand new little company brought out.

Each chapter represents a doorway through which any ambitious writer, salesperson, or businessperson can enter the world of publishing at the head of his or her own company—with all the satisfaction and financial security that comes with owning your own business.

A Publishing Revolution

There is a revolution taking place in the publishing business today. One aspect of this revolution is a matter of scale. The large publishing companies are getting bigger and bigger, leaving the very lucrative local, regional, and specialized markets open to all comers. The big New York publishers have become "blockbuster" oriented, abandoning the sure but (for them) relatively modest profitability of the short-run book or magazine to what used to be known as the "small presses," which are now referred to more and more frequently as the "independent publishers."

The Real Opportunity: Periodicals

But this is just the beginning. The real opportunity for greater and more immediate returns lies in the publishing of advertising-rich periodicals: city and county magazines, newcomer guides, tourism guides, weekly newspapers, free circulation shopping guides and other publications of this type.

The Tools That Make It Possible

Coupled with this restructuring of the publishing business itself is the truly revolutionary appearance of desktop publishing technology. Thanks to the equipment that this revolution has spawned—in all its forms and permutations—independent publishing companies can now be run from the kitchen or a spare bedroom in your own home.

RECOMMENDED RESOURCE! To understand how you can build a publishing business, I recommend reading the stories of those who have done it themselves. Emmanuel Haldeman-Julius's *The First Hundred Million* is a great place to start. Then take a look at Al Neuhart's autobiography, *S.O.B.*, and Bill Henderson's *The Publish-It-Yourself Handbook*.

One of the most successful independent publishing companies I know of is run from a small apartment built in a former dry-cleaning shop in a town of 200. My own office is in a 150-square-foot spare bedroom, a former child's nursery. There I preside over my worldwide electronic empire. I routinely receive and transmit manuscripts by modem. I fax contracts and requests for quotes on publications in progress. I write, lay out, and design more than 20 publications each year with a $2,000 computer and laser printer. I do business with printers in Ann Arbor, color separation houses in Colorado, and book wholesalers in California. In publishing, the much-heralded "electronic cottage" is very much a reality. *And it works!*

Immensely powerful and ever more affordable microcomputers, driven by very sophisticated page layout and typesetting software, have put into the hands of the hometown, entrepreneurial publisher the tools needed to control planning and production of the product at every step of the way. With the new "publishing on demand" technologies, books are not even printed until the orders come in.

These new methods give the entrepreneurial publisher advantages that were unheard of just 15 short years ago. Their use produces great savings in pre-press production costs and, as a result, a substantial increase in profitability. Projects which once might have been financially marginal are now quite profitable.

A One-Person Business

Since it does so much so well, desktop technology creates the possibility of operating a business single-handedly. One person can do almost everything. It permits more efficient schedule management. You are doing everything in-house, so there are no outside people whose work schedules, holidays, and down time you have to accommodate. It creates more efficient general operations, since the same computers that produce your books and maintain mailing lists can send bills and do all other necessary accounting operations, from accounts receivable to general ledger.

The SOB Factor

Another great benefit of the new technology is what I call the SOB factor. When you develop a new business there are three ways that you can finance yourself during the start-up phase. You can use OPM (Other People's Money), by going to the bank and getting a loan which you immediately have to start paying back. You can use YOM (Your Own Money) by raiding the reserves of your hard-earned savings. Or you can use SOB (Sweat of Your Brow), by doing all of the work yourself until the business is up and running. It used to be that before you could get a publication on the street you had to pay designers, typesetters, paste-up people, and printers. Now you do it all yourself. It takes longer, but it's much easier on the pocketbook. You are converting the Sweat of Your Brow into equity in your business.

Getting into Publishing

There are many reasons for going into any business, including the publishing business. The most direct and easily understood of these is the desire for financial gain. Most of us who give in to the entrepreneurial urge and crank up our own enterprises share that basic goal.

Whatever other motivations there may be, we all want to turn a profit. But our other, more personal, motivations are important, too. Because of them we turn our attention to this or that opportunity rather than to any one of the hundreds of others that a person with different interests would, perhaps, find more appealing. Strong personal motivations give us the staying power we need to make a go of it.

How I Got into Publishing

In my own case an inborn fascination with words and ink on paper were the powerful motivators that eventually led me into publishing. I don't know where, when, or how it began, but somehow I always knew that I wanted to make my living by working with "words and books," as I remember saying to one close friend on the eve of undertaking my first publishing venture.

Still, for many years, I held back. I became, instead, a college professor—a tried and true way of generating monthly paychecks to finance the hours one spends in the library or at the typewriter. At that time I was totally inexperienced in business and had neither the know-how nor the all-important self-confidence to go directly into publishing.

My First Big Project

But things do take their natural course. Our secret inclinations, strong enough, ultimately find ways to express themselves. One evening I noticed an article in the local newspaper. A steering committee, the article said, had been set up to coordinate the celebration of the town's bicentennial. Such events, I knew, traditionally generated some kind of book. Be it good, bad, or indifferent, a retrospective book celebrating the town's history, people, and places would appear. Most of the ones that I had seen had been very badly and amateurishly done—on cheap paper, with poor printing, and worse writing and design. I knew that I could do better.

I determined on the spot to type out a proposal and go to the committee. For a modest fee, I told them, I would compile, edit, and print a local history. It would be filled with a fabulous collection of old photographs (which I would later have to collect) and the best available writing. My proposal was accepted and I was off on my first big project. I set myself a working schedule that I know now was virtually impossible. I would research for thirty days, write and edit for thirty days, and get the book printed and bound in thirty days. It worked, and at the beginning of the third month I was holding page proofs in my hands.

As I reviewed them my eye fell to the bottom of the title page, where the imprint (name) of the publishing company usually appears. It suddenly dawned on me that I could invent a name for myself, have it printed on the title page and, presto! I would have a publishing company. I would be off and running. And it was, in fact, just that easy. The following year I issued my second book—a reprint of a county history that had been out of print for years and had become a collector's item.

Shortly afterward, I put my new-found publishing expertise to a much more substantial test when I began to publish a regional magazine. This, too, grew nicely and eventually became the statewide, full color, consumer publication: *Tar Heel: The Magazine of North Carolina.*

At this point I gave up teaching altogether to become owner, editor, and publisher of a weekly newspaper, *The Mecklenburg Gazette*, in the college town of Davidson, North Carolina.

Brains, Time and Energy—Not Money

None of this, mind you, cost me one single cent in out-of-pocket cash. Getting into publishing, I found, took its toll in brain power, time, and energy, but required little investment other than that.

As you gain more experience, you may be willing to take on more complicated and extensive projects that require you to risk a modest amount of cash. But in the beginning you need not put up any money at all. When I have made this claim to others, they have found it hard to believe, but it is true. I have never undertaken a publishing project that did not make money from the very first. I have always been able to finance my books, magazines, and newspapers with sweat equity and ongoing cash flow.

Moonlighting: I Highly Recommend It

What about the time required? Is it manageable for someone working at another job?

It is, indeed. In fact your first plunge into publishing will work out better when you start slowly, build wisely, and learn as you go. The fact is that you are unlikely to generate an income to live on from publishing alone until you learn—from firsthand experience—all the rules of the game. You will need an established income for a while yet. Just put in the extra hours until the payoff comes.

> **RECOMMENDED RESOURCE!** On moonlighting your way to success in a home-based business see Barbara Brabec's *Homemade Money*. It's full of practical advice and is a strong motivation builder.

Many individuals will be quite content to continue in this way indefinitely, deriving their major income from a "regular job" and maintaining publishing activities as a lucrative sideline. This is a very workable arrangement, especially for those whose primary employment is so remunerative or so intrinsically interesting to them that they prefer not to give it up.

Others, for whom this is not the case, will eventually discover ways, as I did, to move into publishing as a full-time occupation.

The Three Secrets of Success

The term "publishing business" covers a lot of territory, a good deal of it out of reach for the beginner. It would be nonsense to say that you could start, from scratch, a company on the scale of, say, Harper & Row or Scribner's. You would need to raise millions in capital to fund the publication of fifty to a hundred titles before you could begin to generate the cash flow necessary to cover day-to-day expenses, much less make a profit.

The gigantic undertaking of establishing a truly national circulation newspaper like *USA Today* required the infusion of tens of millions of dollars before the first edition ever hit the stands. Even now, after years of publication, this newspaper is just beginning to return a precarious profit to its investors. But setting aside this high-dollar neck of the woods, there is still a lot of publishing going on out there that is viable for the start-up entrepreneur. How do you recognize the kind of opportunity that is likely to yield success and result in financial reward for the independent desktop publisher?

> **Three—count them, three—keys to kitchen-table publishing success: intensive sales, in a limited geographical area, or to a highly-targeted readership.**

My experience tells me that there are three secret ingredients that you must look for. When one or another of these ingredients is missing, consider it a red flag of warning. You may feel that your publication idea contains other elements that more than compensate for the missing ingredient. And you may be right. There are always exceptions. My advice, however, is to stick with the tried and true, at least until you learn to navigate on your own. To do otherwise can cost you money in lost time and profits.

The secret ingredients of my publishing success formula are as follows: I choose only projects that allow for:

- Intensive sales
- In a limited geographical area
- To a well-defined (targeted) clientele.

Intensive Sales

When a high proportion of the businesses in a given area constitutes prospects for advertising sales for a magazine, shopper, or other periodical, or when a book will appeal to the majority of those who buy books in a given area (a book on Atlanta for Atlantans, for instance), then that magazine or book has the possibility of *intensive sales*. A high percentage of potential customers will be interested in buying an ad or buying a book.

When there is a large enough pool of potential customers that are also easy to reach (see the next section), sales to a reasonable number of them will bring success. A newcomer guide focusing on a metropolitan area is an example of a publication that meets this test.

By way of contrast, let me give an illustration of an idea from another field that does not meet the test of intensive sales. A year or two ago a friend suggested the idea of building personalized doll houses for sale during the Christmas season. The doll houses would be built to resemble the houses in which the family of the child for whom it was designed actually lived. My friend was excited by the idea. The doll houses would be handsomely made and unique, though expensive, gifts. The children who received them would certainly be thrilled by them.

But this business idea did not have the possibility of intensive sales. The prospects for the doll houses, I pointed out, would be limited to those few affluent individuals who could afford such a customized toy. Prospects would, moreover, be further limited to families with female children between the ages of three and ten or twelve. Additionally, they would be limited to those affluent parents of little girls who liked the doll house idea, and whose daughters did not already have a doll house. Looked at this way, our small town had a pool of only ten or fifteen prospects for customized doll houses. It was not an idea worth exploring further.

On the other hand, when you publish a tourism guide to a major resort area, virtually every business there is a prime candidate to purchase advertising, and your ad rep can call on every one of them, with confidence, year after year.

Limited Geographical Area

A single entrepreneur can easily handle a project that covers a limited geographical area, whereas expanding the coverage area beyond the reach of one or two people can create real difficulties.

A city magazine is relatively easy to publish; a regional magazine (the mountains of your state, for instance, or the coast) is more difficult; a statewide magazine requires an entire staff of sales and production people; a national magazine requires all of the above, plus a high-risk investor with several million dollars of idle money in very deep pockets.

When you focus tightly, several good things happen. You or your ad salesperson can make calls and sell the product without traveling anywhere overnight. Circulation and distribution are easily and inexpensively managed. You can do this job yourself, if necessary. In the case of book publishing, all the major booksellers can be called on personally. Your own advertising becomes more affordable and your name recognition more readily achieved.

A Well-Defined (or Targeted) Clientele

It is difficult for a small publisher to market a general interest novel because those who may want to buy it represent a diverse group of people spread across such a wide area that it becomes prohibitively expensive to reach them all. A typical book of this kind, even when successful, will sell relatively few copies in each of a large number of bookstores nationwide. A company that does not have a national sales force simply cannot make the calls necessary to get the title on the bookstore shelves. When a few people in a great many communities constitute the potential pool of buyers, the small publisher has a problem.

The successful desktop publisher will bring out books and magazines that have a large number of potential readers in a very limited area. When I brought out my bicentennial history, 99% of all sales took place within a fifty mile radius of the town. No one in Detroit or Denver or San Diego was interested in a picture history of Greenville, NC. But a great many people in Greenville were. Enough, indeed, to sell out an entire first edition.

Analogous to the concept of the limited geographical area (and an acceptable substitute for it) is that of the targeted, specialized, and easily identifiable readership. This is the domain of the so-called "niche" publications, each of which has a highly specialized readership. If you bring out a magazine called *Gum Disease Today*, you know that it will appeal to every periodontist everywhere. Mailing lists of targeted readerships are readily available, so that even though this group of individuals may be spread across many geographical miles, they are still easily reached by direct mail or by telephone. They are targeted in such a way that even the small publisher has a chance of hitting the mark.

The following chapters will take you step-by-step through the process of starting and publishing a wide variety of periodicals and specialty books that meet the success criteria described in this introduction to the business.

The Magic Circle of Success in Periodical Publishing

A well-conceived and implemented periodical, which appeals to and is read by....

Most people in your trade area, people who will benefit from and can afford to buy the products and

Businesses, which, in turn, will buy advertising space in your well-conceived and implemented periodical to reach those readers.

This diagram illustrates in graphic form the lesson I teach over and over again in this book. No matter what project you start, no matter where you start it, success depends on the completion of this circle of energy. If the positive and negative terminals of a battery are not connected, no current will flow. Similarly, if any one of these three elements is missing from your project, the process will be interrupted wherever the weak link occurs. Remember that your publication project will not work if you can't get it into the hands of your targeted readership; your project will not work if that readership, once you do get your publication to them, finds nothing of interest inside it; and it will not work if your advertising prospects are too widely scattered, too difficult to reach, and too expensive to call on. Don't let wishful thinking mislead you. These three elements must be present for you to succeed. Nothing happens when the circle is not complete.

2

Setting Up Shop

Afriend of mine who is a very successful hometown entrepreneur says that all you really need to get into business is an idea and a pack of business cards with your name and address on them. Then, he says, you go out and get started. There is a great deal of truth in this observation. Many potentially great businesses never get off the ground because the idea person put off the start-up until he was totally prepared. But that moment of total preparation never seemed to arrive.

The middle road of wisdom lies somewhere between these two extremes of winging it on a pack of business cards on the one hand and mind-choking over-preparation on the other. You must plan carefully, to be sure. Just don't get so bogged down in the planning stage that you never move beyond it.

A Gradual Process

In my experience, setting up to do business has been a gradual process. There are the bare minimum space and equipment requirements, of course, but a great many decisions can, and should, be put off until your needs become clearer and more well-defined as you go along. And as work comes in you'll create a flow of cash that will help you acquire some of the niftier and more expensive things that you need.

In my own start-up phase I found many substitutes that I pressed into service until I could afford the real thing. I did layouts on the dining room table and used wooden fruit crates for files. As the work flow began to build I went beyond these homespun arrangements for two reasons. The first was that I knew that I could work better and faster with the proper equipment. The second was that I simply enjoyed myself more and felt better in more professional surroundings.

I believe that you will feel that way, too. And I must confess to a third reason. I am in publishing as much for the love of the business as for the money I earn by engaging in it—as important as that is. The truth is that I simply enjoy the paraphernalia of writing, typesetting and production. I assemble it, use it, and care for it out of pure pleasure.

Finding the Space

When you set up as a publisher in your own home, the first challenge is to find a convenient and usable place to work. I have found that 150 square feet of tightly-organized space can be adequate for a small publishing company. This is especially true if you utilize odd spaces in the rest of the house for order fulfillment, wrapping and mailing, fax transmission, conferences, etc.

I firmly believe that any business that can be started in the home ought to be started in the home. You will need to nurture your start-up capital and your initial income from publishing projects, using it to build your business. There is no sense at all in leasing expensive office suites that you do not need. And once you are up and running there is really no reason to move out into rented space unless you grow to the point that you can't do without it. A seldom-used, spare bedroom is the perfect start-up space. Your business can be located there, and you can still unfold a roll-away bed when company comes. A garage that is closed in to the weather and heated (or capable of being heated) is even better. The relative quiet and privacy that such spaces offer are always welcome. They come close to being necessary if you have small children running around un-tamed.

Some conditions—rarer than you might think, though—can make a home-based business unworkable. If for various reasons, it is difficult to create an atmosphere conducive to work you may have to set up elsewhere. Maybe you are blessed with ten active children, all under the age of twelve. Maybe you just have two of them, but they are as noisy and rambunctious as twelve would be. It would be a miracle if you could keep them out of your hair for the unin-terrupted hours of work and concentration that you will need. If the children are older and under control perhaps you can commandeer a seldom-used for-mal dining room or parlor, often found in older homes. Used only for the visits of wealthy maiden aunts, these rooms readily serve the needs of the home-based entrepreneur. It is unlikely that the rest of the family will miss the use of them at all.

No such rooms available? Then take over the corner of a den or any other reasonably large room where you can install your computer and other equip-ment with at least relative permanence. Leave them up and ready to go when you finish a work session. Otherwise you will spend all your time setting up and tearing down your apparatus.

There may be a space problem that, even with the best of wills, you just can't solve. Maybe you share a studio apartment with a spouse and a child, and can't muster up even a closetful of real privacy. If so, you can rent a small space in a budget-level office complex or in a "business incubator" center. Check the business development office of your local community college or the Chamber of Commerce for leads.

Space Utilization

There are some ready-made (but quite inexpensive) cabinets that go a long way toward getting the absolute maximum use from limited corner spaces. I bought one just yesterday at a discount office supply store near my home. A miracle of tightly-planned organization, this work station utilizes the corner of a bedroom or den and six feet of wall space on either side of it. The computer station is in the middle, at the corner. To the right and left are spaces for printers, fax machines, telephones and other peripheral devices.

The cabinets, shelves and storage spaces are arranged so as to give the greatest flexibility of use. You can buy one for $250. It comes disassembled, and you put it together yourself. You can also nail a work station together on your own if you're handy with hammer and saw. Begin with an old hollow-core door with a two-drawer file cabinet on each end for support. Bought separately, though, these items are expensive, and costs will run up rapidly. Unless you have the materials on hand, the store-bought version is probably the cheapest way to go.

You can scatter other office items around the house, if need be. Your copy machine might be in a bedroom or a hallway. A piece of 3/4-inch plywood, cut to size and placed across the clothes washer and dryer, will provide work table/mail-out/production space. Another piece of plywood, with its base on your worktable and top leaning against the wall, can act as a paste-up board or layout table. It is true that computers do so much of what was once done by hand on layout tables that they have almost become almost, but not quite, extinct. I do not use mine often, but when I do need it, I find that it is indispensable.

That Flood of Paper

There is no doubt about it: business is done on paper. Following is a list of the basic paper items that your publishing business will need. Check your computer first. Invoices and statements appear on the list below, but they can

RECOMMENDED RESOURCE!

An important one: you can buy first-class business cards, stationery and other paper goods at wholesale by becoming a vendor for companies like Carlson Craft, Mankato, Minnesota or Admore (presentation folders and PR materials). Resale of these items at retail prices can also become a nice secondary profit center for you. Other suppliers advertise in the classified pages of the *American Printer* and other trade magazines.

The Value of a Customer

A satisfied customer will generate many more of the same kind. Many businesses fail or do far worse than they should through simple failure to recognize this basic fact. Your customer—whether an advertiser in your magazine, a sponsor of your county history, or a Chamber of Commerce executive—is your most precious asset. This is true not only for the income you currently derive from meeting his needs, but from all the future business you will derive from him and from everyone to whom he recommends you. A good customer recommends you to two friends, who also recommend you to two friends and so on into the future. It's a geometric progression. It takes a while to land the first client or two but after that, if you do your work well and deliver as promised, it becomes much smoother sailing. An ill-served, dissatisfied customer, on the other hand, represents a dead end and, at worse, a dead weight that you will drag along behind you for years to come.

Always go the extra mile to make your clients happy, even the smallest among them. Put the same effort into thoughtful advertising design for the guy who takes the one-twelfth page ad in the back of the book as for the bank that takes the back cover. Write your clients. Thank them for their business. Deliver complimentary copies. Refer leads to them when they come your way. Do business with them yourself. Send Christmas cards. Maintain positive contact in every possible way. When you have a complaint, go overboard in trying to resolve it in a way that will meet your customer's needs. Big businesses can be built on the solid, sound base of satisfied customers.

also be generated by a variety of accounting software packages. Other forms can be designed using your database program.

You can also buy ready-made forms of various kinds at your office supply store. You will just insert the name and address of your business in the proper place with a rubber stamp. While these preprinted forms may be good enough to get started with, they are too expensive to serve over the long run and, of course, they are not very professional either. They don't do a thing for your image.

Most of the items listed here can be bought from suppliers like Carlson Craft (this company will give you wholesale prices when you ask to be set up as a distributor) and NEBS (the Wal-Mart of business form companies). You will have a wider choice of business cards and letterhead styles and quality with Carlson Craft than with NEBS. The addresses of both these companies are given in the Resources Appendix. Other forms (such as the advertising approval forms and sales management forms) can simply be photocopied from the blank forms provided in this book.

- *Business cards.*
- *Letterhead and envelopes.* I usually buy these in two grades—a smaller quantity of good bond for special uses and "executive communications" and regular white offset for run-of-the-mill use. Both of these items can be created on your computer and printed out on your laser printer.
- *Invoices.* An invoice is issued and sent at the time of sale. Have a separate, numbered invoice for each transaction. These are normally generated by your computerized billing program or accounting package.
- *Statements.* A statement is issued to a regular customer monthly, carrying a line for balance forward, a summary of the month's transactions (with invoice number), and the total balance due. Finance or service charges are added to the statement.
- *Insertion orders.* These are the contractual agreements between advertisers and your company. Samples are given in the Appendix.
- *Request for quote forms.* You fill out these forms and send them to printers from whom you want to get prices on your publications.
- *Ad approval forms.* You use these forms to get an advertiser's approval of the ad to be run, after you have typeset and designed it. It is his final okay to run the ad just as you have presented it to him. Signed ad approvals are a great help when the time comes to get paid. Some advertisers have a very short memory about what they asked you to do for them and what they okayed. The signed approval sheet jogs such memories very effectively.
- *Other business, sales and management forms.* Templates are provided in the Forms Appendix.

Take Your Time

Take the time to design these paper products well. If you are not an experienced designer, don't be afraid to be a copy cat. Find business cards, letterheads, etc., that you like a great deal and adapt them to your own use. Some computer programs (Pagemaker, for example) have templates which will help you design professional looking products.

These paper goods are important to you. They constitute the first contact that you will have with your clients, whose first impressions will be based on them. And first impressions, as the saying goes (and it is a very true saying), are lasting impressions.

The forms designed for internal use (such as sales reports and advertising manifests) are no less important. They enable you to keep track, on a day-to-day basis, of what is going on in your business. Without careful tracking, the details involved in the simplest publishing project can quickly become overwhelming.

Promotional Materials

The actual promotional materials you need will vary with the publishing projects you undertake. In general, though, your new publishing business will need the following items:

1. *A capabilities brochure.* A capabilities brochure describes what your company is and what it can do for its clients. It is a selling piece designed to lend credibility and support to your salespeople, who will hand a copy to each client at the time of initial contact. The capabilities brochure includes a section on the credentials of the owner and as much additional material about your company as you can come up with. Past and present clients are listed and testimonials are prominently displayed. While the brochure must be cleanly designed and professional, it is not absolutely necessary that you start out with a slick, expensive piece. Using my computer and my laser printer, I designed a very basic capabilities brochure for a recent business start-up that could be produced in-house. I wrote and designed it on my computer, printed it out on my laser printer and duplicated it on good quality 11 by 17 sheets (bought from my wholesale paper supplier) on my office copier. When I folded these sheets over, page-fashion, I had an instant, self-mailing brochure. As soon as you are able, though, go ahead and pay the price for a quality product. It will pay off in the long run.

2. *Ready-to-go business letters.* Writing all those business letters can be a difficult and time-consuming chore, but it need not be. Here again, your computer is your best friend. In business, the details are important, and one of the most important is the correspondence you regularly send out. You write a letter to get an appointment, a letter to thank your client for an appointment, a

follow-up letter of thanks after an appointment, a letter of thanks and acknowledgment for a deal concluded, and a "looking forward to next time" letter when you have not been able to get a signature on the dotted line. As important as these letters are, many business people never get around to writing them. They simply have not organized themselves to be able to do so. When you have harnessed the power of your computer to help you meet all these correspondence needs, you will stand apart from the pack and build your reputation as a solid, dependable business person who attends to details and cares about his clients. As a home-based businessperson, such a reputation is important to you.

Sit down at the keyboard and create generic letters of thanks, of congratulations, of anticipation as well as letters for every other eventuality that you can think of. If you are not confident of your writing abilities, you can buy a book or computer disk of sample letters to meet each of these needs. Any fully-stocked bookstore or computer store will have them on hand. Keep the letters that you write in a special file on your hard drive. When you need one of them, call up the file, insert the name and address of the person to whom you are sending the letter and print it out on your letterhead (also stored in your computer). It's the work of a minute, but the payoff in building long-term goodwill is enormous.

3. *News release form.* You will need a file on your computer dedicated to the preparation of news releases. Your main file will have the blank release form on it, with the appropriate headings. (A sample of the news release form which I designed for Venture Press is included elsewhere in this book.) If you wish to save any release that you write, do so under another file name. Keep the master form blank and ready for the quick preparation of the next release. Newspaper editors regularly sort through the stacks of news releases that cross their desks daily. They include information from many of them in the articles that they publish. Smaller newspapers often run news releases just as they come in, with only light editing; larger papers will usually rewrite the release, or at least rewrite the lead paragraph.

Editors depend on well-written news releases to fill up the columns of their papers. Keep a steady flow of them going out. A published news release is better than any ad you can buy. News releases serve to keep the name of your company before the public and, better still, before your banker, your customers, and the business community in general. Furthermore, news releases don't cost a cent. They are the best free advertising you can get.

4. *Media kit.* You can generate a great deal of free publicity for your company if you have a media kit (also called a press kit) ready to send out on short notice.

The term "media kit" is somewhat misleading, since this packet of PR and promotional materials is used for many different purposes. Yes, it is sent to newspapers and television/radio stations as needed, but it is also your primary selling piece for potential advertisers and all others with whom you wish to establish a profitable business relationship. Your media kit will generally contain a variety of items, arranged in the pockets of a presentation folder. At a later date you can buy custom-printed presentation folders (again from whole-sale suppliers). Until you can afford to do so, the unprinted versions that you can buy at your business supply store will serve your purpose quite well. Among the items to be found in a well-furnished media kit are the following:

- *A fact sheet on your company*: date of formation, publications, activities, trade area covered, capabilities.
- *A fact sheet on yourself as president or CEO of your company*, especially if you have credentials of interest, have published books, held important positions, etc. It is amazing how many great things you can find to say about yourself when you put your mind to it. If you are willing to set out on your own and start your own publishing company, you are by that very fact a fascinating person in the eyes of the general public and, indeed, should be so even in your own eyes.
- *Samples of your publication or publications.* In the case of books, include a flyer advertising each title or a catalog of all your titles. If the first edition of your publication has not yet appeared, include an artist's rendering of the cover, with a full description of the publication itself: design, editorial content.
- *A rate card* for any publication in which a client might wish to place advertising.
- *Copies of any news releases* that may be of interest.
- *Copies of news stories or reviews* that praise you, your company, or your product.
- *A black and white photograph of yourself* whenever you think there is any chance that it may be used. Always attach a cut line (the words to be printed under the picture) to the photograph. An action photo, showing you involved in writing or editing activities is preferred.
- *Your capabilities brochure.*

More details on the preparation and use of media kits are given in later chapters.

The Equipment You Will Need

The power of the new personal computers, laser printers, fax machines and other electronic communications tools makes your home-based publishing company possible. Twenty years ago this equipment did not exist. It was the mid-80's before PC's began to be used in publishing. In fact, the very term "desktop publishing," invented by Apple Computer to market the Macintosh and the first laser printer, dates from that time.

When I published my weekly newspaper in the late 1970's and early 1980's, my typesetting equipment alone occupied almost as much space as my entire home publishing office does now. Times have changed. The Macintosh that occupies the place of honor on my desk today has more power and does more things far more cheaply than two rooms of ruinously expensive phototypesetting equipment used to do.

Which equipment will do the job you need done? What are the best buys? Here's your shopping list:

A Personal Computer and Modem

The fairy tales tell about a mythical goose that lays golden eggs. As far as your publishing company is concerned, your computer is truly that magic goose. As you learn to use it more and more efficiently, it will do the work that would have required a team of four or more people in the old, pre-computer days. Now you can do it all yourself, far better, far faster, and much more cheaply than it was done before.

Nothing changes as quickly as the type and price of computer equipment. You may be reading this chapter shortly after publication or a year or two down the road. Just remember that the kinds of equipment you will need will not change, although the available capabilities and prices surely will.

This machine will be your typesetter, graphic arts and layout person, page designer, bookkeeper, communications specialist, secretary and all-around best friend. It takes the place of three or more employees, yet never needs a vacation. It never asks for a raise and never, ever shows up late for work. It is perfectly reliable and ever-faithful.

Which computer should you buy? You will choose between Macintosh computers with their own operating systems and one of the many computers that run on a version of Windows. Prices are tumbling as I write this. In the past twelve months they have fallen as much as 50%. This includes laser printers and fax machines as well.

Which Computer Should You Buy?

I use Macintosh computers in my business, for several reasons. First, they are very user friendly. It is possible to have a reasonably competent typist doing word processing chores after a half-hour's training. Furthermore, the Macs are great for graphic designers. If you're going to do a lot of advertising design you will find their versatility and ease of use helpful. However, there is no doubt that much more software, especially for Internet marketing, is available for Windows.

Macintosh computers are somewhat more expensive than comparable Windows machines, but are much less so than they once were. I recently bought a G-5 Macintosh with 512 megs of RAM and a 40-gig hard drive for $1600. This machine is a powerhouse. I have used a Macintosh for years (beginning with the prototype Mac Plus) for publishing books, magazines and apartment guides, including all typesetting, ad design, and page layout. I also use it for correspondence, bookkeeping, and billing.

Nowadays, the Windows machines are really not that much more difficult to use. The development of the Windows program has simplified operations immensely, although it requires a longer learning curve than the Mac to get a new worker up and going. The computer business is fiercely competitive, so I am not going to recommend computers by name. I will just specify the capabilities you need in whatever computer you buy:

- *The speed* with which a computer processes the information you feed into it and completes the task you ask it to do is measured in megahertz. You will want to buy a computer with as much speed as you can afford. As I write this (though by the time you read these words even higher speeds may be available) you should be able to find a computer running at 500 megahertz or more. Some faster ones are now available at rock-bottom prices. For simple word processing and black and white page layout, speed is not of the essence. It becomes more important as you begin to ask your computer to perform color work, create and place halftones, and perform other memory-intensive operations.
- *Random Access Memory (RAM)* allows your computer to manipulate data and programs as you work. The more RAM you have, the more tasks you can undertake simultaneously and the more programs you can keep open and active simultaneously. In the beginning you may be able to get by with as little as 128 megs of RAM, but you should go ahead and get more RAM capability at the outset. It is cheaper to buy RAM when you purchase your machine than to add it later on. I recommend a RAM of at least 256 megabytes. Photographs require an enormous RAM memory and program updates use more and more RAM in every version. If you are routinely processing photos, especially color photos, get the maximum RAM available to you and your pocketbook.
- *Storage memory.* Storage memory refers to the space available on your hard drive to store information that is not currently in use. Storage memory is measured in gigabytes. Computers become sluggish when

you are operating at or near the capacity of the hard drive. Just a few years ago a 500-megabyte hard drive was considered adequate for most purposes, and prior to that, most personal computers were not equipped with hard drives at all. Today a storage memory of 500 megs is considered a mere dab in the bucket and virtually unusable. Your computer should have a hard drive capacity of 20 gigabytes at the very least. Since hard drive memory capacity is inexpensive when you first purchase your computer, get one with as much storage memory possible.

- *External storage.* You will need a device for storing publications on portable disks so that they can be easily shared with others—your printer for instance. Zip drives (now virtually replaced by CDs) and read/write CD burners are usually built in on good computers, and they work well. If you are buying new, get these along with your package.
- *Modem.* A modem, internal or external, is necessary for e-mail and internet connection. Modems are built-in on all computers sold today.

External Storage

As you continue to do business, you will accumulate ads, articles, photographs, art, and even whole publications that you will want to store electronically. You will be unable to store them all on your hard drive, since, over time, they will require a great deal of space. And even with a hard drive of enormous capacity, you will risk losing everything in the event that it crashes.

The wiser course is to back up your work regularly to zip disks, CDs, or to an external hard drive. If you are buying a computer, you can find one that has the capability of creating the disks you need. If your computer does not have this capability you can buy external zip and CD-burning drives for a couple of hundred dollars or less (as I write this).

Your Laser Printer

So what do you need in a laser printer? Who makes the good ones? How much are they? Here are the features you should look for:

- The laser printer you buy must be a "Postscript" printer.
- The laser printer you buy must produce type at a resolution of at least 1200 dots per inch (dpi). Add memory to your laser printer to bring it up to 32 megs or more if you wish to work with photographs. In the early days of desktop publishing I published many full-color, slick-paper magazines with type output that came directly from an Apple LaserWriter Plus, a first generation workhorse, and a 300 dpi machine. If you are going to do tabloid newspapers, buy a printer that handles "oversize" pages. You can buy used and reconditioned laser printers by calling the

companies that advertise in the back pages of most computer magazines. I did this recently to replace a laser printer that had been stolen from my office.

Paying for Your Computer/Printer

The base, so-called "street" price for your computer and laser printer used to be set by the mail order dealers who advertise in the computer magazines. Today, you can buy computers at near street prices in discount stores almost everywhere.

There are still some good buys by mail order. I have often dealt with these businesses and found them to be very reliable and their warranties rigorously honored. Some of them, as I have said, deal in "used" equipment, too. I use the quotation marks because some of these machines are actually overstocks and are delivered still packed in their original cartons.

Credit Cards, Leases and Discounts

You can put your equipment on your credit card, or you can lease it. Apple and other computer companies routinely offer business leases that will be available to you if your credit rating is average or better.

Investigate the so-called "educator discount prices." These sometimes save you a sizable percentage off list price. Student stores on university and colleges campuses often offer computer equipment for sale at mail-order prices. The purchaser must be a student or a member of the faculty, of course, but this obstacle is one that you can usually find a way to get around.

Your Fax Machine

You will need a good fax machine. The fax has ubiquitous because it is so useful. Immediate quotes can be given via fax, and immediate pricing received. Advertising proofs can be faxed to your customers and approval faxed to you in return. It used to take days—even weeks—to get these simple chores done. Now they can all be taken care of in a few minutes. Fortunately, faxes are no longer expensive. Be sure to get a fax that has "broadcast" capabilities. That way you can use it for marketing purposes. A fax broadcast sends a single fax to scores of preselected telephone numbers.

Your Copy Machine

Copying machines, too, can be bought used. I don't think it makes sense to buy them any other way, so long as the machine in question has been under a continuous maintenance contract. Actually, between your laser printer output of proof pages and your scanner's ability to make at least some copies, you can put off this purchase until you get up and going, if need be. But if you do decide to go for a copier, what kind do you need? Look for the following capabilities:

- Enlargement and reduction capabilities in one point increments. The lower price machines will reduce and enlarge, but at four or five fixed percentages. You want to be able choose any percentage that you need. This capability is particularly useful to you in designing ads for newspapers, tabloid shoppers, or magazines.
- Very good and dense blacks. Run a document with large areas of black in it through the printer you are thinking about buying. Do the black areas on the copy you made have thin, faded areas in them? If so, ask your salesperson to adjust the machine for the best possible blacks. If they don't get markedly better, look at another machine.
- When you buy a used machine, you often get optional features for very little extra money simply because the option is already in place. Options that will be helpful to you are an automatic document feed and a "duplex" capability that will allow you to print on both sides of a sheet of paper. Neither of these features, though, is worth the higher price that you would have to pay if you bought them off the shelf.

Your Scanner

I got along quite well without a scanner for many years, but now that I have one I wonder how I did it. As I write this, good scanners can be bought for as little $150. The best of the lot in this price range seem to be made by Hewlett-Packard and Epson. Software to run the scanner is usually bundled with it. In addition, you will need a program for text recognition and another for photos and graphics. I recommend OmniPage Pro and Photoshop. Your scanner will have to perform the following tasks:

- Scan printed pages and read the type into one of your word processing files so that you can edit and print it out again in a new format without having first to retype it yourself.
- Copy, resize, and paste into a new document all line art and logos that you may wish to have on file.
- Create halftone screens of photographs.
- Scan color photographs for the production of color separations.

Additional Equipment

You may find that you need additional equipment to help you work in the specialty that you choose for yourself. If you do a lot of hands-on paste-up, you may wish to buy or build a portable light table. If you bind documents for clients you may wish to buy an inexpensive GBX plastic comb binder or some similar machine. Since I am now publishing a great many books in loose-leaf type binders, I have a small, table-top shrink-wrap machine to keep the books closed and the pages in place. The plastic shrink-wrap dresses up the product for marketing purposes as well.

Software

As a publisher you will utilize your personal computer to perform the many tasks that your projects call for. There are a great many software programs on the market to help you do these jobs. Which ones are the best for you? You will need three basic programs: a word processing program, a page layout program, and an accounting program. The first rule of thumb is to stick with what is most widely used. Program compatibility will often be a boon to you.

1. *Word Processing Programs.* Two word processing programs dominate the market today. These are Microsoft Word (originally written for the Mac but now available for windows machines as well) and WordPerfect (originally written for DOS machines, but now available for the Mac). Each of these programs has its champions and aficionados. I prefer Microsoft Word because it seems far simpler to utilize and learn. On the Macintosh it is the only real choice.

   WordPerfect is a very strong program with a wide range of capabilities. But since you will be using a page layout program to do many of the tasks that you have to get done, WordPerfect's array of features sometimes just gets in the way. My recommendation to you? If you use Macintosh computers, use Microsoft Word for your word processing needs. If you run Windows computers, use either Microsoft Word or WordPerfect. If you have previously learned either of these programs, then stick with the one that you know best.

2. *Page Layout Programs.* There are two major players in the page layout market: InDesign and QuarkXpress. I prefer InDesign. It is very nearly as good as QuarkXpress at graphic arts, but has strong text handling capabilities that Quark lacks. The program will perform every task that the homebased publisher is likely to ask of it and a good deal more besides. It is the all-around champ in the text-handling and layout fields, and it is getting better all the time.

3. *Accounting Programs.* You will need a computer program to help you send out bills, collect the money that is owed to you, register payments and credits, and print monthly statements. These chores can easily get out of hand when you try to do them manually.

Niche Markets: What
They Are and How to Find Them

Entrepreneurial publishers identify and exploit niche markets. But what is a niche market? How do you recognize one? How do you estimate its potential for profit? A niche market is composed of individuals or businesses:

- That have similar interests and needs,
- That can be readily identified, and...
- That can be easily targeted and reached.

A potentially profitable niche market will also have one other indispensable element: *a broad base of businesses ready and willing to buy advertising space* in order to reach the individuals who comprise the niche readership.

One entrepreneur in my area just cranked up a very successful tabloid called *Hospital Business News*. He publishes this biweekly in the Miami-Fort Lauderdale area, a massive metropolitan market. He had identified this niche himself and had seen that he had virtually no competition in it. He also recognized immediately that he could target both readers and advertisers with great precision. Furthermore, the potential advertisers he had in mind all had a great deal of money budgeted for the purchase of advertising space.

The more specialized your niche market, the better off you are. A specialized market can be more easily mastered by a small organization. Every nook and cranny of it can be ploughed and farmed, like a small, fertile plot of land. A niche market is important because it is manageable: you can easily get your mind around it, your pocketbook around it, and your hands around it. It is also much easier to create the necessary visibility for your own company within a limited segment of the business community. Do you see niche market opportunities around you? Is there a well-defined group of readers that advertisers want to reach? Can you devise a publication that will appeal both to these readers and to your base of potential advertisers? If so, you may have discovered the opportunity you are looking for. There is much more on this important subject in Chapter 11.

I do not advise you to do all of your bookkeeping yourself. You can keep your day-to-day journals and records, but then go to an accountant at year's end. This professional will enable you to slim down your taxes and stay even with all the reports that Uncle Sam will require of you. The fees for these services are quite reasonable. I have usually found that when I went to an accountant I saved far more in taxes than I ever paid out in accounting fees.

I bring this up because there are two types of accounting programs on the market. One type does everything possible for you, from your general ledger, to your profit and loss statement, to inventory control. In fact, these programs insist on doing far more for you than you need or want them to do. Furthermore, it can take a person with considerable accounting background and skill to set up and use these programs. You are far better off leaving all of this work to your accountant.

**RECOM-
MENDED
RESOURCE!**
You can buy a very useful collection of ready-made business letters from Quicken very inexpensively. If you are inexperienced in business correspondence these can be very helpful to you and can save you a lot of valuable time.

These comprehensive programs have a drawback. They are all-or-nothing packages. You cannot easily use part of them without using all of them. You will want to buy one of the *s*impler programs, like Quicken or Quickbooks. If you decide against this, then I recommend one of the *modular programs*. These programs permit you to purchase a certain portion of the overall package and utilize it independently. You can then add further modules if and when you need them. To begin with, you will probably need only the *accounts receivable* module. This will enable you to keep up with the greater part of your record-keeping chores, such as billing and collecting. Your accountant-bookkeeper will do the rest. I once tried to shift over and do all of my own accounting on my computer. It was a disaster. I simply was not well enough informed in accounting practices and procedures to do it properly, and it took an enormous amount of time at the computer. I gained a new respect for my accountant's staff and marveled that he was able to provide his services to me so cheaply.

Organization: Sole Proprietorship or Corporation

You will hear a good deal of discussion about company organization. Is a sole proprietorship best? Should you incorporate? I prefer the corporate structure for several reasons, all of which I believe to be sound. It is true that under today's tax laws incorporation will not save you money; indeed, it may cost a little more because of the increased accounting costs. But it can be very useful in other ways. Above all, the corporate structure will protect your personal assets in the unlikely chance that things go awry, either financially or legally.

Publishers are more open to lawsuits than many other businesses are. You publish materials about other people, their lives, and their businesses. You could find yourself looking down the muzzle of a very unwelcome lawsuit. This is not common. I have never, in all my years in this business, been sued for any reason, and I don't know many who have. In all likelihood your own common sense will keep you miles away from any lawsuit, too. But in the remote event that you were brought into court, and you lost, only corporate assets would be at risk.

In the financial realm, it is true that no bank is likely to lend money to your corporation without your personal guarantee. But your suppliers—printers, color separation houses, and others—will do work for your corporation and bill the corporation. In the event of bankruptcy, such creditors can obtain liens on your corporate assets. Your personal property, however, would not be in danger.

The corporate structure is more easily marketed, should the time come when you wish to sell your business. As a "subchapter S" corporation, you can avoid most of the double taxation snares of regular corporations. Your accountant will guide you through all these details.

Your Management Team

You will want to locate an accountant and an attorney with whom you can work and feel comfortable. Consult them, and especially the accountant, early in the organizational process. A friend of mine, a CPA who specializes in business start-ups and funding, has a favorite saying. "If you want me in at the landing," he tells entrepreneurs, "then get me in at the takeoff."

There is some good sense in this. Many of the first decisions you make will affect the way you do business over the long haul, and you want to make the right ones. You do not need to seek out the most expensive people in town, just good, competent professionals who take an interest in your needs. Shop around. An initial interview costs nothing. Ask what the rates are and what services are provided. Get a feel for the personalities involved. Can you work with this person? Keep looking until the answer you give yourself is "Yes, certainly."

I do not advise you to keep your books yourself, nor should you prepare your own quarterly and year-end tax returns. Accountants have bookkeepers on staff who can handle these matters for you at very reasonable hourly rates. Utilizing an accountant's staff for such routine matters can save you the cost of a staff person during your start-up phase. And when income tax time comes around your accountant will have everything in order and spend much less time doing your return than would otherwise be required. In addition, if you are like many of us, failure to use an accountant or his bookkeeper will probably result in the levy of at least some fines against you because of the late filing of required tax reports. It takes a special mind to keep up with these things. I confess that my own is not one of them.

The attorney will be less necessary in the beginning, unless you decide to incorporate. In that case, although you can do the necessary paperwork yourself, an attorney can be called in to help. Thereafter, he will take on the responsibility of keeping your all-important corporate minute book up-to-date and in compliance with the law. In my state it costs anywhere from $400 to $500 to incorporate. I paid a lawyer the first time I formed a corporation and thereafter did it myself, paying only the $50 fee required by the North Carolina Department of State. If this is your first time around, and if you do not have a clear understanding of the legal requirements of incorporation, you should certainly use an attorney.

Management Know-How

As you progress in your publishing business you will learn more and more about business management. Success or failure in business is as much a result of effective management as it is the result of a good product. Even the best product can bite the dust if management (in this case, you) doesn't do its job.

You will read constantly. There are a number of good books out on small business management. Titles, authors, and publishing companies of some that I can recommend are given in the back of this book. You will attend seminars that look useful to you. My first full-time business venture was the publication of a weekly newspaper. For several months I went to every seminar on newspaper management, advertising sales, and page design that I could find and fit into my schedule. I might sit all day long in one of these sessions and glean just a single new idea. But often this idea made a major difference in the way I ran my newspaper and greatly enhanced its profitability.

Let me be more specific and tell you a few of the most important things I have learned about management over the years.

Develop a Business Plan

The first item you should generate on your new computer, if you haven't already done so, is a business plan for your desktop publishing company. This plan will be your point of reference, your road map to success.

Spend some time on your plan. Write it carefully. Be realistic. Don't be afraid to set challenging goals for yourself, but bear in mind that you've got to get there from here. The plan will detail both desired accomplishments and plans for achieving them. Review the plan with your accountant and other trusted advisors. Pay attention to any concrete and specific difficulties they may notice, but don't let them throw cold water on your plans either. Your accountant is not the entrepreneur. You are.

When you're satisfied with your plan, take it down to the nearest quick copy shop and have it duplicated and spiral bound. Your banker may need a copy—and definitely will, if you seek a loan of any kind for your business—and so may others with whom you will work. Remember, too, that no business plan is written in stone, including yours. It exists to guide you, not to hamper you. As early as six months into your business, you may well glimpse new opportunities, rule out ideas that now seem less profitable, set new financial projections, and make other basic changes. If these changes grow out of experience in your business and not out of mere vacillation, simply call up your business plan file on your computer, amend it, and print out new copies. Here are the basic items that I include in my own mini-business plans.

- *Define the concept.* Tell precisely what your business is and what you will do.
- *Outline the qualifications of the principals.* Here's where you tell about yourself. Put down on paper those elements of your background, education, and experience that support you in starting your business.
- *Define your market position.* Analyze the market for your goods or services. Name and analyze the competition, if any. Specify how you will position yourself in the market so as to capture your share of the business.
- *Outline marketing strategies*—the ways in which you will seek and obtain business.
- *Prepare a pro-forma.* The pro-forma is your detailed projection of income and expenses. Most business plans do a pro-forma for at least three successive years. Obviously, the pro-forma is not expected to be absolutely accurate, but it does represent your best guess concerning the financial progress of your firm.

In all of these areas be simple and direct. Do not worry if you don't feel comfortable with what you turn out. Do the best you can. Six months from now you will know a great deal more, and your plan can be revised.

The Importance of Schedules

Work out reasonable schedules for yourself and then stick to them. For publishers, time is money. If you publish a magazine twice yearly you will make twice as much money as you would if you published it only once. It is very easy, especially if you are working at another job, to let your schedule slip. You go a week over in closing advertising sales. You give yourself an extra weekend to get an article in. The photos come in a week or two late. Consequently, you lose your place in line at the printer's and publication is six weeks or more behind schedule before you know it.

Not only do you lose credibility with your clients and customers when you are late, you sabotage your own bank account. It does not take a mathematical genius to understand that if you make $15,000 in three months you are earning at the rate of $5,000 a month. If your schedule slips and it takes you four months instead of three to get your magazine out, your personal earnings fall to $3,750 a month. You have given yourself a nifty cut in take-home pay. Was that weekend off worth it?

In setting a schedule, always work backward. Decide when you want the completed project in hand. Then work out a plan to finish on time.

Hitting (and Surviving) the Wall

You hear long distance runners talk about the "hitting the wall." They will be running well, they say, over quite long distances. Then, suddenly, they feel that they can't go on, that they have reached the limit of their endurance and they can't continue a step farther. At this point some give up and drop out. But the real winners, those who have and reach their goals, understand about the wall. They know that if they continue on, stride by stride, and do not give in to the strain, they will pass through the wall, tap into unexpected reserves of energy and strength, and carry the race through to its conclusion.

In business, too, we often hit the wall. Things are going well, according to plan. Suddenly, difficulties arise. You can't meet a deadline, ad sales just don't develop, the hoped-for contract doesn't come through. You feel so overworked and worried that you are tempted to say the heck with it and throw in the towel. This often happens just when your business seems on the verge of real and substantial success. It is a critical moment. If you will persevere in following your plan—writing the next page, selling the next ad, making the next presentation—you can break through. The wall is gone and there's smooth sailing ahead. Often your base of satisfied customers will carry you through. At other times, a new idea or opportunity will suddenly surface and come to your aid.

Very often, if you keep on keeping on, you will break through the wall. You never know just when or where your next great success is going to come from. After all, you can only see as far as the horizon. But when you reach that point there is always a new horizon, one that becomes visible only as you tough it out and continue—at whatever the cost in effort and dogged determination—to make forward progress toward it.

3

Preliminary Money Matters

Rich in ideas but low in capital? You may be better off than you think. You can get into the publishing business on a shoestring. After I had assembled my basic equipment, I often had nothing more to invest in a new project than my ego and my time. I worked hard to make publishing time and brain intensive rather than money intensive. The only real equity I invested in most of my projects was sweat equity, and most often that was enough. You've certainly got every bit as much of it as I have.

The up-front cash layout for the start-up publisher is the lowest of any business I know. Yet the profit potential can be far greater than that of most businesses. Anyone who can beg, buy, borrow, or lease a good personal computer, a laser printer, and a few odds and ends of peripheral hardware and software, can set up as a publisher. Combine these basic tools with enough imagination and ambition and there's no limit to what you can accomplish.

Don't Spend Too Much

Limited funds? Great! Flat wallets can actually bring some very real benefits into your publishing ventures. I advise you not to spend too much, even if you have it. It can be bad for business, just as a diet overly rich in sugar and fat can be bad for the heart and the circulation. Obviously, anyone with deep pockets can spend enormous amounts of money starting any business, and I often see people do precisely that. Although it sometimes works, it is often a mistake. Even the biggest publishing companies on the scene today had modest beginnings. Dick Simon and Max Schuster got Simon & Schuster Publishing Co. underway when they brought out a series of inexpensive crossword puzzle books. They then expanded the business with the cash flow that this early project generated.

A limited bank account, far from causing concern, can be a positive advantage. When cash is scarce you get the most out of every dime and dollar. You plan carefully. You find ways to pay writers after publication, to get printing ten or twenty percent cheaper, to use the family car for business rather than that fancy new van you have your eye on, to do the billing on the kitchen table rather than in an office suite you really can't afford.

Maybe you have just $500 in the bank for your start-up and not $50,000. Don't worry about it; revel in it. Run a tight ship. Stretch your resources to the very limit. Such financial discipline can produce a sound working base: a business built on what is good and necessary, rather than on what is wasteful and strictly for show.

Many a new business has needlessly failed because the principal (or principals) couldn't resist driving that "image-building" Mercedes and filling closets with $500 suits and fancy Italian shoes. They bought mahogany desks and conference tables when a homemade table would have done just as well.

On Resisting Temptation

Some years ago I was involved in a start-up of my own. Apple Computer had just reduced prices and come out with a new line of products (a development which is becoming disgustingly familiar to all of us who buy and use computers), all of which I loved. I could have paid out $5,000 and had the computer of my dreams. Instead, because I simply didn't have enough cash on hand to do that, I bought a lowly Mac Classic. As it turned out, the Classic was quite powerful in itself, and I wrote, typeset and designed five books on it in two years' time. I turned out work for others, including top-of-the-line, four color capabilities brochures and direct mail packages. After a week or two I was totally acclimated to the small Mac Classic screen and seldom even gave a thought to what I had *not* been able to buy. I was too busy making money with the computer I had. The Mac Classic, it turned out, was all I really needed at that time. It cost $1,000. The $4,000 difference between the computer I wanted but did not really need and the little workhorse I actually bought was put into building my business. In addition, I had no monthly payments hanging over my head to keep me awake at night.

The same things are true for your copying machine, your fax, your furniture, your car—even the pictures on the wall. Limited resources wisely spent will buy (or lease) what you need. And they will prevent you from wasting valuable cash resources on things you don't need.

Why Big Is Not Always Better

It is also true that big is not necessarily better. I learned this while publishing real estate guides in a large southern state. I started out with three of them, and I was taking home about $50,000 a year from this activity. I kept adding more guides and taking in more money. I was also meeting higher payroll and printing bills and coping with vastly more difficult management problems—and I was still taking home just $50,000 a year.

I would wake up in a cold sweat in the middle of the night praying that my ad revenues in a very distant city, from a publication I had necessarily put into the hands of someone else to manage, would equal or surpass the five-digit printing bill that was coming due. I had to let many other opportunities pass me by. I had successfully expanded to the point where I grew unhappy with my business, and when a willing buyer came along and offered me a substantial profit I was only too happy to sell out.

This kind of thing is just not necessary. Don't create an empire unless you're a natural-born emperor. Just create a profitable enterprise. There is a certain healthy joy in a lean, small, profitable business. You can play the niche markets and build one of your own. Remember, success is not measured by the amount of money that flows *through* your pockets or your bank account, but by how much actually *sticks there* for you to use as you see fit.

Where the Money Comes From

How do you generate revenues for your publishing business? These come from three sources:

- Product sales
- Advertising sales
- The sale of services

If you are a book publisher, for instance, your income is primarily *product-based*. You publish a book that costs you $1.50 to produce and sell it for $18.95. After paying your printing bill and giving the necessary wholesaler and bookstore discounts you hope to retain at least 40% (on the average) of the retail price as gross profit.

If you publish a newspaper, magazine, or any type of guidebook, your income is chiefly derived from *advertising sales*. You send out a sales rep to sell advertising to businesses who believe that they can earn a profit from the exposure they will get in the pages of your publication.

You may or may not charge for the publication itself. Most small publishers do not do so unless they have heavy mailing costs, as in the publication of a magazine of state-wide circulation. Very little, if any, net profits are generated from direct sales of the publication itself. The profit comes almost exclusively from the sale of advertising.

Considerable income can be generated by the *sale of services*. In magazine publishing, for instance, the client may be charged back for advertising design and layout. Sometimes a client with whom you do business will ask you to design a brochure, a direct mail flyer or even a product catalog. Your advertising salespeople will often encounter such needs and bring home requests for quotations from their customers. You can handle such an assignment with the equipment you have on hand. Such service-based revenues can constitute an important secondary profit center for your company.

Cash Flow Strategies for the Small Publisher

When you're trying to start a business with no money down, cash flow becomes a major challenge. After all, you will have to spend some money before your first publication comes out. But where will it come from? How do you pay the suppliers, free-lancers and others who must do work for you when you still have not cranked up a flow of money coming in? Since I often faced such problems, I have developed various strategies for dealing with them.

RECOMMENDED RESOURCE

You can't operate your business without careful record-keeping. In fact, the law requires that you do so. Bernard Kamaroff's *Small-Time Operator* will give you the bookkeeping basics—in clear and easy-to-understand language.

You will, of course, do everything you can yourself. In addition you will keep a sharp eye on expenses. Do not order expensive stationery. Your laser printer will turn out excellent letterheads. All you have to do is to buy the blank paper, and if you shop around for that at paper wholesalers or at discount office supply houses, you can get hold of it very cheaply. You can buy envelopes at $3.50 for 500 at WalMart or similar stores. Invoices are generated by your bargain basement accounting program. Envelopes, again, are addressed and generated by your computer and laser printer. Sign up with Carlson Craft or one of the other business card printers to the trade, and get your business cards at half of retail or less. By working at home you eliminate business-related rent, telephone, and utility charges. Still, even after doing everything you possibly can to limit expenses, sooner or later you will have to pay out some funds to people who provide services for you.

Four Functions of Publication Management

What services will you pay for? In any publishing company there are four main functions (or jobs) to tend to. These are:

1. The management function
2. The editorial function
3. The production function
4. The sales function

Fortunately, you do not need a separate person to handle each of these functions. I have often done all of them by myself, and doubtless there will be such times for you. Realistically, though, when the business gets going and the work begins to pile up, you will certainly need some help.

The actual demands of these four functions vary from project to project. The editorial function consists of writing, editing and proofing. The production function consists in typesetting, design and production. The sales function sells ads for periodicals or sends out the books for review, contacts bookstores, sells subsidiary rights, etc. The management function sees to it that all the other functions get done in such a way as to make a profit.

You, as owner of the publishing company, will bring your own bundle of talents and skills to your projects and pay others to provide those that you lack. I am good at writing and editing, and I can easily do typesetting, design and production. As the publisher of a struggling weekly newspaper I quite literally had to do everything to survive the first lean months. When the printing was done I still did not go home. I bundled newspapers, stuck mailing labels on them and delivered them to the post office. Then I made the rounds of the racks, put fresh papers in and collected the quarters from the coin containers. (Lest you consider this work too demanding and demeaning I hasten to add that I paid myself a quite livable salary, and sold the paper after three years for a $200,000 profit.)

If you are good at writing but a dud at sales, you can hire someone to go out and sell advertising. If you are terrific at sales but not so hot at the editorial part of it, you hire someone to do the writing for you. You will certainly exercise the management function yourself and probably the production (exclusive of printing) as well.

Nine Ways to Generate Up-Front Cash

In my own publishing activities I have found that there are several effective ways to generate upfront cash:

1. I send an invoice as soon as an advertising contract is signed. The amount shown on the invoice is not strictly due and payable until my publication actually appears, and my invoice makes this clear. But many of those who receive it, especially the larger businesses who routinely put such billings in the hopper for action, will pay on receipt.
2. Further, I offer a two-percent discount to advertisers who pay within 15 days of the invoice date. Many large businesses routinely take advantage of such discounts.
3. I offer a five-percent discount to small advertisers who will pay on the signing of the contract.
4. On agreements for the sale of services, such as designing and producing a book, a brochure, a direct mail piece, a product catalogue, or some other such project, I require one third of the agreed contract price on the signing of the contract, one third on approval of preliminary proofs

(galley proofs), and one third on approval of final proofs (page proofs).

5. My agreement with those who sell advertising for me specifies that no payment of commissions will be made until the invoice is paid. This arrangement encourages salespeople to try to get a check on the signing of the contract. Often just asking for the check is enough. A surprisingly large number of advertisers will pay in advance if asked to do so.

6. In book publishing, I try to sell a large number of books through prepublication and direct mail promotions. Often, the revenues from these campaigns are sufficient to pay all production expenses and overhead.

7. I work hard to sell advance subsidiary rights to books: book club rights, reprint rights, translation rights, and any other rights I can.

8. In some publications (a county history, for instance), I contract with a local bank or industry to provide a "collector's" version of the first edition, along with a preface by the CEO of that institution, for use as a promotional and public relations tool. I once sold an entire edition in this way to the president of the R. J. Reynolds Tobacco Company.

9. In such a book, I will also sell full page ads to the larger business concerns in the community.

All of these and similar ideas are discussed in detail in the pages that follow. For the moment, I just want to assure you that it is, indeed, quite possible to generate the income you need and do real, substantial business on a pay-as-you-go basis.

Publisher's Perks

Publisher's perks are hardly a part of the central financial management of your home-based publishing company, but they are very pleasant benefits nevertheless. Small publishers do not benefit from any tax breaks not available to the business community in general, but due to the nature of the business, publishers are able to use these laws in very flexible and interesting ways. No single one of these benefits is substantial when taken alone, but taken together they constitute a welcome cluster of tax-sheltered earnings.

When you work at home you do not increase your mortgage payment or rent. You work out of the same space as you lived in before, but now a percentage of the cost of that mortgage has become a deductible business expense. You can write off a portion of the rent proportional to the floor space that you use exclusively for business purposes. And you shelter not only the mortgage payment itself, but the same percent of the insurance, property taxes, utilities, and the many other expenses associated with home ownership. You may even take depreciation on this part of your home, although it may not be desirable to do so, since such a deduction will have tax consequences when and if you sell your home. You should check all these matters out with your accountant to see precisely how they will affect you.

In addition, your business can own your automobile and buy your health insurance and even life insurance, insofar as the latter is purchased to protect your business from creditors and other risks in the event of your death. I find that leasing an automobile in the name of my business works best. I pay all auto-related expenses directly from my business account, and simply keep careful records of personal use of the business vehicle, if any, to report on my personal tax return. There is very little travel that you will do that cannot be turned, at least in part, into a business expense. Your interests as a publisher are more general than those of the owners of most other businesses. No matter where you go or what you do, if you survey the products of other publishers, meet with them, look for ideas and ways to better produce your publishing products, then a portion of the trip is deductible.

Other Perks

Other delightful perks come from freebies and barter. When I published *NCEast*, a regional magazine for Eastern North Carolina, I wrote the restaurant reviews and the entertainment and travel columns. When I vacationed on the Outer Banks, for instance, I would call ahead, inform various restaurateurs that I would be on the Banks sampling restaurants for review, and ask them what their policy was. I also shared with them my own policy. My magazine was not in the business of trashing restaurants, I pointed out. It was, instead, promotional. (The magazine was founded with the sponsorship of seven chambers of commerce). If I went to an eatery with clumsy waiters and appetizers apparently made from last month's oysters, I simply did not write about it. On the other hand, when I liked a place I would praise it in the warmest terms and advise my readers to go there and try it for themselves. The result: some very fine complimentary dinners for me and my wife, and a vacation that cost me much less than it otherwise would have. I will add that I am always scrupulous in delivering the publicity that I promise. Many tourist attractions have PR offices with standing orders to accommodate visiting journalists with passes. This is true of the Six Flags and Busch Gardens-type amusement parks. It is also true of Disney World in Orlando, Florida.

The Barter System: The Joys of "Trading Out"

Much more important than the freebies, however, and perhaps even than the tax advantages, is the barter system that will be open to you as a publisher who sells advertising.

How does it work? Let's say that you are publishing a magazine or a weekly shopper in a medium-sized town. Naturally you are going to approach every possible advertising prospect and try to convince them that advertising in your publication will give them profit-producing exposure. With many of these prospects you will be able to conclude normal sales agreements. In other cases, however, your prospects will tell you that they simply can't afford to advertise, no matter how much they would like to. They just don't have the cash.

In such cases you or your sales representative may suggest a "trade-out." You will give the client the advertising space they need. In return you will take a credit at their place of business. At a restaurant you will simply eat out until the credit is depleted. At a motel you will use the credit to provide accommodations for business or personal travel. I once had a large credit at a local motel that I was finding it hard to utilize until my daughter got married and I had to find beds for dozens of out-of-town guests. The trade-out in this case was quite a boon to me.

During one serious downturn in automobile sales, our local Ford dealer was growing desperate. He was paying out large sums in interest for the unsold cars he had on hand and very little cash was coming back in the front door. Yet he needed to run large, relatively expensive ads in my weekly newspaper. I suggested a strategy that would help. My newspaper needed a station wagon, but we did not have the cash on hand for an adequate down payment. The Ford dealer, I explained, could trade out a $4,000 down payment against advertising lineage in my paper. He agreed to this arrangement. He got the advertising he needed while hanging on to his precious supply of cash. I got my station wagon while hanging on to my own precious supply of cash. Furthermore, I was publishing my newspaper anyway. The dealer would not have been able to advertise otherwise. It cost me absolutely nothing to run his ad. My printing cost was the same with or without it.

If you publish a regional magazine, then resort trade-outs can be used for sales incentives (a free weekend at the beach if you reach your goal this month), for client relations and for executive vacations. I have also benefited from trade-outs with bookstores, dry cleaners, office supply houses and many other types of business.

The key, of course, is to trade out only when you do not expect to sell advertising under a normal sales agreement or when you expect only a small ad on a pay-for-space basis and can barter for a much larger one.

4

Looking Before You Leap: How to Do a Preliminary Market Analysis

Success in any publishing project can never be guaranteed, but it can become much more probable when it is based on the hard facts that you will glean from a preliminary market analysis. A market analysis asks and answers the most basic questions, and it does so right at the outset. Among these questions are the following:

- Is there a need for your publication?
- Does a market for the advertising space it contains (a magazine or newspaper) or the information it offers (a book) actually exist?
- Is the advertising base large enough?
- Can potential advertisers afford the prices you will have to charge for space?
- Can you make money at prices that they can afford to pay?
- Is there an adequate demographic base? Are there enough people who will read your periodical and buy the goods advertised in it?
- Can you get your publication into the hands of these people?
- If others are already in the market, is there room for you, too?

The answers that you get to such fundamental questions are as important to you as a map would be to a prospector looking for a hidden gold mine. The prospector is sure that the gold is there, and that it can be his. He can feel it in his bones. But to go directly to the spot marked X, he will need a map. He may simply stumble on his objective, true, but the odds against this happening before his bacon and beans run out and his burro dies of old age are remote indeed. The market analysis you will undertake is your treasure map. But how do you do a market analysis? Isn't the process ruinously expensive? Can the small publisher do his or her own? If so, how does one begin?

How to Do a Market Analysis
Big corporations routinely spend hundreds of thousands of dollars—even

millions—on market analyses before introducing a new product. Whole teams of researchers focus on a product, samples are given out nationwide, questionnaires are prepared, cross-sections of the population are polled, results tabulated.

Fortunately, it will not be necessary for you to spend those big bucks. You can do a thoroughly satisfactory market analysis for a niche market publication—especially a locally circulated one—with the expenditure of just a few hundred dollars, and often with no expenditure at all. Your chief tools will be:

- The yellow pages of your telephone book.
- Conversations with a cross section of potential advertisers, especially with friends and acquaintances in the field who will answer your questions frankly.
- Inquiries directed toward professional or trade organizations in the field, when they exist. Your local Board of Realtors, your Home-Builders Association or your Apartment Association are such organizations.
- The mastheads of competing publications.
- The media kits of competing publications.
- The business calendar.
- Economic activity and forecasts in the field in which you wish to publish.

Importing an Idea That Seems to Work in Other Places:

If you live in a community where a type of publication that you *know to be successful elsewhere* does not exist, you may well have a profitable publishing opportunity on your hands.

Possibly, but not necessarily. There are still important questions to ask and answer. You have an initial market analysis to do.

- First, ask yourself why this market niche is open in the town where you live or where you wish to publish. Is there some factor that you have overlooked that would make the publication a difficult one to promote and make successful?
- Look closely at your model publication. Is it really as successful as it seems? Is anybody really making any money? You can get a line on this by calling its larger advertisers. Say that you are considering advertising in the publication. Ask them if it comes out on time; if service is good; if ad rates have increased in past months, etc.
- How many potential advertisers does this publication have? You can calculate this figure roughly by studying the yellow pages and counting the businesses that could benefit from advertising in it.

- How many *actual* advertisers does the model have?
- What percentage of the potential market does the publication convert to regular advertising orders? You can get this number by calculating the average number of ads in a run of three successive issues and dividing this number by the number of potential advertisers that you have calculated.
- Send for the media kit (see below) of this publication. Find out how much ads cost. Calculate maximum possible revenues from each issue. Discount this figure by 15% to allow for discounts and special deals. Now subtract the cost of printing and the cost of sales. The sales cost, in total, will run approximately 20% of gross. The resulting figure is your model publication's gross profit before overhead and taxes. Does this figure seem to be a profitable one to you?
- Now that you know how much money the model publication is making, ask yourself whether it would be a profitable use of your resources to start a similar publication.
- Look at your own projected market. How many potential customers are available to you? It's back to the yellow pages again.
- Can you make a profit if you sell the same percentage of your customer base as your model publication does?
- Has anyone in the past attempted a similar publication? If so, why is it no longer published? If not, why has the market been overlooked? There may be factors present that you are unaware of.
- Once you have counted the number of potential customers (in a niche market this is always an identifiable number), calculate roughly what it will cost you to sell the advertising and produce and distribute your publication. This figure will constitute your out-of-pocket costs.
- Next, add to this base figure the minimum gross profit that will give you a return adequate to pay you for your time and effort. This total figure is the amount of advertising you must sell. In the beginning, even if your project is well-conceived and marketed, you will probably not sell more than 20% of your potential customers. How much will you have to charge each of them to reach your minimum goal? Is this a realistic figure? (If your project is a strong one, and the niche market really does exist, you will sell a greater and greater percentage of available customers and thus increase your profits as you go.)

Start-up entrepreneurs, however, generally do not have the capital to finance a losing business until it is able to cross the line, in some more or less distant future, into profitability. I certainly didn't. And even if, for whatever fortuitous reason, the capital is there, would it be wise to risk it in this way? My own inflexible, absolutely rigid rule of conduct is never to go into an enterprise that will not break even or make a modest profit from the very first issue. Relax this guideline and you deal in hope, not reality. I will add that I have never been at a loss for projects that fit my rule. Whenever I have deviated from it (usually because I had money in the bank from some other successful publication and so felt that I could "afford the risk"), I have been sorry that I did so.

Develop a worst-case scenario. Underestimate your potential ad sales. If you can still break even and make a small profit, go ahead. You can then build gradually to more acceptable levels.

Market Analysis Where There Are Competing Publications in the Trade Area

When you are out fishing and not pulling much in over the side of your boat, you scan the horizon. Way off to the east you spot another fisherman who just can't seem get his hook baited fast enough. Spanish mackerel, sea trout, grouper... he's pulling them in right and left. So what do you do? Do you sigh, reel in your line, and conclude that the other guy has cornered the market in fish? No, you crank up your outboard, position yourself as close as you can to where the other guy is, and begin pulling them in yourself.

In the same way, the presence of a competitor in the market is not necessarily bad news. It can mean that the market is an active one—that there are plenty of financial fish out there for everyone. Probably.

To find out for certain, do a market analysis. If your market analysis can convert this probability into a near certainty, then it may well be worth the risk of dropping your publishing line into those same waters.

Marketing specialists, for instance, tell us that the wise entrepreneur entering the mail order field will not invent a new product. He will survey the market to see what is selling for others, regularly, over a long period of time, and develop a strategy for selling the same thing himself. He will do everything he can to put a new spin on his advertising, offering new benefits to his customer and melding new qualities into his product. But essentially he will have discovered:

- That there is a certain product that sells to a broad base of customers,
- That it can be sold by mail, and
- That if the next guy can sell it, he can too.

It is your market analysis that will tell the story. In carrying out this analysis with respect to competitors already in the trade area, ask and answer the following questions:

- Does the competitor own a newspaper, printing press, or possess some other material advantage that will allow him to print and circulate his product much more efficiently and cheaply than you can?
- Does he have any other built-in advantages that you will not have?
- What advantages do you have that your competitor does not have?
- Can you convert your advantages into better service and more afford-able prices so as to be more attractive to potential customers?
- Has your competitor saturated the market to the degree that every customer you get will have to be taken away from him? This may be difficult to do unless you offer very strong and competitive benefits to the advertisers.
- Is there a large enough customer base so that you can, through strong selling and market positioning, create additional clients?
- Does the competition's media kit reveal to you enough about their operation so that you can develop an effective and competitive market position for your own product?
- Can you price your product so that you can be modestly profitable—or at least operate at break-even—from day one?

Market Analysis for Books

So far we have been talking about publishing projects that make their money primarily through the sale of advertising. But what of books? Aren't books profitable, too? Can't the home-based publisher make money publishing books as well?

Yes, he certainly can. Often one or the other of your activities—advertising-based periodical publishing or product-based book publishing—will constitute a primary profit center and the other a secondary profit center. While I was publishing my apartment guides in seven North Carolina cities, I also published books. I did this as time permitted, and I found book publishing to be an important source of revenue (and satisfaction) to me. Today, my new, home-based company, Venture Press, is primarily a book publisher. But I expect to develop at least one, and possibly two, secondary profit centers in advertising-based publishing. I am currently surveying the market where I am now located to see what its needs are and what niche I can identify and develop a publication to fill.

Publish for the Market

Market analysis in book publishing is much less concrete than the analysis you can do for advertising sales, but it is certainly no less important and, clearly, it can and must be done.

It is a sad but very true fact that thousands of books are published each year—especially by small publishers or self-publishers—for which there is no discernible market at all.

The publishers of such books have usually put the cart before the horse. They had a book idea that interested them. They published the book. Then, with 5,000 copies of their brainchild piled in the hall closet and stacked behind the sofa they began to think about possible markets.

Too late. Much too often, there just aren't any. Or, just as bad, any markets that may exist are so vaguely defined and untargeted that the periodical publisher has no practical way of reaching his potential readers.

Got a Book Idea? Get Answers to These Questions

To evaluate the chances for your book's success, get good, firm answers to the following questions. Each of them is important, and each of them must generate a positive response. One weak link in the chain and you risk disaster.

1. Does your book fulfill a distinct and definite need? Rule number one of home-based book publishing is this: identify a widely-felt need; then produce a strong product to satisfy that need. The front cover of my Venture Press catalog clearly proclaims the following motto: "Books that help people solve pressing problems or satisfy strongly-felt needs." As long as I live by that motto, target my readership, and produce books that deliver precisely what they promise, I will be able to sell them and make a profit. To the degree that I stray from that purpose I enter a very high-risk area indeed. The question in the mind of the potential book buyer is simply this: What will this book do for me? How will it help me change my life and reach my goals? If the buyer comes up with strong, positive answers to these questions, everything else, including price, becomes a secondary consideration. What are these basic human needs that cry out so loudly for satisfaction? The following constitute my basic list:

- People want to lead more self-fulfilling, meaningful lives.
- People want love and companionship.
- People want a strong self-image.
- People want better health and longer lives.
- People want financial security and, beyond that, wealth.
- People want sexual satisfaction.
- People want to be self-sufficient, including owning their own businesses.
- People want to understand their place in the overall scheme of things.

The more of these needs you fulfill in a single book, the greater will be the number of potential buyers who will see strong benefits in the book for them. This book, for instance, tells how to start a business that will bring personal satisfaction, provide financial security, build a strong self-image and more. It satisfies basic human needs. Yet it remains, at the same time, a highly focused book on how to start a successful publishing company while working out of your own home.

2. Is this need shared by a large enough group of readers? Never overestimate the number of people who buy and read books, even when those books might solve pressing problems for them. Be sure that your book can be profitable at the sales levels that you can realistically expect. *How to Keep Your VW Alive* had a readership that was limited to the owners of certain cars, and to the owners of the older models of those cars at that. Yet the potential readership was broad enough for the author to sell tens of thousands of books and build a very successful publishing company on the foundation of this one title. Had he written a book called *How to Regrind the Valves on Your 1949 Studebaker,* however, he might not have been so successful. Even if he had written the definitive book on the subject the potential reader base might have included only himself, his best friend and one elderly gentleman in Toledo who happened to have that very model on blocks in his backyard. Bill Henderson, founder of Pushcart Press, points out that to build a book publishing company all you need is one strong title that will sell again and again over the long haul.

3. Can you reach the people who will want to buy your book? But there is an even more fundamental question: Are the readers you target people to whom you can market your product with the means at your disposal? Your targeted readership should have either of these two make-or-break characteristics:

- Extensive, general sales potential in a limited geographical area (a picture history of a town, for instance). The local market is the easiest to reach. Personally I have had great success publishing for city, county and regional markets. In such a market you can handle all sales yourself, eliminating much of the normal sales expense.
- Extensive sales possibilities to a specific, identifiable segment of the population nationwide that you can reach through the use of specialized mailing lists or specialty retail outlets. If your book has a targeted but geographically diffuse market the problem is not so simple. Marketing will take more time and a greater investment of money in a direct mail campaign. Can you afford to reach this potential readership?

4. Can you sell your book at a price that will make it profitable for you? What will the cover price of your book have to be to produce a satisfactory profit? Fortunately, in information-intensive and how-to books, the price is keyed to the benefits the reader expects to derive from the book he is buying. So prices tend to be higher, on the average, than those of books that are bought merely for purposes of entertainment.

Still, there is a limit to what you can reasonably expect to get for your book. Will you make a profit at a price your reader is willing to pay? And even if you can, is this profit adequate to pay you for your time and effort in bringing this book out?

5

How to Publish City and Regional Magazines

City and regional magazines are very attractive projects for home-based publishers. They are especially tempting for those who, like me, went into publishing primarily because they wanted to make their living through "words and writing" (as I once told a friend) and who want to be associated with first-class magazines.

Such individuals derive a lot of their satisfaction out of the quality of their product. The money is important, of course, but the public visibility, the leading of the literary life and other intangible but personally important benefits are highly valued as well.

As editor and publisher of a "real" magazine (as distinguished from the promotional Chamber of Commerce variety) you will be courted and admired by writers and artists and be featured as speaker at many a civic club dinner. You will have a showcase for your own writing, and even begin—over time— to wield a bit of influence in molding and mobilizing opinion in your community through the articles that you publish.

As editor and publisher of a city magazine you are indeed a businessperson; the life of your magazine and your own economic well-being depend upon that. But you are also a literary person. Your magazine will publish book reviews, restaurant reviews that actually tell the truth and even an occasional short story or poem. Then, of course, there are all those personality profiles, features, interviews and maybe even a controversial piece or two.

The Magazine Publishing Facts of Life

That's the good news. The bad news is that the survival record of city and regional magazines is not reassuring. You can enhance your own chances for long-term success by studying and meticulously accepting the seven magazine publishing facts of life described below:

1. Business comes first. Some city magazine editors tend to be literary people and not business people. They may have inflated expectations of income and disregard some of the caveats and tips that I gave you when discussing preliminary money matters.

2. A city magazine can't support everybody and his brother in the style to which they would dearly love to become accustomed. When too many people have to make a living out of your magazine you create a built-in money drain that you just can't support. City magazines produce money on a gradually increasing scale. They start small and grow gradually. But even when the money does start to come in, secondary profit centers (see my chapter on that topic) are normally required to keep the ship safely afloat. These additional profit centers and the more commercial aspects of running a magazine are too often neglected through inexperience or out-and-out disinterest.

3. City magazines are more expensive and time consuming to produce than travel and tourism guides or quality of life magazines. You have to pay better writers, spend more editorial time developing attractive articles issue after issue and print a lot of expensive color photographs. There is seldom any repeat material printed issue after issue. The content of each magazine must be created anew.

4. The ads are a bit more difficult to sell, issue after issue, than the ads in some other publications. Most city magazines are published at least six times a year. Businesses that buy space in the first issue may drop out of successive issues, buy every other issue, etc. This is due to the relatively high cost of ads in your magazine. The company that places a half-page, $1000 dollar ad will pay out $12,000 a year to stay alive in a monthly magazine, $6,000 in a bimonthly and $4000 in a quarterly. Costs will be proportionately higher for the two-thirds and full page ads. Not too many advertisers in most medium-sized towns can fit that kind of expense into their ad budgets, which were established long before you and your magazine came along.

5. It takes time to get into advertising budgets, which are usually set a year in advance by the larger corporations and enterprises. Even when a local bank wishes to advertise with you, it may be several months or more before you can be worked into the budget on a regular basis. You will not face this problem with the Chamber of Commerce magazines, for instance. The funds for an ad in this publication will already have been allocated by most of those who appeared in last year's issue. All you really have to do is to call them and renew the order.

6. It is expensive to sell subscriptions to any magazine.

7. It is difficult to guarantee circulation to your advertisers when you attempt to sell, on the newsstand or to subscribers, some or all of the magazines you print. Fortunately, once you are aware of these potential problems, my experience is that you can overcome them.

My own introduction to publishing was as the editor of a regional magazine. Over the years I have started a number of them from scratch. I have found workable solutions for each of the seven problem areas listed above. These solutions will become clear as you read the remainder of this chapter.

Types of Magazine

The phrase "city and regional magazines" could be a bit more specific. There are, in fact, at least four varieties of these magazines. All of them are not suited for the entrepreneurial, home-based publisher.

- A "city magazine" focuses on the people and interests of a single metropolitan area. Such a magazine is entirely urban. This fact requires that the trade area be active and affluent enough in the business sector and also large enough to support a magazine such as yours. If publishing a city magazine is to be the main activity of your company, then you need a growing metropolitan area with a sizable number of major banks, S&L's, corporate headquarters, top-of-the-line retailers, decorators and other service providers, etc. I hasten to add that if your magazine is one of several profit centers from which your company derives income and profit, you can successfully publish in a smaller trade area. I once published a city magazine in a town of 15,000 persons. I felt that even within the limits that its economic environment imposed it would work. It was slick, but had less color than big-city versions. I could saturate the area with fewer copies. It came out annually. It produced an annual net profit of about $8,000. That is not much for a magazine that is your only enterprise, but it is a pleasant sum to earn in addition to the other profits you are bringing in.

    Will your magazine work on the scale that you have planned for it? Only a thorough market analysis will answer that question for you. Remember that only a small percentage of potential advertisers will become actual advertisers. The pool of prospects must be deep enough so that a limited number of them will be adequate to meet your advertising needs. Notice that I put advertising sales needs first. It is a great, but very common, mistake to look for a potential readership, and, finding one, to assume that will make your project a success. But it is not readers who guarantee success. It is advertising sales, and advertising sales alone that produce profit in magazine publishing. Remember these words. Put them in petit-point and hang them on your wall. Give a copy of them to everyone who works with you or for you. Great magazines have failed for lack of sufficient advertising revenues; none that I know of, however, has ever failed for lack of highbrow literary content.

- A city-county magazine covers not only a metropolitan area but also the suburban and even rural areas outside the city as well. Such a combined area makes an effective editorial format more difficult to work out, since you are trying to cater to the tastes of two different readerships. Yet, in the right circumstances, such a magazine can have a lot going for it. A city-county magazine works best when the city itself is relatively small, so that the disparity of interests between the "inside" and "outside" readers and advertisers is less than it otherwise might be. Indeed, the beauty of this dual purpose magazine is that it can make publication viable in areas where one would not have thought successful publication possible. I published my *Washington and Beaufort County Magazine* in a county that had only 49,000 inhabitants, which made it one of the least populous in the state. Yet I was able to publish this magazine annually, making a substantial 50% profit. The total sum of money involved was not enormous, and ad rates were low. But people liked the magazine and regularly advertised in it. Since it was annual it did not make serious demands on my time. Yet it contributed steadily to the gross profit margin of my publishing company. The eight thousand dollars it earned was peanuts, perhaps, in the overall scheme of things, but it was certainly not negligible.

- A multi-county regional magazine goes a step farther. It targets a readership (and an advertising base) which covers a homogeneous area of a state. Many states have such regions. In Virginia, for instance, there could be a magazine called *Northern Neck* (there may be one) or in Maryland *The Eastern Shore*. North Carolina, where I lived for many years, is divided into the mountain region to the west, the industrialized Piedmont Plateau in the central portion of the state, and the Atlantic Coastal Plain and seashore to the east. Each region has its own characteristics, cultural tastes and needs. Each constitutes a fairly well-defined trade area. I published, at various times, two magazines for eastern North Carolina, *The New East* and, some years later, *NCEast*. Both were sold at a profit after I had established them and built them up.

With each step along the road of expanded coverage, however, the publisher encounters more and more difficulty carrying off a project profitably. Remember the golden rule for the independent publisher: stick to projects that have a *well-defined readership in a limited geographical area*. The city magazine was most clearly limited. The city-county magazine, still manageable, was nevertheless made more difficult by the modest expansion of the trade area to include outlying districts.

The multi-county, regional magazine (*NCEast*, for instance) was most difficult. The regional magazines that I published, while successful, were less profitable than others with more limited coverage, and they required enormous time and attention. Selling ads was more expensive, since I had to keep salespeople on the road. Distribution was also more expensive. The trade area was so broad that it was difficult to satisfy every part of it with the editorial coverage in every issue. Advertisers kept looking for articles on their specific geographical areas and, of course, I simply could not regularly satisfy all of them. The multi-county magazine is on the far edge of the reach of the small publisher. There are usually much more profitable projects closer to hand.

- The state-wide magazine. And for the same reasons, state-wide magazines (*Texas Monthly, Tar Heel: The Magazine of North Carolina; Florida Trends*) are definitely beyond any reasonable reach for the home-based publisher. These magazines are expensive and risky. A good deal of capital is required for start-up. No longer labor-intensive, they quickly become very hungry, money-eating machines. They will take all your time and all your funds, too.

How Often Should You Publish?

Choose a city or regional magazine that you can comfortably handle, keeping in mind that it is not going to be the only enterprise that you will be involved in. Once you have made this choice, you will have to answer another question, one that is more complicated than you may think: How often will you publish your magazine?

There are three main points to consider:

- How often are you capable of bringing out a quality magazine? No fudging here, please. Don't be misled by what you want to do. Take on only what it is possible for you to do. Personally, I have never attempted a publication schedule more frequent than six times yearly. I was able to handle that schedule with the use of free-lancers and one other person on my payroll for a limited number of hours. I could have handled quarterly publication even more easily. Monthly publication, on the other hand, would have projected me into an entirely different arena. I would have had to hire an editorial assistant, a secretary, a typesetter, and an art and layout person, as well as twice as many sales representatives. There would be two or three issues in progress at any given time. This is a killing work load (probably impossible) for the one or two person firm. Forcing yourself into too-frequent publication can be damaging in another way, too. It can hamstring you, tying up your time to such a degree that you cannot do any of the other (frequently more lucrative) projects that inevitably come along. It puts all your eggs in one basket—a dangerous position for any business person to be in. And it is especially dangerous for the meagerly-capitalized home-based publisher.
- How often can your customers afford to advertise with you? There is no sure way to answer this question, but I'll wager that for many of them it will not be more often than four times yearly, unless you are in a major market like Atlanta, Dallas or Chicago. Even if they love your magazine, interior designers and other boutique businesses may simply not have

RECOMMENDED RESOURCE!

One of your early challenges will be that of designing a magazine that looks professional and that is, at the same time, very readable. Alan Hurlburt's book *The Grid* will give you an irreplaceable tool for overall design. See also Roger C. Parker's *Looking Good in Print*. Details are given in the resources section in the back of the book.

the money to appear on a more frequent schedule. Trust your most conservative instincts. Remember that ad rates in a slick magazine are necessarily high. How many people can pay them, and how frequently? It is folly to come out more frequently than your advertisers can afford.

• What is the most profitable publication schedule for you? Think carefully about this one. It is not simply a question of how much advertising you can sell in a single issue. You will have to average advertising over a twelve month period. There are a number of factors operating here. More frequent publication may increase expenses at the same time that the per-issue total of advertising revenues is shrinking because everyone can't afford to stay in all the time. The result will be a reduced margin of profit. You may even be spending more money to make less of it.

You will also have to determine whether taking on a variety of publications, of which your magazine is only one, will not in the long run bring in far more money. This is money that will stick in your bank account and not simply pass through on its way into the coffers of printers, salespeople and all the others whom you will have to pay. In the case of *Washington and Beaufort County Magazine* I found that annual publication was most profitable to me. I often thought about increasing the frequency of publication, but experiments with biannual and quarterly publication fell flat on their faces. The advertisers just couldn't afford it.

If you are in doubt, I suggest that you begin with a publication that comes out less frequently rather then more. If things go well it will be easier for you to increase frequency of publication than to decrease frequency if you discover that the advertising base just isn't there.

With a year or two of experience under your belt you will have developed the know-how that enables you to get the magazine out more easily. In addition, an increase in frequency will send a success signal to your readers and advertisers. Cutting down on frequency—going from a six times to a quarterly publication or even an annual—sends the opposite signal. Readers and advertisers will wonder, "What's going on here? Is this magazine in trouble?" And this is a reaction that you clearly do not want to encourage.

Circulation

To satisfy your advertisers you must get your magazine into the hands of the people who can and will buy their goods and services. In doing this you can't use the saturation circulation approaches that the local newspapers or television stations use. They print or broadcast messages for all kinds of advertisers and put these messages into the homes or into the hands of virtually every living person in the community. They are indifferent to demographics. They reach the wealthy, the get-by's and the penniless, across the board.

Your magazine is too expensive to enable you to do this. A newspaper costs just a few cents a copy to produce. Your magazine could cost a dollar or two per unit, depending on the paper you print on, the amount of color that you use, and the size of your print run. You must find a better way to do the job, a way that fits your product.

Target Your Readership

This need not be a drawback if you successfully target your readership. After all, a newspaper ad offering $50,000 automobiles gets results only when read by persons who can afford to buy $50,000 automobiles. The tens of thousands of copies that go to the homes of poor and middle-class families are totally wasted circulation as far as these car dealers are concerned. If the newspaper's circulation is 100,000, only two or three hundred of these readers will actually be in the market for a high-end automobile. If you can target and reach the majority of these high-income readers you will have done as good or better job for your advertiser as the mass circulation newspaper can do.

And your advertising may get even better results, for the following reasons:

- Since you target educated, affluent readers, your entire magazine will reflect this fact. The auto dealer's ad will benefit from the prestigious environment in which it is placed.
- A newspaper ad is here today and gone tomorrow. It has a life span of a single day. A television or radio ad is even more ephemeral. It is nothing more than an electrical impulse on its way to the planet Jupiter just seconds after it is broadcast. Your magazine, on the other hand, has a life span of two months, three months or even a year. It is read in library reading rooms, at newsstands, on airplanes, in lobbies, day after day and week after week. It goes on selling as long as the issue is current, and

even after. Such magazines are often not thrown away but kept for later reference. And at each perusal your advertiser's message comes to life again in the reader's mind.

- The people who pick up the magazine are those who are intrigued by the cover art and the editorial slant. And these are precisely the people who have the discretionary income to spend money buying the advertisers' products and services.
- Magazines are great image builders among the people whose opinion counts: your targeted readership of individuals with discretionary income.

Each of these observations is a strong selling point that you and your ad reps must define, elaborate on, utilize and adapt endlessly.

Free Circulation

There are two categories of circulation in the periodical publishing business: free circulation and paid circulation. As a city/regional magazine publisher you will utilize each of them.

Free circulation refers to those copies of a magazine or other periodical simply left available for anyone to pick up free of charge or mailed free of charge to the inhabitants of a town or neighborhood. The apartment guide magazines described in a later chapter were free circulation, for instance. Magazines are left in places where qualified individuals will see them and pick them up.

The list of free circulation outlets is quite wide for apartment guides. For city magazines it will be far less so, but still broad enough. Some important opportunities for free circulation of your expensive city magazines are the following:

- First class lounges and frequent flyer lounges of airports. Airlines have such lounges at many major airports.
- Seat-back status for your magazine on commuter airlines and charter airlines. This is not easily achieved, but perhaps you can smooth the way by trading out free advertising for the commuter airline in exchange for the seat-back circulation privilege that you desire. You can place a full-page ad for the commuter airline at no charge with the understanding that your magazine will be placed in a readily available spot in the passenger sections of its airplanes.

I have always tried to work out these arrangements and have sometimes succeeded. It is always worth the effort; airline seat-back status is a powerful selling point for your advertising salespeople. This sales pitch can actually set you in a class apart. (If the airline does not have a seat-back magazine of its own, why not offer to design and publish one for them? Always keep in mind those secondary profit center opportunities.)

Here are more opportunities for targeted, free circulation that sells ads:

- Newcomer kits from banks, chambers of commerce, county economic development offices and major employers. You can easily get your magazine in many such kits, which are mailed out to people who are moving into your trade area. Simply furnish free copies to the institutions that send the kits out.

- Mailing lists that you assemble of key individuals, political leaders, community leaders and opinion molders. In the beginning, especially, you want everyone who is anyone to see, hold, feel, and, with luck, actually read your magazine. You can do this by assembling a mailing list of individuals who, in your opinion, will constitute a valuable reader base for you. Readers will be in a position to create great word-of-mouth interest. Many of them will also be in a position to buy ads somewhere down the road. Who will be on your VIP mailing list? Be sure to include publishers and appropriate editors of newspapers; news directors and key reporters of TV stations; heads of programming at all radio stations; leading members of the Chamber of Commerce; CEO's in your trade area and their marketing executives; civic leaders.

- Collect the names of leaders among the membership of organizations like the Board of Realtors, Bar Association and other professional groups. Include also service-related social clubs, such as the Junior League, Arts Guild, Opera Association, etc. Include heads of civic clubs. Contact program chairpersons and offer to give luncheon talks. On such occasions always distribute cards which one may fill out to receive a free subscription. Let the audience know that there is a subscription price and that the price is, say, $18 per year, but that they can receive an introductory year free of charge by filling out the card. The card will have a space for a business address, type of business etc. In giving away subscriptions remember that you are building the worth of your magazine, enhancing its image and increasing sales. It is a given that you will be making your money on advertising, not subscription sales. You can offer a deal to convert some of your free circulation subscriptions to paid status at the end of a year. It is essential that your advertising rep be able to say, "This magazine will be in the hands of every artistic, media, business and political leader in this community. It is read and talked about. Your ad will be seen by the people with the money to buy your product."

Paid Circulation

At the same time, though, you will be selling all the subscriptions you can. Even though the bulk of your revenues will come from advertising sales there is no need to completely overlook the potential dollars to be gleaned from paying subscribers.

But how do you get those subscribers? Do not buy a mailing list and send a mail order solicitation to all the names that you have gathered. As a small, start-up publisher you can't afford this approach. Its down-the-road payoff is years away, when renewals come in. Those unfamiliar with mail order often have a very unrealistic notion of the return that a mail-out will produce. The average of a successful direct mail promotion will be a 1% return. A mailing to 5,000 names, then, will cost about $300 for onetime use of the mailing list, $900 for postage. On top of that will be the cost of design and printing. A 1% return will net 50 subscribers. The cost of your mail out was, say $1,800. Fifty subscribers (less 5% no-pays, about average for magazine subs) will bring in $855. This represents a loss of just under $1,000. Unless you have a great deal of money and have no other ways to garner subscribers this is obviously not the way to go. But what else can you do? Fortunately, you can do plenty:

- Promote subscription sales as a fund raiser. Schools, clubs, children's groups and a great many other organizations will sell subscriptions as a fund raiser. You supply the sales materials. They supply the prospects and leg work. Since your magazine is one that is community-oriented, each salesperson will have little difficulty placing two or three subscriptions with family and friends. Promotions should be on-going. Stay alert for possibilities. When you read that the junior high school band needs new instruments or new uniforms, call them. They can earn a good deal of the needed funds selling your magazine. Rules of the game? Offer a discount to the subscriber to make a "yes" decision easier; give very generous commissions (up to half or more of the proceeds) to the salespeople or selling organizations; and always have your sales people collect the subscription fee. (When utilizing adult groups you can make Mastercard or Visa payments possible, if you have them available.) When it comes time for renewals you can have these individuals do the contacting again, for a lesser commission, or you can bypass them and do it all yourself.
- Recruit a crew for telephone solicitations. Retired women with lots of friends make excellent telephone salespersons. Those who are outgoing and who enjoy and approve of the magazine will get a real kick out of it. Give such people a title that will please them. Ask the more active ones to recruit others; then pay each of them an override on the sales of her personal sales group. Make a subscription sales agreement with as many

such people as you can. It is a numbers game. The more telephone calls that are made on your behalf the more subscriptions you will sell. *The State* magazine, a popular and long-lived North Carolina publication, recently honored an elderly woman who had done subscription sales for more than two decades out of her home. She had added thousands of new names to the subscription list over that period of time and accounted for many more renewals. There are more like her out there. You need them working for you.

- Hire a subscription sales rep. I say "hire," but this person would be an independent contractor, paid entirely on a commission basis, and only when subscription monies actually come in. Some people are very good at this kind of work and take it on enthusiastically. Look hard, do not be discouraged easily, and you will find the right person to represent you. Sometimes they may be repping for other fund-raising products and simply add you to their list of clients. They are often very active and will get results for you. It may take a while to find exactly the right person, but keep trying. It will be well worth it when you do settle on a good one. Sometimes these reps may want to solicit others to work for them, including school groups, and be paid an override on these sales as well.

The Hardest Question, and How to Answer It

At some point in a sales presentation, your ad prospect will turn to you (or to your salesperson) look you squarely in the eye and ask, "What's your circulation?"

You've got to understand this question before you answer it. It's not as simple as it sounds. My experience has been that most business people simply want to know how many readers you have. At any rate, I assume this to be the meaning of their question. In their minds they are comparing you with television, newspaper and radio. In your answer point out that:

- Your readership is highly targeted to their prime prospects. There is no waste circulation.
- The magazine gets into the hands of 95% of the people in the community who are likely to need and be able to buy their product or service. Point out that no one can give them any better coverage than that. If there are one hundred people in town who are, at any given time, hot

---

RECOMMENDED RESOURCE! Everybody loves a picture. The way you use photographs in your magazines and other publications will be a key element in their success. A great resource for using photos is *Editing by Design*, by Jan V. White.

---

prospects for their product or service, and if your magazine reaches all of them, no one can do any better. Neither the newspaper with its 500,000 circulation nor the TV station with its 200,000 viewers can do more than you and your magazine can do.

• Your readership numbers approximately four times the number of magazines actually printed. This figure will include first readers and all initial readers, all household members, and all "pass-along" readers.

Counting Households

Answers such as these will satisfy most of your potential advertisers, and they will be accurate. Some clients, though, may say that the actual number of copies printed seems small compared to the total population in your area. And it will, in fact, seem small when you look at this number without understanding its meaning.

First, get the facts yourself. Read through the latest census figures for the trade area of your magazine. You can also ask the county economic development office or reference librarian for a distillation of the census data as it affects your trade area.

The census data will reveal two interesting points that you can put to great use. In its pages you will find an economic profile of your community. You may discover, for instance, that 40% of local families have incomes of less than $20,000 a year.

Moreover, you will find a figure representing the total of the number of households in the trade area. Few people ever think of circulation in terms of the number of households, yet it stands to reason that each of them will need only one magazine. There will be far fewer of these than anyone might guess.

An example: let's assume that you are publishing a magazine in a city of 100,000 inhabitants. In that town there will be an average household size, say, of 4.5 people. This means that you have approximately 22,000 homes. The census also tells you that fifty percent of these homes bring in incomes of $20,000 or less. It also points out that many households operate below the poverty level, and it gives a precise number for these.

This means, in a hypothetical situation and based on my experience, that of the total of 22,000 households in this representative city, only half, or 11,000, will have the discretionary income to permit purchases beyond that which is absolutely necessary to day-to-day needs. Far fewer will have the discretionary income which will permit the purchase of even the most limited items or services that might be considered "luxuries." So if you print 11,000 magazines you can, in absolute truth, tell your advertisers that you have one magazine in circulation for the household of every potential buyer of his goods or services in the entire trade area.

Unless your advertiser is in the food business and makes a living selling turkey necks and liver pudding to masses of people each Saturday, he will be unlikely to accept your presentation as valid. He may never have clearly understood just how few households he was depending on to generate a profit.

Newsstand Sales

You will also be selling your magazines on newsstands. This will bring in a little cash, but not too much. Revenues will likely be modest.

You will, however, benefit from the exposure. Having your magazine visible on the stands gives it credibility with your advertisers. This is not theoretical circulation; it is visible, tangible circulation. When your sales rep approaches a new client who has already have seen the magazine in the supermarket, drug store, or elsewhere, the sale becomes easier.

To get on the stands you will make a deal with a wholesale news distributor. There are one or two of these in every area. In North Carolina each of them covers one or more metropolitan areas, and often several nearby counties in the more rural parts of the state. These agencies will normally take your magazines on consignment at a 50% discount.

The news agencies are definitely not run by literary types, and they couldn't care less about the qualities of any individual product. They will not work very hard to place your magazine on the particular newsstand where it is likely to do best. Furnish them a list of the spots where you want to see it on display, and hope for the best. Without the list, even that slim hope is largely futile.

Keep careful records. Since you are providing magazines on consignment to the dealer, you will not be paid until returns are collected and charged back to your account. Wholesale news distributors are typically very sloppy in the handling of very small accounts like yours. Though they will agree to handle your product, you are more a nuisance to them than anything else. If you want to get paid for the magazines sold, you will have to take the initiative. Have the agency sign off on the number consigned. When returns are credited, have them sign again and then send an immediate bill. Keep after them until they pay.

Ask for "Whole Copy" Returns

One word of caution: news agencies usually do not return full magazines. For most publications this would be too expensive, both for the publisher and for the distributor. Magazines like *Playboy* or *Home Office Computing* do not want the leftovers of last month's issue sent back to them freight collect. So the normal routine is for the distributor to tear off covers of returns and send these back to the publisher as proof of non-sale. The remainder of the magazine is dumped.

But you are not *Playboy*. You have paid dearly for your magazine and you can use back issues for promotional purposes. Tell your news agency that you want "whole copy" returns. When they protest, as they likely will, tell them that you will come by and pick up the returns so that they will not have to bundle them up and ship them back to you.

Design for Newsstand Sales

Your cover should always be designed with an eye to newsstand sales. The photograph or art on it should have strong appeal to the widest possible readership. The sell lines (the blurbs telling what's inside) should be readable from a standing position on the lowest shelf of the rack.

Other Retail Sales

The newsstands are usually controlled by the news distribution agencies, and it is virtually impossible to get on the racks without going through the distributor. But you can place your magazine in shops and boutiques, book stores, gift shops, card shops of the Hallmark type, locally operated drugstores (the chains use the distributors), and elsewhere. In the beginning, especially, you want to get into every possible location to increase visibility to the maximum. If you can afford it, provide a stand-up cardboard rack for point-of-purchase display for your additional retail outlets. If this is not possible, find the next most advantageous position for your magazine and place it accordingly.

How to Develop a Strong Editorial Format

When I say "editorial format," I refer to the nature and slant of the stories that you will publish in your magazine. The slant is important. A story on a new dam and recreational reservoir will be treated quite differently in different magazines. *Audubon* magazine will focus on the environmental effects; *Fortune* on its significance for the business community; *Texas Monthly* will try to find an expose to do on the shenanigans and financial manipulations of the developers of surrounding properties. *Inland Boating* will focus on water sports. And so on.

To begin with, get hold of every successful city/regional magazine you can find. Analyze articles for length, content, slant, illustrations, type, etc. Analyze the editorial format with respect to the character of the readership.

Pay attention to the letters to the editor to see what kind of reader response articles are getting. Be absolutely shameless in borrowing and adapting ideas for your own magazine. Note how badly some magazines are edited and designed. You'll learn what to avoid, too.

After as much of this as you can stand, look at the community where you are going to publish your own magazine. What is its nature? What are the people like? What will interest them most and sell best? Ask yourself how can you develop a magazine whose personality matches the personalities of potential readers.

There is room for much trial, error, and adjustment as you go along. Some people seem to have a sixth sense about what will work editorially, but you can't count on this.

Start with a game plan of some kind, even if you intend to adjust it at the halftime break. When a free-lance writer calls in to ask what kinds of material you are looking for, you will have to tell him. Most magazines publish a "writer's guidelines" flyer, consisting of just this kind of information. (I often answer that what I am looking for is good ideas, and ask the writer to send me a list of articles he or she is prepared to develop and write about.)

Here are some decisions you will have to make:

- How long will your articles be?
- What kinds of articles do you want: service, profile, recreation, history and nostalgia, roundup, self-improvement, etc.?
- What is the slant: expose, lifestyles of the rich and famous, how Susie decorated her home for less than $1,000, down-home?
- What kinds of art, illustration and photography do you need?

Article Types

The following is a list of the major kinds of articles found in successful magazines. Your start-up article format should include a mix of them in each issue. This is a great help in planning. If you know that you are going to need— say, an interview, a service piece and a profile in every issue—you can plan ahead.

You have a number of slots to fill before a magazine can come out. When you fill all the slots you are ready to go:

- *Personality profile.* Such articles recount the accomplishments, personality, likes and dislikes, projects and achievements, friends, and relations of an interesting personality in your community. Profiles should be written with rich detail and wit and include both characterization and dialogue. In most city magazines, profiles are friendly appraisals, although they are not simply puff pieces. In more hard-nosed and aggressive magazines of the muckraker variety, profiles can be quite unflattering. What is your slant? Make sure your profiles fit it.
- *Interviews.* Some of the same people who will make interesting profiles will be right for interviews, but not all of them. A subject for an inter-

view will be articulate and be involved in specific activities that readers are interested in. He or she will be an initiator of important activities or a major player in these activities.

- *Roundups.* Got a problem in town? A controversial issue? A challenge? Get the opinions of ten (or fifteen or more) leading citizens and do a roundup article.
- *Service pieces.* These nifty articles are sure reader pleasers. You can't have too many good ones, and you want at least one in each issue. Service articles tell readers how to get the goods, do the things, or achieve the goals that interest them. Typically set in a numbered, how-to format ("Ten Ways to...."), they are always sure sellers.
- *Things to do and places to go (as well as things to avoid).* These articles can be written from a first-person viewpoint or in the third person. The first person, when it works, has higher reader interest. Sidebars give details on costs, accommodations, restaurants, etc.
- *The way things were.* Local history, with old photos, always has high reader interest. The subject matter of these articles will fit your editorial profile.
- *Your regular departments:* editor's notebook, book reviews, art and performance reviews, calendar of events, restaurant reviews, gardening, decorating, cooking, etc.

One warning here: when a writer comes to you with a column idea, and you like it, ask to see ten sample columns. There are many short-winded writers who take on long-winded commitments, and the mix is disastrous. These writers lack follow-through, and you can't afford to deal with them. Just when they are beginning to develop a following, they fail to send in next month's piece. Readers like to see the same departments, issue after issue, right where they are supposed to be. Toying with your departments makes readers uncomfortable. They like predictability and permanence. If you have doubts about the long-range commitment of the author of a column, don't begin publishing the item. If you are a good writer with wide-ranging interests you can always write a number of columns yourself under various pseudonyms. I once wrote the entire contents of a magazine that I published just to see if I could do it.

RECOMMENDED RESOURCE!

For detailed, easy-to-understand information on the types of magazine article you can include in your magazine, see *Magazine Article Writing*, by John M. Wilson. Slanted toward writers, it is very useful for inexperienced editors, too.

The Importance of Sidebars

Sidebars are powerful tools for creating and holding reader interest. This being the case, it is astonishing how many local magazines seem to neglect them, whether through ignorance of their value or lack of writers who know how to construct them.

Sidebars, for those of you who might not be familiar with the term, are those little featurettes—usually set apart and highlighted by a border or box—that amplify the contents of, give further details about, give instructions concerning, or otherwise comment on the contents of the article they accompany. An article on blue birds in the Carolina mountains might be accompanied by a sidebar, "How to Build a Bluebird House." An article on hurricanes Andrew or Hugo might be accompanied by a sidebar listing the most destructive storms of the century, their paths, strengths, etc. An article on Caribbean cruises, for example, might be accompanied by a sidebar, "What to Take Along."

Why are sidebars so important? They attract and hold reader attention. Most people don't read magazines cover to cover. They browse through, looking for items that interest them. They look at article titles. They look at photographs and read the cutlines (which is why I always insist on long, fact-filled cutlines under any pictures in my magazines). They especially look at sidebars. In the age of TV soundbites, the average reader's attention span has been whittled down. People look for and enjoy easily-digested nuggets of useful, compelling information. Most often it is the sidebar that leads the casual reader to plow through the entire article rather than the other way around. There is an excellent article on the structure of sidebars in *Writer's Digest* magazine for September, 1993 (pages 32-34). This issue will have long disappeared from the newsstands by the time this book appears in print, but you will find a copy among the back issues in most public libraries. Popular sidebar types include the following:

- *The list.* Ten most powerful storms; Ten most beautiful women; Ten best cruise buys, etc.
- *Tests and Quizzes.* How do you rate as a lover?; Can you take these deductions?; Ten questions on good nutrition; Do You Understand Women?; Men?
- *Definitions.* Definitions of unusual words or phrases related to the subject of the article, *i.e.*, "Understanding Software Jargon."
- *How to Do It.* As a sidebar to an article on sex in marriage, a list of "Ten Ways to Be a Better Lover."
- *Information Sources* (A subdivision of the list sidebar.) Where you can get more detailed information on the subject at hand.
- *Maps, graphs, graphics.*

Editorial Integrity and Editorial Support

The newcomer's guides, the tourism guides, and the quality of life magazines described in other chapters are openly and unashamedly promotional in nature. A city magazine is a different animal. It is an honest-to-goodness, real magazine. Editorially, it must maintain its objectivity and integrity, or it will lose the confidence of its readers. You will not publish an article in praise of a particular enterprise simply because its owners have bought an ad. Your city magazine presents itself as unbiased in its viewpoint, and unbiased and objective it must remain. This does not mean, however, that you leave your sales force without support. You support them in every way possible, consistent with editorial policy. Here are a few examples:

- Do you want to sell advertising to the banks? Do a cover story on banks and financing (not on a single bank) in your community. Schedule this article far enough in advance that your sales force can let banks know about it and considering advertising in the issue that contains it.
- Do you want to beef up advertising from Savings & Loans? Do a feature on home building, buying and financing. This should bring many of them in, along with building supply firms, real estate firms, and others.
- In addition to such *ad hoc* projects, which can be implemented at virtually any time to meet virtually any need, plan an entire editorial calendar for the coming year. Feature one segment of the business community or another in each issue. Let the ad people know this calendar in advance. They can build sales around it. In this way you provide editorial support for advertising sales without compromising your magazine in any way.

Develop a Physical Format That is Easy to Produce

The companion to the editorial format is the physical format. Like the editorial format, the physical arrangement of the parts of the magazine will remain the same issue after issue. The articles' headlines, the overall page design, the column width, the type-style and size, the column heads—all these things are constants.

Graphic designers can do many things. Left to their own devices, they can specify exotic type fonts, splash color across two page spreads and do wonderful things with pictures. The trouble is that there is not likely to be a graphic designer in your kitchen closet. You're going to have to do it yourself. Besides, it is just too expensive to start from scratch every time you publish an issue. You do not have time to redesign your product over and over again, and, to tell the truth, your readers do not want you to. They like their favorite magazine to look like it is "supposed to look."

I published this city-county magazine for five years, utilizing all the features discussed in this chapter in the small town of Washington, NC. The magazine was well received and quite successful. I discontinued it only when I sold my business and moved to my present location in Fort Lauderdale.

Study the magazines on the newsstand. With the exception of very few—magazines like *Vanity Fair* and *Vogue*—these publications will have a format that varies little from issue to issue. The *New Yorker* looked the same for more than fifty years. *Time* magazine and *Newsweek* are heavily formatted. Most regional magazines—*Mid-Atlantic Monthly, Yankee, Southern Living*—have a format that varies very little. Research these magazines. Using them as a base, borrow from them.

Here are some elements you will have to design:

- The name of the magazine on the front cover. Remember that it has to be dramatic and readable, but that it has to coexist on the page with art or a photograph.
- The masthead on page two or three, listing the publisher, the other editors, contributing writers, photographers and artists and giving the address of the publication's administrative office.
- The look of the table of contents.
- An "In This Issue" feature.
- Headings for all departments, including back of the book advertising sections. These should be consistent in design, giving a feeling of unity and permanence to the publication.
- The page layout, the margins, the columns. Three columns per page is preferred by the vast majority of magazine editors. It is more dynamic and provides a wider variety of layout options and ad sizes.
- The width of columns, the space between columns, the name of the typeface for the body copy, the name of the typeface for the headlines. These typefaces will remain the same for every article, in every issue. If you happen to be a gifted designer, you can vary the headlines, but the body typeface will remain the same always.
- The title page for articles. An easy-to-use title page which readers seem to like and that anyone at all can lay out by paste-up or computer consists of a headline, a subhead (leading into the article) and a

by-line. See the accompanying illustration for an example of this title page. You may design two or three standard variations of this format.

- The typeface and type style for the cutlines, the words that accompany pictures and tell what is to be seen in them.
- The blurbs. Blurbs are small excerpts enlarged and separated from the main body of the article by rules (lines). These very useful devices serve to assist in the layout of the magazine, providing filler when copy needs to be stretched.
- Remember that your goal is to create a very professional looking magazine, but one that anyone can put together following the guidelines that you set.
- Once you make your decisions, stick to them. Readers like familiar features. They like to see what they expect to see. Stick to your decisions, too, because they simplify your life. It may take some doing and a lot of looking at other magazines to come up with your publication style sheet, but you only have to do it once. It is clear sailing from that time on.

Selling the Ads

Three main motivations will move people to buy advertising space in your magazine (and in almost any other publication you decide to do). Needless to say, these motivations are not mutually exclusive. They often exist in rather interesting mixtures.

- *Image enhancement.* These advertisers don't expect any immediate, measurable return. They would not even know what to measure if they tried. They just want to get their name and the nature of their business before the reader. If, at the end of the year, they find that their bottom line is improved or if, in recessionary times, they find that they are still doing better than their competitors, they know that they have done something right. Whether it was your magazine that did it for them, the new sign on their building, or the full page newspaper ads—they don't have the foggiest idea. Such advertisers include major banks, hospitals (surprisingly faithful advertisers who buy expensive ads), educational institutions, manufacturers, civic-minded corporations, etc. This is the bedrock of your advertising effort. It is essential that you sell as much as possible of this market.
- *Ego satisfaction.* There will be some advertisers who simply want to be associated with the prestige product that your magazine is. They can often be sold when you suggest that "We will come in and take some photos of you and your people, letting our readers know something of the basic human reality of your business." Ego-centered clients go for the photographs. Still, they must have the funds and at least enough of a

need to rationalize this ego-stroking. These are, by and large, individuals who are spending their own money as opposed to the City Exec who is spending the bank's money.

- *The development of immediate business.* The hospital that has just bought a new, million-dollar magnetic resonance imaging outfit wants people to check in and use it. It wants to instill confidence so patients won't go to the university hospital fifty or a hundred miles away. The developer advertising a new subdivision or shopping center is seeking to develop business as well. The interior designer, a high-percentage sell for city magazines, is looking for those few clients on whom a prosperous career can be based. These and others are looking for fairly immediate results, and if they get those results they will continue to advertise with you.

In your market survey you will list every possible advertising prospect. You will place them in one or more of the categories given above. You will prioritize them as to their likelihood to buy and their importance to the financial health of your magazine. Ask yourself how many of the businesses you have listed you can reasonably expect to sell, and calculate what you think you can charge them for space. Can you make a profit at that level?

Those Money-Making "Little" Ads: Treasures in the Back of the Book

What about all those individuals and businesses who would like to advertise with you but can't afford the big bucks for the larger ads? Do you just write them off as bad advertising bets? Not at all. In fact some of the most lucrative page rates that you have will come for the special advertising sections that you develop for just such clients.

Most lucrative? How is this possible, with the First National Bank paying $2800 for the full page ad opposite the table of contents? It's possible because small ads cost the client more per unit of space that larger ads. If a full page ad pulls in $2,800, that same page full of small ads at $290 for two column inches

RECOMMENDED RESOURCE!

One of the very best books I know on designing effective advertising for magazines is David Ogilvy's *Ogilvy on Advertising*. Your success depends, in the long run, on the satisfaction of your customers. Get Olgivy's book and study it from cover to cover. Combine this with John Caple's *Tested Advertising Methods* and you will get a super education in writing print media advertising that works.

brings in much more. You can get fifteen of these on a typical page, grossing $4,350. Furthermore, if well-designed and positioned, these ads can pull even more powerfully than their larger cousins elsewhere in the magazine.

Examples? Open *Better Homes and Gardens, Entrepreneur* and many other magazines. The back pages are chock full of tiny ads, each containing an amazing amount of copy and graphics, advertising fascinating and useful products and services. These ads constitute a buyer's paradise. In fact, I bought the Apple computer on which I am presently writing this chapter from one of the small ads in the bargain basement section at the back of *MacWorld* magazine. So interesting are these ads that many readers habitually open the magazines from the back cover and read through from back to front. A glorious extra is that, because they get results and because they are so affordable, these ads are easy to renew. After a few issues some advertisers will simply tell you to keep them in the magazine until they give you the word to pull them out.

There may be several of these back-of-the-book sections. One might be for specialty retailers; another will be for hotels, motels and accommodations; a third may be for schools, colleges and specialty educational opportunities ("Double Your Income! Become a Dental Technician!"); a final section will contain ads for restaurants, along with restaurant reviews. Each section will have its own, easily identifiable heading: *New East Bazaar*, *Bed and Board*, *Who Can do It*, etc. In addition to the advertisers to whom they are ideally suited, these back-of-the-book sections are your fall-back ads for virtually everybody. When a larger firm can't take out a big ad don't fold up your tent and stop selling. Instead, extol the wonders that the $190 back-of-the-book mighty miniature will work for them. Often they will be so relieved not to have to spend $1000 that they will say "yes" out of sheer gratitude. So develop those special advertising sections. There are no limits to the business you can do in them.

Running a Tight Ship

Publishing a magazine is a complicated process. There are many opportunities to miss deadlines, stretch production time and fail to have your magazine out on publication date. It is very easy not to be on time.

Unfortunately, late publication makes readers and advertisers very unhappy. The designer who took the full page ad in your Spring "home and garden" issue had a big sales promotion set up to break when you said that your magazine would come out. The promotion breaks as schedules. If your magazine is not out as scheduled, your advertiser is going to be very angry, and rightly so.

In the publishing business, deadlines are sacred. They are not to be missed. Things must be done the way you promised they would be done, and they must be done on the date that you promised that they would be done. Set up a production schedule and follow it to the letter. Don't let a single deadline slip or the whole process will begin slipping. Be sure that every member of the team knows what the deadlines are and what his or her individual responsibilities are.

Do the following things with *all* your publications:

- Set a clearly defined date when each task must be accomplished.
- Include each and every task that will have to accomplished in publishing a magazine: articles assigned, articles edited, articles typeset, etc.
- Have a meeting with everyone youe entire staff. If this consists of yourself, your spouse, two sales reps and a part-time layout person, so be it. If it consists of just you and your spouse, you still need the meeting. Everyone's responsibilities must be defined individually, with deadline dates made clear.
- Get to the printer on the day you promised to be there, at the time you promised to be there. Get your magazines to the newsstand agency on the date promised. Get magazines mailed to subscribers on time so that they will receive each issue at the promised time.
- Keep in mind that your goal is to do several publications, not just one, plus some work in other profit centers. To keep all these balls in the air simultaneously requires rigorous timing.

Failure to do these things can have serious consequences. If you are lucky, you may be able to muddle through with a single project, but it will cost more than it should, will satisfy fewer people than it should, be far more time consuming than you can afford, and monopolize your energy to the point that you can do little else but ride herd on the chaos and hope for the best. In periodical publishing, scheduling is everything. The other way, madness lies.

Getting Started

Once everything is in place, the surveys done, the media kit complete, the sales people in place, your production schedule ready, and a stable of writers (your local free-lance friends) ready to produce copy for you, you're ready to go.

The only problem is that, unless you tell people about it, no one will know it but you. To spread the word, you will be a luncheon and dinner speaker every time the opportunity comes your way. You will flood television news directors, newspaper editors and radio stations (especially public radio and other stations interested in "cultural" news) with news releases. There will have been a release to tell that you were planning the project, a release every time you found someone to work with you on the project, and releases on every other conceivable subject, all carefully written to be publishable and to heighten awareness of your new magazine. Finally, there is a news release announcing that the project is actually under way.

Awareness of your new city magazine will grow gradually. You may be surprised to learn that the project that has so dominated your own life is not particularly central to the lives of others in the community. So you help them become aware of it in every way you can.

If you have a good product, if you have organized a lean, hard-working and detail-oriented publishing company, if you are profitable—even marginally—from the very beginning, then the outlook for success can be very good.

Issue after issue, more and more people will see, read and appreciate your magazine. Calls will begin to come in from potential advertisers who contact you on their own to ask for a media kit. When this begins to happen, rejoice! The future is yours to make.

6

How to Make Money Publishing Newcomers' Guides

We are a mobile nation. The average family in the United States pulls up stakes and moves to new cities, towns and neighborhoods every five years. This means that twenty percent of all families in America are on the road at any given time. We are also a nation of consumers. We need things. We need people who can do things for us. And when we move we need them all at once. Last week, securely nestled in our old home, we knew which doctor to go to. When we had a toothache, we knew which dentist to call. We knew where to go to buy a car or the insurance on our car. We knew where to shop for clothes, go to the movies, eat a good meal, buy a book. We knew how to register the children for school, where to get the electricity turned on and how to subscribe to cable TV.

Yes, last week we knew all of these things. But this week we don't know any of them. We are in a new home, in a new neighborhood, in a new city— maybe even in a new state. We need to find these things out all over again.

This is precisely what a newcomer guide helps us do. In conception and even in format, a newcomer's guide is very similar to a tourism guide, except that it is for people settling permanently in a community rather than for two-week visitors. The advertising base is much more extensive than the base for a tourism guide. The tourism guide focuses only on entertainment/pleasure activities. In the newcomer magazine everyone from plumbers and electricians to interior designers and new car dealers are prime targets for your sales force, and many of them will choose to advertise in your pages.

For this reason newcomer guides are a staple of the independent publisher. Every metropolitan area of more than 30,000 is prime territory for such a publication, but newcomer guides can be quite successful on a smaller level in much smaller towns. I published one successfully in a town of 14,000.

Your Sales Pitch: Customer Creation

Why are newcomer guides so successful? Because aggressive business people realize that when newcomers come to town and buy goods or a service from one or another of the suppliers they find there, they will in all likelihood continue to buy from that same supplier as long as they reside in that town.

The businessperson who is alert and attracts these new families does well for himself. Not only does he make that first sale, but dozens of additional sales thereafter. If you go to a hair stylist who does a perfect job on your hair, in an attractive shop that is a pleasure to be in, you will more than likely go back to that shop time and time again. If you buy insurance for your home from a knowledgeable, friendly representative, you will go back to that person when you next need automobile insurance or health insurance.

The census figures will help you sell ads. These reports will reveal that there are far fewer families in a town of 50,000 inhabitants than most people realize. The report will call them "households," and in a town of 50,000 there are likely to be just 15,000 of them. If you are in business you've just got to replace the households that are constantly leaving with the new ones that come in.

If the total number of persons residing in the town does not change, and if 20% of the families are moving each year, then 3,000 new families are coming into town annually. Year after year. The businessperson who doesn't get his share of this new business is truly courting disaster. The businessperson who does get his share cannot fail to do well. That's why the biggest businesses with the most sophisticated marketing programs—the banks, for instance—all have a newcomer representative whose job it is to attract newcomer business. This is your sales pitch for your newcomer's guide, and it is a very strong one. It is strong because it is absolutely accurate and true. Indeed, it is virtually irresistible for the business owner with any marketing savvy at all.

What you are doing for them is actually creating their future generations of customers.

My First Newcomer Guide

My introduction to the world of newcomer guides came when a major real estate developer in a large North Carolina city decided that he needed a slick, high-quality magazine to feature his subdivisions. He hired a graphic arts firm to do such a magazine, commission the writing, sell the ads, etc. He succeeded in publishing a first issue, and it looked very good. What the developer learned, however, was that publishing a magazine—as he was doing it—was very expensive. He also decided that he would do far better to spend his time tending to his real estate business, in which he was expert, than in supervising the production of a newcomer magazine, in which no one was less expert than he.

I heard of his indecision over whether to go on publishing and called him. He was delighted to hear from me, and I made a deal. I would buy the magazine from him for a very modest amount of money, which would be paid back to him as a percentage of the gross advertising sales in future issues. If the magazine, for any reason, failed, I would owe nothing. If the magazine succeeded, it would automatically repay the purchase price.

I bought this magazine only because it was already there, because it was so inexpensive and because it was, to whatever limited degree, established in the market. The first issue looked good. But I could just as easily have started my own. I could have come out with a full color magazine, done the graphic arts work and the writing in my own bargain-basement ways, and increased the profit margin many times over that enjoyed by my developer friend.

The cover of *Welcome to Wilmington* magazine, my first newcomer guide. This slick paper, full-color magazine was an annual publication. It took about six weeks to produce and contained $40,000 worth of advertising.

This magazine was so easy to do and so profitable that I planned a series of "Welcome to...." magazines all over North Carolina. At that very time, however, my wife and I, having grown up on the salt creeks and rivers of the Georgia coast, were bitten by the sun bug and decided to make a change. I sold my half of the business to my partner, moved down to Fort Lauderdale, where I now live, and bought a 34-foot, ocean-going cabin cruiser. Another four feet and I could have run my publishing company from it. I still work just as hard as I used to, but I now spend weekends on my boat in the Keys, diving for lobster when I feel like it and lying around in the sun when I don't. And I am about to start my next annual "Welcome to..." right here in South Florida.

Defining the Product

What does a newcomer magazine look like? What kind of articles and information do such magazines contain? What makes a newcomer magazine successful? Here are some answers, based on my experience of what really works. Not every newcomer magazine will contain all of these features and reference guides, of course. But the best of them, the ones that really do a job for their advertisers, will do so.

Your newcomer guide should be full to overflowing of detailed information, so practical and useful to new people in town that it will be utilized by them for weeks and months, getting more and more results for your advertisers every day. Your magazine should contain the following sections and many more like them:

1. A reference guide to community institutions and facilities. Reference guides are consulted, not thrown away. They are thumbed through again and again; they are mined for the kind of detailed information that the new resident can't find gathered together anywhere else. And since the reader comes to rely on the accuracy and completeness of the reference material in the magazine, he or she also comes to rely on the products and services offered by the advertisers. In a sense, these ads are validated by the reliability of the reference material.

- The guide will tell the newcomer—in brief, outline form—what the school system is; what the school calendar is; where and how to register their children; what documentation to bring with them when they register; what private schools are available; what unusual opportunities the school system offers (pilot schools, experimental schools, schools of science and mathematics, schools of performing arts, etc). What about athletics for boys, for girls, etc.? What are the fees to be paid? Give the precise amounts. Are checks OK, or must you have cash? What is the tuition in private schools? What are the school district boundaries? Deal with these and every other question on this subject that you can imagine. Do so in an absolutely thorough way. Treat all other subjects just as exhaustively.
- Your newcomer guide will contain hours and locations of public facilities such as libraries, parks, physical fitness facilities, auditoriums, concert halls, museums, etc. What are the rules governing the use of facilities? Include details; readers love them. Where is the museum? What is the art collection like? What kind of swimming pool does the city own? What documentation is required to get a library card? Are there any fees? How large is the library's collection? Do they have talking books or audio tapes for the hearing impaired? If so, how large is their collection of tapes and what kinds of books does the collection include?
- What about drama groups, orchestras, chorales, writer's clubs, and other cultural activities? What about radio clubs, stamp clubs, dance clubs, and other specialized interest organizations? What about computer user groups? It will take some digging (and constant updating) to build this section and keep it up to date, but it will be a very valuable addition to your magazine. Give details, details, details.
- Where do you go to get the lights turned on, the gas connected, the water running? What are the current rates? What deposits will be required? Does everybody have to pay deposits, or are there exceptions? Give details. All addresses and telephone numbers should be included, along with directions to any office that is unusually difficult to find. Can the whole thing be handled by telephone? How? Etc., etc.
- Emergency services and hospitals. Tell how to call an ambulance, how to

call the rescue squad for emergency medical services, how to call the police.

- Where do you list your property taxes? What is the tax rate? When are taxes due?
- What about a zoning map? Where can you consult one?
- Fill the newcomer in on city government. Where and at what time does the city council meet? Where is the agenda published? How does one arrange to be sent an agenda? Who do you contact to become active in political party activities? Who are the precinct captains, and where can you find them?
- Include lots of photos illustrating all of these activities and facilities.

Every town or city will have all these special areas to cover and many others besides. The key here is to organize the information in concise, useful ways. Give tons of detailed information and specific, step-by-step instructions wherever possible. Postage stamp-sized maps that show locations of buildings are a big seller too. Remember, the more you do for your readers the more your readers will utilize your magazine and shop with its advertisers.

All of this information will be repeated issue after issue. It will grow more and more complete and thorough. Ideas for new sections will surface after the first issue hits the streets and you begin to get some feedback. Be sure to take careful note of them and to implement them.

2. The newcomer guide will contain articles introducing the reader to the more interesting sites in the community. How about a walking tour of the historic district, complete with photographs? First-person narratives work very well. Always provide a friendly, folksy map of the tour.

3. How about a list of day-long activities and visits that the whole family can enjoy? I once did a very popular feature on this called "Sunday Drives." The ground rules were that the location had to be close enough that you could drive to it with all the children in the car without a squabble breaking out among them. It became a reader favorite. Include maps and features describing the pleasures and beauties of the countryside surrounding the town. Be sure to include details such as that nice little place to eat, where rest rooms are and the name of the country store where a do-it-yourself lunch can be bought at an affordable price.

4. The newcomer guide will have personality profiles of cultural leaders, writers, artists, etc. It will profile interesting people in other fields who are doing interesting things. It will introduce recent newcomers who have solved the problems of settling in with great success, and it will tell how they did it.

These profiles will change from issue to issue, giving a different look to successive magazines.

5. The newcomer magazine will contain articles on the history and character of the town or city which it serves. The idea here is to give the town you are writing about a depth dimension that the newcomer, who initially encounters only the surface of things, would otherwise miss. I am one of those individuals who feels disoriented when moving to an entirely new town, and there are many others like me. I felt that way when I moved to Greenville, NC, from the larger city of Charlotte. But shortly after arriving I wrote an illustrated history of the town. What I learned in doing that project made me feel much more at home. When I crossed the main street I knew that beneath the asphalt were cobblestones laid down in the early 1900s. And I knew that beneath the cobblestones was sand dredged from the Tar River a score of years earlier. I learned where the first brick store had been and about the winter in the 1890s when the Tar River froze over to a depth that would support ice skaters. I even published a photograph of those skaters.

Such three-dimensional knowledge makes one feel more comfortable, a little more at home. In all the magazines I have published, the historical articles, with their accompanying drawings and photographs, have consistently been among the most popular.

6. Then there are all those service articles, pieces that tell people any number of definite ways to get things done: "Ten Ways to make Your Home Look Like a Million on a Bargain Basement Budget"; "Seven Things to Look for in the Resale Value of Your Home"; "The Secrets of Physical Fitness: How to Be in Top Shape at Any Age"; "Newcomer's Guide to Outlet Stores and Bottom Dollar Shopping," etc. The topics are endless, but they will all interest newcomers *and they can all be tied in to advertising sales*.

Advertorials

Advertorials are a relatively recent development in periodical publishing. While you normally won't find them in the average over-the-counter consumer magazine, the chamber of commerce publications, tourism guides and newcomer guides will be full of them. An advertorial is sold to the customer like advertising. The advertiser buys, say, two black and white pages and one color page at regular advertising rates. Sometimes a single page is purchased. This is an expensive package, and you must give good value in return. You write a full-fledged magazine article about the customer and his or her business. You use anecdote, characterization, dialogue and all the other stylistic devices that would be found in any other first-rate article. You assign the advertorials to your very best writers, or, if that top writer is you, then you write it yourself.

To work well, the advertorial must be as interesting to the reader as any other article in the magazine. This is not difficult to do, since readers love stories about individuals who have built businesses, worked their way up to success, and overcome all the odds to achieve their goals. The benefit of the advertorial to the person paying you for it is that in the article you are able to make the business come alive, make it human, give the reader a feel for the way the firm does business, and its ability to satisfy its customers. Advertorials are powerful promotional pieces, and when well written can delivery virtually guaranteed results to the advertiser. I have written advertorials that have put new businesses on the map overnight. These articles are always accompanied by top-notch photography, in color or black and white—or both.

Two Choices of Format

Some newcomer guides are very slick, four-color magazines that come out once a year. Ads are expensive, articles carefully written and photography of the highest possible quality. These newcomer guides look like the best magazines on the newsstands, and the most fastidious and image-conscious advertisers feel at home in them.

But you could also choose to do a monthly, inexpensively produced publication of the highest possible circulation, targeting travelers and casual visitors as well as true newcomer families. Ads will sell for far less money, but since you publish more frequently you make as much money in the long run—though you probably work a good deal harder for it.

Both of these approaches will work, though they are quite different projects in terms of format, quality of finished produce and advertising gross per issue. Each has its own strengths and weaknesses.

The Monthly Newcomer Guide

Let's begin by contrasting the annual newcomer guide with the monthly version. The annual is full magazine size, printed on slick, enameled paper with lots of fine photography in both color and black and white. It is laboriously produced and, in detail, quite impressive. Nothing is left to chance. It will stand up well against any magazine anywhere in appearance and design. Because it is produced annually you and your small group of free-lancers can get it out handily. You would never be able to publish such a magazine monthly without a very sizable chunk of capital to support a staff three times the size that you presently have. You would always have two or three issues in preparation simultaneously.

The monthly newcomer guide, on the other hand, borrows its techniques from newspapers. It is probably printed on 40 lb. newsprint, quarter-folded, and held together with a staple or glue, whichever your printer can provide. The TV guide in your local newspaper is a sample of a quarter-fold publication. (See the chapter on printing and on tabloids for further technical details.)

Color ads are few, because many newspaper presses still don't handle color

Cost Analysis Form

Throughout this book we have talked about setting profitable, competitive advertising rates. There is a good deal of intuition in this—good old seat-of-the-pants-flying. Yet there are some facts to take into account. This work-sheet will help you define them. If you get results you don't like—if your prices are too high or your profits too low—you will have to reduce your sales and production costs or find some value-added features (such as becoming a seat-back magazine on commuter airlines) to justify your necessarily higher prices.

Itemization of Costs per Issue	Price
Printing per issue	
Distribution per issue	
Writer's fees per issue	
Layout and design per issue	
Ad sales commissions	
Prorated rent and utilities	
Miscellaneous	
TOTAL COST PER ISSUE	

CALCULATIONS

$$\frac{\text{Total Cost per Issue}}{\text{Number of ad pages sold}} = \text{BREAK EVEN COST PER PAGE}$$

$$\frac{\text{Cost per issue plus desired profit}}{\text{Number of ad pages sold}} = \text{RETAIL COST PER PAGE}$$

easily or well, and many of the smaller ones do not handle full color at all. Color also runs up the cost considerably and is very time consuming to design into your publication. Some spot color is about all you will ever want to use.

One way to look colorful is to print a separate cover on light weight, cheaply coated stock and saddle stitch it in place as an outside wrap to the newsprint interior pages.

Ads are simple and straightforward. Most newspaper ads that your clients are running elsewhere can easily be adapted for the monthly newcomer guide— or simply picked up and used as is.

Articles are quite short, with the average running 200 to 350 words. The directories and other information are organized very succinctly. Since you will distribute these monthly guides in motel rooms as well as elsewhere, more of the materials will be slanted to the weekender and traveler who is in town for a brief period.

Layout and design are attractive, but need have no fancy, expensive special effects.

Cost of Ads

Ads in the monthly newcomer guide are much less expensive than those in the annual guide. In pricing your ads in the annual guide, follow the guidelines given for the quality of life magazine in the chapter devoted to that project.

Rates are lower on a monthly basis because the advertising budgets of most merchants will not support anything higher. Your base rate will be one-twelfth that of the annual guide. Then raise that sum as much as the market will bear. In determining the final ad rate for the monthly guide, go through the same process as recommended for use with the tourism guide. Remember that at this level you will also be competing with the local newspapers, so your rates should probably not be higher than the newspaper's, and if they are lower it is a strong plus for you.

Pros and Cons

Which should you do, the annual or the monthly? The annual guide brings in a much greater sum of money once yearly and leaves a generous amount of time free for other publishing activities. This is the option I have always chosen.

Yet there's much to be said on the other side. The monthly guide brings in a steady flow of cash all through the year, and this is very desirable. However, the constant pressure of selling, writing, and producing twelve issues per year may leave you little opportunity to do other things. Since annual guides are much more expensive to print, you can't distribute them as freely as you might otherwise want to do. You can't, for instance, afford to put one of them in every motel room in town. For distribution, follow the guidelines outlined for the quality of life magazine.

The monthly guide, printed on newspaper presses, is dirt cheap. You can produce as many as you can possibly use and offer your advertisers saturation circulation. You will use the same distribution techniques used by publishers of tourism guides, putting free magazines in every available place.

Big firms (those selling an image or upscale products and services) will prefer to place ads in slick, annual magazines and pass up on the monthly guide opportunity. On the other hand, because of the low price of your ads in the monthly guide, you will have a wider base of advertising prospects who can afford your space.

Analyze both projects. Which will produce the most profit? Which will enjoy the better market position in your trade area? Which would you prefer to do? Which project fits your capabilities and experience? Put it all down on paper then choose. Either way, you can't go too far wrong if you take care to produce a good product.

7

How to Publish a Tourism Guide

Tourism guides are big business in both primary and secondary tourism markets. Some versions of them—like the *TravelHost* Magazines—are franchised. You purchase a franchise, and you get instructions on how to put your magazine out, monthly features on travel that are not tied to any particular market ("The Ten Best Discount Airfares"), a format, and an operations manual. You may also get some nationally-placed ads which will be sold at the home office and sent out to you for insertion. Naturally, on such ads you kick back a generous share of the revenue to the franchise organization. But there is really no need to go the franchise route. The tourism magazine is too easy to do on your own, starting from scratch.

What They Are

Tourism guides take many forms, from tabloid newspapers to full-sized, extra-slick magazines. The most popular format is the digest-sized (5.5 by 8.5 inches), saddle-stitched, full color publication. It is generally printed on economy enameled stock. The tourism guide has very short, pithy articles on things to do and places to go. It is filled with little maps that help readers find their way around. It lists restaurants and their specialties, nightclubs and every other possible kind of vacation or travel activity, including everything from the miniature golf course built to resemble the Aztec Empire to true golf courses, parks, flea markets, sight-seeing guides, specialty shopping, and other entertainment possibilities too varied to catalog here.

What to Put in Your Guide

The editorial content of a successful tourism guide focuses on the character, history, amenities and attractions of the trade area it serves. Usually the written articles constitute less than 20 percent of the guide—just enough to interest a casual reader and carry him and his attention through the pages of the book. The editorial part of the publication is very easily done. Much of it— especially the guidebook type features and how-to articles—remains virtually unchanged from issue to issue, since it always finds a brand new readership as hotels and motels fill up with brand new travelers. There will be only a few very short feature articles to write for each issue after the first one, mainly to present what will appear to be a fresh magazine to advertisers issue after issue. Local free-lancers can easily handle these features for you. You will probably gather the information articles yourself.

Tourism guides are chock-full of ads. Readers study these eagerly, looking for precisely the right restaurant, the very best golf course, the perfect excursion. The ads are an essential part of the information the tourism guide contains. In successful guides the ads are carefully designed and written to be as attractive and interesting to the reader as the editorial copy is.

The cover of the North Carolina Travel and Tourism Guide, published by my company. The broad scope of its coverage made it more difficult (and expensive) to market than a guide targeted to a more narrowly defined trade area would have been.

Why Travel and Tourism Guides Can Be Profitable

Vacationers normally do not know their way around the areas where they go to relax. Generally they have a good deal of money to spend. They eat out at every meal. They want to be entertained every evening. They look for daytime attractions that will give them pleasure.

To find out just how to do all these things, they utilize the tourism guide that they pick up in their room or in the lobby of their hotel or motel. Businesses that want to reach travelers and tourists will not hesitate to advertise in your tourism guide if the price and the circulation are right. If there is a competing guide in the area, work carefully to develop a market position that will set your guide apart from, and above, the others. I refer you to the pages on developing a market position elsewhere in this book.

Successful tourism guides go on bringing in the cash season after season. If your magazine is attractive in appearance and is circulated effectively, advertisers will get the results that keep them coming back to renew their contracts, issue after issue.

Tourism guides possess the three essential ingredients which make for success in any publishing project. They carry the possibility of intensive sales to a targeted clientele in a limited geographical area.

Study the Successful Guides

The next time you check into a motel in a major metropolitan or tourism area, sort through the publications on the bedside table. Tour the lobby and collect the free publications there, either at the front desk, on free-standing racks or perhaps on the top of the vending machines. Chat with the desk clerk and the motel manager. Find out what you can about his knowledge of the publication. Does he, or his motel, advertise in it? Do they get results? Has it been around a long time?

After having done this two or three times at different locations you will have gathered several travel and tourism guides. Open each of them, find the name, address and telephone number of the publisher. Call or write the publisher and ask for a rate card and a media kit. Tell them that you are interested in placing some advertising in their trade area for one of your clients. Your purpose in doing all of this is to identify the most long-running, successful publications among the lot.

Look over the best publications carefully. Answer the following questions:

- What is the ratio of editorial copy to advertising?
- According to the figures on the rate card, how much advertising (in dollars) does each issue contain?
- What special departments (featured sections) seem to appear in the most successful guides?
- What is the frequency of publication?
- What is the format of the most successful publications (trim size, number of columns, size of type, type font, amount of color, etc.)?

A Case History

While vacationing at Atlantic Beach, North Carolina, I picked up a tourism guide that we will call the *Atlantic Vacationer*. In format it was digest-sized, with the ads and editorial content pretty much as described above. I immediately began to leaf through it, not only because of my professional interest in the publishing business but because, like any other tourist, I wanted to find a good restaurant for dinner that night.

I began to ask around about the *Atlantic Vacationer*, and, when I had a chance, I dropped in to meet the publishers, Sam and Sandra Wade (fictitious names). Like most independent publishers, Sam and Sandra were glad to meet with me, talk about publishing and exchange stories of triumphs and occasional near-disasters. I learned that their publication was in its fifth year. They had started it, they explained, working out of their own home.

With Sam out selling ads and Sandra at home doing layout and design,

Publication/Production Schedule

Whatever publication you are producing, the schedule is of the first importance. The following list constitutes a simple, step-by-step production schedule similar to many that I have used. To set up a schedule, work backward from your planned press date and assign a completion time to each task to be done.

- Hold conference with sales force to decide on topics in the editorial format: profile, interview, how-to, etc. Insofar as possible, keep sales needs in mind when filling article slots.
- Assign articles to freelancers and in-house writers, if any.
- Contact columnists and department editors to learn the contents of their pieces for the upcoming issue.
- Assign photographs.
- Assemble manuscripts of completed articles.
- Assemble manuscripts of columns and departments.
- Edit articles.
- Close ad sales.
- Produce ads.
- Proof ads.
- Ad approvals in.
- Proof and correct articles.
- Send proofs to outside writers for correction.
- Assemble art and photographs.
- Hold conference with advertising sales force.
- Prepare dummy.
- Prepare camera-ready copy.
- Send color work to color house or service bureau.
- Final proofing of bluelines.
- Final proofing of color keys.
- Press date.
- Distribute magazines.

the magazine took shape. At that time there was little competition, and it was immediately successful. *Atlantic Vacationer* chugged along year after year, bringing a very nice profit into the publishers' household. Then temptation struck. In 1989, the publishers decided to make a change and put their magazine on the market for sale in the high five-figure range.

A Reminder: The Importance of Thinking Small

What happened was that Sam made a serious mistake in judgment. If *Atlantic Vacationer* were profitable in a small trade area, he reasoned, wouldn't a national magazine be just that much more lucrative in a larger one? Alas, it doesn't work that way. As is so often the case, the more widely circulated magazine brought along with it massive costs that swamped Sam and cleaned out his own bank account as well as the accounts of several backers. Sam never recovered from this disaster.

Small publishers need manageable publications that even a single salesperson can handle. They should avoid printing and circulation expenses so large that, at the first misstep, the whole project comes crashing down on you and sweeps your business away with the rest of the rubble.

Publications with regional and national trade areas are not just larger versions of local publications. They are different animals altogether, with an entirely different set of financial and management costs and requirements. For the small publisher it is always better to zero in on the main market. Leave overambitious expansion to others.

In the tourism guide business the word to the wise is, "Think small. It's the royal road to success."

Your Publication Schedule

As with most advertising-intensive publications, your publication schedule is directly linked to the advertising budgets of your advertisers. Advertisers can spend only what they can afford to spend. You may wish to come out weekly, thus immensely increasing the amount of money you take in. You may soon find, however, that most advertisers cannot or will not pay your high advertising rates that frequently. If you want to publish weekly you will have to come way down on your rates. This may well be self-defeating.

In my view it's best to keep the rates up and publish less frequently, unless the market position you have carved out for yourself requires you to do otherwise. This way your printing costs go down, too. Most tourism guides appear monthly, bimonthly, quarterly or even annually. If there is an off-season, publication may cease entirely during that time, with leftover copies of earlier editions kept on the stands to maintain your presence in the market.

I suggest a quarterly publication schedule. It is easily managed by you and your spouse or principal helper. It is infrequent enough to maintain a reasonably high level for your advertising rates, and it will result in some economies in printing. With fewer issues coming out, you will be printing more of each issue. It is far cheaper to print two runs of 30,000 each than four runs of 15,000 each, since on longer runs the per unit price falls sharply. In addition, on this schedule presses are set up less frequently, ads designed less frequently and the publication written and laid out less frequently. The time thus saved can be devoted to maintaining the highest quality circulation, thereby winning the thanks and confidence of your advertisers, or to taking on additional publishing projects.

What Size Print Run?

The print "run," in the jargon of printing and publishing, refers to the number of copies you print when you go to press. When you print fewer copies you have a "short run." When you print more copies you have a "long run." What is a good print run for your tourism guide? In the beginning, of course, you'll just have to rely on educated guesses. Later you can be more precise. But even your initial educated guess will require some analysis. To begin with, gather the following information:

- The number of hotel and motel rooms in your area. You will want to keep fresh copies of your guides in these prime locations.
- The number of copies that the Chamber of Commerce thinks that it can circulate to newcomers and drop-ins at its Welcome Center, etc.
- The number of retail and other outlets where you will put your magazine for visitors to pick up and take with them.
- The number of copies any competing publication claims to print. You will have to meet this competition. (See the important discussion of "readership" versus "circulation" later in this chapter.)
- The number of copies that you can afford to print. Have a printing and production estimate in hand.

There are a lot of variables here and some decisions to make. I suggest the following guidelines to get you started.

- Print one book per motel room for each month of the life of your magazine. For a quarterly publication this means three copies per room. If you count 5,000 motel rooms in your survey, and the life of your magazine is three months, you print 15,000 magazines for the motel market.
- Print the same number (an additional 15,000) for distribution at other outlets.

• Add the number of magazines that the Chamber of Commerce and the Visitor's Center will distribute (let's assume 5,000).

This will give you a total run of 35,000 magazines. Is this enough? If the competition is actually distributing far greater numbers you will have to increase your run to meet the competition. Add to this your own intuitive feeling about the number you need to print to keep the magazine in active circulation until the next issue comes out.

After your first edition you can check actual needs against the size of your print run. If you collect a lot of leftovers, then you can decrease your print run. If a great many of your distribution points have run out of copies you will increase the run. In general it is better to err on the side of too many copies, especially on the first issue. You want it to be seen everywhere. Nowhere is the old cliché about first impressions being lasting impressions any truer than in the field of publishing. You want to start with a bang, make the biggest possible splash, go for the gold. The reputation earned by your first edition is one that you will have to live with for a long, long time.

How to Distribute Your Tourism Guide

As a publisher of an advertising-intensive magazine, you succeed to the degree that you get results for your clients. Wherever tourists and travelers go, your magazine must go, too. If readers have your magazine in hand as they enter a shop or restaurant, so much the better. It does not take many of these grand entrances to convince a business owner of the efficacy of your book.

And as your base of satisfied, repeat advertisers grows, you can expand your activities to include hunting down marginal advertising prospects, improving the quality of your guide, taking care of the details that set you farther and farther ahead of your competitors or solidifying your hold on the market.

Sound good? It is, and it will happen, if you take pains to get your book into the hands of every possible purchaser of your advertiser's goods and services. This takes planning and constant attention. Never neglect the servicing of magazine outlet sources and prospecting for new ones. Since your magazine is free, most business owners will be happy to let you leave copies for customers to pick up and browse through. When you do get permission to leave your magazines in a particular location, find a visible spot and put your magazine there time after time. Check frequently to make sure magazines remain available. Replenish supplies as soon as they are exhausted. Leave fewer magazines at circulation locations where the action is slow and more copies where activity is more brisk. You will soon have a pretty good idea of how many copies to leave where.

Every trade area has special places where copies of your magazine should be placed, and you should know of these and take advantage of them. But mostly you will leave magazines at the following places:

- Convenience stores.
- The Chamber of Commerce.
- The Visitor's Center or the Welcome Center, if any.
- Real estate offices.
- Restaurants, where your magazine makes excellent browsing while vacationers are waiting for their meal to be served.
- Hotels and motels: leave one for every room after agreeing with the management to see that magazines will be placed in the rooms. Replenish the supply regularly.
- Places of business of your advertisers.
- Banks. Ask them to include your magazine in their newcomer kits.
- Savings and Loans. Again, ask to be included in newcomer kits.
- Mass transit locations, especially airports, tour and charter bus companies, car rental agencies, etc.
- Service stations.
- Gift shops, souvenir shops, newsstands, bookstores and other retail outlets.

Here's one important tip on circulation: circulation must be very visible. All of those magazines the Chamber of Commerce distributes at its headquarters and that the banks stick into their newcomer kits for mailing to out-of-town inquirers are doubtless valuable circulation avenues. The only problem is that they are invisible to your clients.

You must not only *do* good circulation, but you must also be *perceived to be doing good circulation*. Make very sure that you have your magazines on every available and visible shelf, rack, or counter, especially those in places where your advertisers are likely to see them. The sight of all those magazines with their advertisement right there on page 27 is very reassuring, especially on the days when they reconcile their bank accounts.

Circulation and Readership

Here is an item that you will have to deal with whenever you have competition, and it is true for every type of publication: the problem of readership versus circulation.

The word "circulation" has a precise meaning. It is the number of actual magazines that you get into readers' hands. You print 50,000 copies of your April issue, for instance. Is that your circulation? Strictly speaking, it isn't. Some copies will be spoiled in packing and handling. Subtract these. Others will be left undistributed in the office. Subtract these. Another batch will be picked up from outlets when the new issue appears. Now, subtract these. The number you have left is your actual circulation. Since this number, in a free circulation magazine, is usually very close to the number printed, most publishers simply list the print run as circulation.

The real problem comes with the term "readership." This word has no precise meaning at all. In determining readership publishers estimate how many people might read each individual copy of their magazine. These estimates are more self-serving than scientific. A publisher might calculate, for instance, that every magazine placed in a motel room remains there for two weeks, on the average. During that time 14 people will have inhabited the room. So, while the *circulation* of a single copy is one, the *readership* is 14.

On a run of 50,000 copies, then, you can claim, by this line of reckoning, that your circulation is approximately 50,000. But your readership will be far greater. For the 25,000 magazines placed in motel rooms, the readership will be 25,000 X 14, or 350,000. If the remaining 25,000 magazines are read by 1.5 persons each, the readership is 37,500. The total readership of the 50,000 run then is 387,500 individuals.

Obviously readership figures are more impressive than circulation figures. But since any publisher is free to define readership in any way he or she wishes, it is not a very objective figure. Many advertisers, unsophisticated in such distinctions, will confuse these two figures. If you have a competitor you must be sure to meet him on an equal basis. If he is stressing the readership of his publication you must do the same.

One of my salespeople recently told me that she lost a substantial sale to another magazine because, in the words of the prospective advertiser, "It reached so many more people." I managed to get hold of my competitor's rate card and sales material and discovered, as I suspected, that they were claiming a readership of 50,000, whereas we were reporting a circulation of 20,000. Closer inspection showed that the competing magazine was printing only 12,000 magazines, a full 40 percent fewer than we were. The other 38,000 came from their rather inflated notion of readership. Calculated on this basis our own readership would have been nearly 100,000.

Because of these confusions, the circulation of all major magazines is audited by such organizations as the Audit Bureau of Circulation (ABC) or one of the newer agencies that audit free-circulation publications. These agencies report only circulation. Advertising agencies expect audited circulation figures for larger magazines, but they are aware that for the smaller fry—you and me—such audits are not economically feasible.

If ad agencies or other clients insist on some proof of circulation, you can often satisfy them by showing them a copy of your invoice from the printer, which will have the number of copies printed clearly spelled out.

How to Know How Much to Charge for Your Ads

In my seminars for publishers I get one constant question: "How do I know how much to charge for my ads?"

To set the advertising rates for your tourism guide (or any other publication, you must first come up with two key figures:

- The smallest amount you can charge and still break even.
- The highest price that the traffic will bear.

Let's begin with the first item. Begin by setting a reasonable number of pages for your publication. If there is competition in the area you can use their example to do this. If not, use you best guess.

Next, decide (arbitrarily) on an average print run and the average number of color pages you will use. With these two figures in hand you can get a quote on the cost of your printing.

Now estimate the following costs:

- Printing costs per issue
- Distribution costs per issue
- Writer's and artist's fees per issue
- Layout and design costs per issue
- Rent and utilities (overhead) for the time required to produce a single issue
- Miscellaneous costs per issue
- Cost of sales (commissions and expenses) per issue

When you add all of these costs, the total will tell you how much each issue will cost. (Note: You may personally provide some or all of these services, but add in a cost for them as though you were paying someone else to do the work. Success will eventually force you to hire people to help and you want your rate structure to be high enough to make this possible.)

Next, make a guess as to the number of advertising pages you think you can sell. Divide the total cost by the number of ad pages that will be in your book. The resulting dollar amount will give you your break-even point in advertising cost per page. If it will cost you $20,000 to produce your magazine, and you expect to sell 34 pages of advertising, your minimum page rate will be approximately $600. This $600 page rate is your break-even rate. At this level you are not losing money, but you are not making any, either.

The next step is to decide on the profit you would like to make on each issue. Remember that profit is defined as money left over after paying all costs, including your own salary (or what the salary would be if you had to hire someone else to do what you do). Add this figure to that of the costs per issue.

Now divide this new total by the number of anticipated ad pages. The result of this calculation will give you your maximum advertising rate per page.

Now apply some marketing strategy and some common sense. How does your rate fit the market? Is it out of line with the competition, the radio/TV rates or the newspaper? (In comparing your rates to those of the electronic media and the newspaper, remember that you are giving exposure over a longer period. The newspaper ad is current for a single day, while your ad will be current for a full three months if you are publishing on a quarterly basis.)

After this comparison, you may find that your page rate seems a bit high. In this case adjust it downward a bit. Check to see if your profit is still adequate. If it is, all well and good. If it isn't, perhaps you can reduce costs in some way to make up the shortfall. You may also find, happily, that your costs are far below what the competition and competing media are charging. In this case you can raise your rates a bit (still keeping your "low-cost" marketing advantage) and increase your profits thereby. Play some games with your pricing, testing various scenarios. What happens if you fall short of your advertising goals? What happens if you sell ten additional pages of ads and have to print more pages? What is the optimum size magazine for you?

Pricing Smaller Ads

Once you have set your page rate, add a reasonable amount to it for color. If the base black and white page rate is $1,000, the color page will sell for, say, $1,495, plus the cost of the color separation. Now use these figures to calculate the costs of smaller ads: three-quarter page, one-half page, one-quarter page, one-eighth page, etc., in a two column format. In a three column format your small ads will be two-thirds page, one-third page, one-sixth page and, if you desire, one-twelfth page.

The thing to remember is that smaller ads are proportionately more expensive. If a full page costs $1200, three quarters of a page might be $1,050, a half page, $800; a quarter page $600 etc. The rationale for this is that it takes just as much time to design and lay out a small ad as a bigger one, not to mention the costs of billing and collecting. And, of course, you want to encourage the purchase of larger ads.

A Profitable Project

A tourism guide can be a very profitable project for the entrepreneurial publisher. These guides are easy to produce, easy to sell (because of the well-defined trade area) and easy to edit (because of the limited amount of new editorial copy in each issue). Such a guide, if reasonably successful, can provide the cash flow which will make a great many other projects possible.

8

How to Publish a Quality of Life Magazine

If you are planning a move to a new city and you write the Chamber of Commerce for an information packet on the area, you will soon receive a packet of maps, pamphlets and other materials. Among these will be a publication that looks like a magazine, with a strong mix of editorial and advertising. These are the so-called "quality of life" magazines that virtually every Chamber of Commence in the country publishes annually. It is not a real magazine, of course, like the ones that you would buy on a newsstand. It is a strong promotional piece dressed up to look like a magazine.

Most of the hundreds of quality of life magazines I have examined have been colorful, slick and expensive as far as advertising is concerned, but dry as dust editorially and often poorly designed. The articles in them, ostensibly written to project a dynamic, desirable image of the Chamber's trade area, usually read like the back of a cereal box. With close attention to writing and design you can make a name for yourself in this area of the publishing business.

There is no regular publication date, since each issue is good for as many as two or three years, and does not constitute an onerous commitment to an ongoing publication—unless you want it to. If you do a fantastic job you'll be asked back. You can decide at that time whether you want to do the magazine again or not. Usually the money is very good, the time commitment reasonably small, and the public recognition for you and your new company both gratifying and valuable—a combination of benefits that is hard to resist.

Again you have the three key ingredients going for you: intensive sales, in a limited geographical area, to a highly-targeted clientele.

I won't say that ad sales are ever easy, but with the quality of life magazine they are as easy as they are going to get. The businesses and industries that are Chamber members have been conditioned to "participate," issue after issue, year after year. There may be a grumble or two, but most of those who bought last year will buy again this year.

Ad rates are traditionally higher than those for any other regional or local magazine: up to $3,100 for a full page, full-color ad in a magazine I recently did in a city with a population of 35,000.

Profile of a Quality of Life Magazine

What is a "quality of life" magazine? The best way to answer that question may be to describe to you the one I received a few weeks ago from a local chamber of commerce. It is a 112 page, perfect bound magazine (squared at the spine, with the pages glued in) and the size of a standard magazine (81/2" x 11"). The cover, in full color, has been made extra glossy by the recently developed process of liquid lamination.

Inside, inserted between the cover and page one, is a threefold brochure on the city of Greenville. More about this brochure later. The first forty pages, as well as the front and back covers—inside and out—are filled with mostly full page, full color ads for major industries, financial institutions, a university, an ad agency, some commercial building contractors, etc.

 I developed this quality of life magazine for a group of five small-city chambers of commerce in eastern North Carolina. We edited it with great care, and when it appeared it was so well-received that, with the blessing of the chambers, we continued to publish it on a quarterly basis for the following year. This is most unusual for a quality of life magazine.

These ads, which cost from $3,000 to $4,500 each in this book, are interspersed with editorial material in the form of short (about 700 words, tops) articles on such breathtaking topics as (and I quote the table of contents) "Recreation; Growth and Development; Education and Health Care; Real Estate; and Shopping." There are also a few pages of "useful names and addresses."

Seventy additional pages are filled with a membership directory, giving the name and address of each member of the Chamber, alphabetically. With some entries there is a mug shot, for which there is an extra charge. Judging by the number of these postage stamp-sized photos, there are enough hungry egos around to make this little profit center of more than passing interest to the publisher.

Following the alphabetical listing is a listing by profession or business specialty. A large number of fairly simple black and white ads in one-third, two-thirds, and full page sizes appears in this section.

The Publisher

I note on the table of contents page the name of the publisher. How did he get the assignment? Very simple. He walked into the office of the Chamber executive and offered to do his next quality of life magazine.

"What's in it for the Chamber?" the executive asked. The publisher told him, outlining a generous profit-sharing plan. Then he sold the ads, wrote the copy, laid out the book, had it printed, and collected the money for the ad sales. I calculate that total sales reached the $45,000 level. It cost $15,000 to sell the ads and print the book. Probably $5,000 went back to the Chamber. Profit: $20,000 plus. Not bad for two months' work.

How Quality of Life Magazines Are Used

How does a Chamber of Commerce use its magazines once it has them? One copy will be given to each member, with additional copies going to the larger businesses and industries that buy the expensive full page ads. This local circulation is the main basis for the claim of the publication to be an effective vehicle for advertising the products and services for the membership. (This may not be a very strong claim, but it is apparently enough to raise advertising sales to profitable levels.)

The remaining copies will be held in the Chamber offices and perhaps the offices of the county development commission (as it is usually called). These may be sold to casual inquirers. But the more important use is as the lead item in the packet of community information that the Chamber sends out to professionals, businesses, and industrial enterprises expressing an interest in locating in the area. The quality of life magazine, in fact, becomes a mainstay of the town's or the county's media kit and is used for civic advertising and promotion purposes. It must, therefore, be as handsome, slick, and professional in appearance as the publisher can make it.

Background Research

Do you need some secret knowledge to do one of these books? Is there some hidden lore secretly passed on from generation to generation about how to make money and succeed in publishing quality of life magazines? Not at all. You just need to follow a simple, basic rule that has worked time and time again.

To find out what has worked, assemble the largest possible collection of recent (there are fashions in these things and you want to be up to date) quality of life magazines from Chambers of Commerce in your area, including large, small, industrial and resort towns. Study them. Make inquiries about the cost of advertising space. See what works—in terms of design and format—and what doesn't. Start a notebook of ideas that you find particularly interesting and that you think you can improve on. Keep a file of tear sheets of design ideas that you think you can use. Analyze the organization. Read and study every word.

Chambers don't usually give their quality of life magazines away. You may have to pay a few dollars for each copy or perhaps you can strike a deal for outdated copies of older magazines. But it is worth the investment. When you have finished your cram course in this specialized niche of publishing you will know what a quality of life magazine is all about, how it is put together, and what writing you are expected to supply. You will have the all-important product knowledge necessary to sell yourself to a Chamber executive as someone thoroughly familiar with the quality of life field. You stand as good a chance as the next guy of getting the assignment.

Chambers of Commerce, and How They Work

What is a Chamber of Commerce?

There are so many misconceptions, even among those of us who should know better, that I will answer the question in some detail. After all, you're going to be dealing with a Chamber of Commerce on a project involving major sums of money. You need to know who your partner in business is.

The most popular misconception, I suppose, is that a Chamber of Commerce is a public organization, a department of the municipal government. Nothing could be further from the truth. A Chamber of Commerce is a private organization, with its own director, its own aims and goals, its own agenda. While these aims and goals usually coincide with those of a progressive mayor and city council, it has no official relationship with them and, more important, usually receives no financial support from them.

A Chamber of Commerce is made up of members drawn from the business and professional community of a town or city. In non-metropolitan areas many Chambers of Commerce, while centralized in the largest town, also include county-wide membership.

The Chamber membership then hires a full-time executive director (sometimes he or she has other titles) and an office staff. It houses them in commercial space which is as upscale as its budget will permit. The function of this paid director and his assistants is to promote the growth of the business community through community development, industrial development, population growth, etc. The Chamber mounts campaigns to achieve these goals and supports those that others may mount. For the community at large, the Chamber of Commerce becomes identified with its offices and its salaried, full-time director. It seems to have a life of its own and is often mistakenly perceived as an organ of government. When well run it has high visibility and is a major asset to the community at large. The Chamber's budget is met by dues paid in by the membership, but these are never adequate for all the activities it wants and is expected to carry on. In order to make ends meet, the Chamber itself begins to operate as a small business enterprise, doing what it can to generate additional funds for its operating budget on the one hand, and seeking out cost-cutting measures on the other.

The quality of life magazine is interesting to the Chamber for these very reasons. Without investing a cent, the Chamber is able to have a publisher deliver to its offices several thousand expensive, full color magazines for use in its work. It could never find the funds to pay for such publications directly. Furthermore, in return for its endorsement of the project, the Chamber receives from the publisher a percentage of gross advertising sales paid back into its own treasury.

How to Write Your Proposal

Once you get an initial expression of interest from the Chamber with which you are doing business, write up a draft proposal and present it for review. There will be some negotiating and some give-and-take, and the draft proposal serves as a base-point for your discussion. When the details are ironed out, write up the final version. If the executive secretary of the Chamber likes it, he will then present it to his board of directors. Once he has their approval, he will sign, you will sign, and the business of making the magazine can get under way.

What is in such a proposal? In general, a proposal includes two major parts. Part one specifies what you will do for the Chamber of Commerce and part two specifies what the Chamber will do for you. Although every proposal will be tailored to fit the circumstances at hand, you will be in good shape if you cover the following points:

Part 1: What You Do for the Chamber

- Specify that you will sell the advertising, typeset, write and publish a quality of life magazine in accord with specifications agreed to by the Chamber.
- Specify the type of paper, cover, etc. that you will use. Any printer can look at your sample copies and tell you what kind of "stock" (paper) it is printed on.
- Specify that you will prepare editorial copy in the amount of, say, 1,000 or fewer words on such topics as history, community characteristics, education, real estate, industry, retail climate, growth & development, transportation, etc.
- If a membership directory is to be part of the project, specify that you will include this directory in your book in both alphabetical order and in listings by trade or specialty.
- Specify a schedule for completing the project. This depends on your publishing and managerial experience—if any. Don't make it too hard on yourself. Ninety days is a tight schedule. On your second time around

you could pare that down to six weeks. Never guarantee a publication date. There are too many things that go wrong and cause delays, and some of them undoubtedly will do so. You can include mention of an "estimated publication date," but nothing more firm than that.

- Specify that your company will do all selling, billing, and collecting.
- Specify that you will pay to the Chamber 10% (or whatever percentage you negotiate) of gross revenues actually received by you. I say that 10% is "standard." That has been the agreed on figure for the deals I have made or know about. However, if your overhead is low, or if it is worth taking fewer dollars in profit to get a start in the quality of life business, you may offer 12% or even 15%. This will certainly give you a leg up on your competitors. The Chambers are interested in whatever course of action will maximize income to them. When you offer them more money, you become more interesting. But put pencil to paper and calculate costs carefully. Offer to share as much of the profit as you can, but no more.
- State that no percentage will be paid on bad debt accounts (yes, you will have some) or on filler pages. Filler, as you probably know, is used to provide copy, public service advertising, or other material for pages where no advertising has been sold and which would otherwise remain blank. I once ran into a problem when a Chamber wanted me to pay them a percentage on a page which I had filled, for lack of anything better, with a house ad for my company.
- Specify the number of copies that you will print and the maximum and minimum number of pages. Specify the number of these that you will distribute, free of charge, to the Chamber and to the advertisers.
- Specify how you will sweeten the pot—the extras that you can throw into the deal. Earlier in this chapter I mentioned a brochure that was included in the quality of life magazine distributed by my own Chamber of Commerce. This brochure was a freebie thrown in as an incentive by the company that did the magazine. Other popular pot sweeteners include a promotional slide show and script on the town that can be used in oral presentation to industries looking for a spot to locate or, if you have the know-how required and can do it easily, a video on the town. Easier to prepare is a slide show of, say, 100, 150, or 200 color slides that the Chamber executive can use for oral presentations.
- Include an escape clause. How much advertising do you have to sell to make a go of it? Calculate this figure and specify that if this amount of advertising is not under contract at the end of the selling period, then you reserve the right not to publish the magazine. This is almost never a problem when a magazine has already been done several times.

Part 2: What the Chamber Does for You

- Specify that the Chamber of Commerce will endorse your publication to its membership. This is an essential part of the agreement, and it is built on a solid community of interests. You, as publisher, and the Chamber are after the same thing: increased business—you for yourself and your advertisers, the Chamber for its community and its members. As publisher you are interested in building a profitable business and generating cash flow into your own bank account. The Chamber, dependent on income from any source it can scare up, is interested in generating cash for its own coffers.

- Specify that the Chamber will share with you information about ad sales in previous editions, who the top prospects are, who the contact people are, etc. It may even agree to make some calls on behalf of the magazine to heads of industry whom you may have difficulty seeing. The Chamber should help you with problem solving at every stage of the game. But remember that the Chamber executive, who has to go to his membership frequently for money to support this or that activity, probably does not want to get directly involved in ad sales. That is what he has you for.

- If you are working in a distant town, you may ask the Chamber to furnish a desk and telephone during the sales campaign.

- The Chamber should agree to furnish complete information about advertising rates in previous editions. It will be difficult for you to go up by more than 5 or 10%. Rates for quality of life magazines are already far higher—on a per page and per reader basis —than any other print media advertising your clients are likely to buy.

- The Chamber will agree to furnish complete membership lists and to be responsible for proofreading and approving these after they have been typeset.

- The Chamber will review page proofs and give final approval to print.

When you have these items written up in duplicate originals, signed both by you and by the Chamber executive, you are ready to begin.

The Sales Campaign

The sales campaign will be tightly organized. You have fewer ads to sell in this book than in other publications, but each will cost considerably more. Since you don't want to "burn a prospect" (a salesperson's term for losing a sale or account through poor planning or bad salesmanship), you will plan carefully, day by day and week by week. You will review the history of each company. What ads have they bought in Chamber publications in the past? Ask

The Endorsement: What's in It?

What does an endorsement consist of? In general you will find the following parts:

1. A prominent write-up in the monthly Chamber newsletter announcing the project and introducing you as the person undertaking it. (The Chamber executive will want to tell his membership that you, too, are a member of the Chamber, so you will have joined up. The dues you chalk up to the cost of doing business.) You would do well to write this note up yourself and give it to the person who edits the newsletter.

2. A personal letter from the Chamber executive to every member which, again, introduces the project. But it also goes further. It suggests that members give you a close and sympathetic hearing when you call on them and consider favorably the prospect of advertising in a magazine that will do so much to generate business and economic development. The envelope also contains a postage-paid business reply card. By filling it in and returning it, the recipient can get detailed information on advertising, rates, circulation, etc. The cards that are returned constitute your first prospect list.

3. Prospects on whom you or your salespeople call often call the Chamber to check on your *bona fides*. When this happens, the Chamber agrees to give you a warm recommendation.

yourself if a prospect has added a new product to his line or a new division to his company. These would be excellent motivators for advertising and getting the message out to the leaders of the community. Show some familiarity with past advertisements placed by the prospect. Knowledgeable talk about such things will build a rapport between salesperson and prospect.

Begin with the biggest, most solid prospects: banks, major industries, big businesses. Present and past boards of directors and officers of the Chamber make excellent prospects. Contact these premium prospects first. This is a good idea for two reasons. When they buy, it builds your morale and whets the appetite of the sales force, which now smells blood. If they don't buy—and with a quality of life magazine that has had good sales in the past, this is, fortunately, very unlikely—you can decide very early in the game whether it is worthwhile continuing or whether you should invoke your escape clause and back out gracefully.

Of course, you need a salesperson with the right appearance, manner, dress, and personal carriage to sell an ad to the president or marketing officer of a bank. The same person who can sell ads all day long to mom and pop retail outlets for the local free circulation shopper may very possibly not be right for this job.

But the bottom line is that you need a good salesperson. Your rep is going to be insistent, to invoke the community good, the necessity for members to support the Chamber, the patriotic duty to advertise in the quality of life magazine that you are selling. If this sounds a little aggressive, it is. But a good salesperson can pull it off without seeming pushy and losing ground.

To get your sales campaign off the ground, make careful lists of those who have bought before, those who have come into the area since the last publication and are good prospects, and those who have not bought but whom you think you can or ought to sell. Schedule these so that when the time for closing sales comes, you will have made all the calls you intended to make.

The larger clients will often have camera ready ads (slicks for black and white, composite film and a proof for color) which have been designed for them by their ad agencies. In these cases all you have to do is pick up the materials and go about your business.

What You Should Put into Your Magazine

It is in the editorial content of your quality of life magazine that you can make a real difference. When you read through the articles in the magazines you gathered, you may well conclude that whoever wrote the copy and whoever approved it knew nothing whatsoever about effective writing.

You would be absolutely right. Remember that these magazines are usually undertaken by specialists in marketing and sales who have no experience in magazine journalism. They do not know what makes for high reader inter-

Get All the Info When You Sell the Ad

Once an ad sale is made, always try to nail down the content of the ad then and there. It can be very time consuming to make several trips back to help the client decide just what he wants to see in print. "We can just pick up this ad from last year. Are the address and telephone number still current?" is a question that will help solve this problem.

But it is not always so easy. You may have to help the client out with suggestions. Always have some ideas ready, culled, if possible, from previous advertising the client has done. Anytime you can repeat an ad that has been run before, it saves you important chunks of time and cash that would otherwise be spent designing new ads for approval. Even when you pass these costs back to the customer—as I suggest that you do—it is far more desirable to settle the matter up front and run what has been run before.

Ads whose content has not been fully defined and agreed to are the main cause of logjams and delay at press time, and a delay at press time is something that you can't allow. A last minute rush leads to errors—typographical and otherwise—and can cost considerable sums of money in customer dissatisfaction and complaints.

est or effective writing. They are, more often than not, quite blind to the quality of writing in the same way that a tone-deaf person is unable to appreciate the quality of a musical performance. The New York Philharmonic or the local fireman's marching band—it's all the same to them. Just a bunch of people blowing on horns.

But some will know the difference, and they'll be the ones who contact you to do other magazines. Furthermore, many readers—although they don't know why—do perceive, for instance, that the *Reader's Digest*, with its personal style, ease of reading, richness of anecdote and example, is more fun to read than the instruction manual that came with their Japanese computer.

Here are some guidelines that I have found useful for creating reader interest. If you are doing the writing, keep them in mind as you proceed. If you are paying someone else to do the work, be sure that he or she is experienced in magazine writing and understands the importance of following these rules.

- *Provide high visibility to facts and figures.* The CEO's of corporations seeking new locations or markets which offer expansion opportunities will want to know the facts about population growth, family size, business activity, and a whole range of other kinds of quantified information. The Chamber executive can provide you with a list and up-to-date numbers. (He can also let you know which items he may not want to include.) Don't hide this material in the body of articles. Combine it, organize it, lay it out clearly. Centralize it on one or two easily accessible pages or highlight it in sidebars.
- *Use anecdotes and examples.* Business writing should not be any less readable or interesting than any other nonfiction writing. Just remember that every generalization, theory, or idea deserves illustration in case history form, within the context of the space available. Success stories are always good. A word of caution, however. In using businesses or business people in your anecdotes, be sure that those you choose to highlight are members of the Chamber of Commerce.
- *Develop strong leads.* Your lead is as important in this quality of life magazine as elsewhere. Work on it. Make sure the reader is motivated to move on to paragraphs two and three.
- *Use sidebars for emphasis.* Sidebars are those small, boxed "featurettes" that accompany and amplify major articles. A sidebar can contain detailed, related factual information or perhaps, along with a mug shot of the principal, a success story that illustrates the dynamic economy (or educational system, etc.) of the area your magazine covers. The possibilities are endless. Read *USA Today*, *Newsweek*, or *Time* for ideas. All three publications make great use of sidebars.
- *Use testimonials when appropriate.* There's no doubt about it. Testi-

monials are powerful selling tools. Ask the Chamber executive to go through his correspondence to find letters that might be useful. I am thinking particularly of the "We looked at your town, you gave us all the help we needed, and business has been terrific since we arrived" kind of comment. Other testimonials might focus on the excellence of a particular sector of the town: education, labor force, health care, etc. Postage stamp-sized mug shots should accompany testimonials whenever possible. Testimonials should be in quotation marks and followed by the name and company affiliation of the person who is being quoted. In the event that no suitable testimonials are on hand, the Chamber executive can usually pick up the phone and generate a raft of good ones.

- *Use "For More Information" items.* Include a "for more information call or write so-and-so" note, usually boxed in with a mug shot of the Chamber executive and copy written in the tone of a personal invitation. A signature over a typeset name at the bottom is an effective touch.

All in all a quality of life magazine is an attractive project. Potential profits are high, and the start-to-finish time is limited enough not to interfere with other projects you may be involved in. If you are already doing business as the publisher of a tourism guide, for instance, you can fill in the fallow, off-season months with a quality of life magazine.

And remember, every Chamber of Commerce does a quality of life magazine at regular intervals—sometimes yearly. So within a day's drive from your home there are some of these money-making projects just getting under way, some just completed, but also some now, today, up for grabs. With the proper preparation and effort on your part, one of them could be yours.

9

How to Make Money Publishing Apartment and Real Estate Guides

You go into a motel in a new town. In one corner of the lobby stand wire racks stuffed full of pamphlets and booklets offering apartments for rent and homes for sale to every eventual newcomer who might be passing that way. These modest publications are chock-full of ads, each of which may cost anywhere from several hundred to a thousand or more dollars a page. Some of theses publications may be tabloid-style, but most will be brilliant, full-color booklets and magazines printed on slick paper. All of them are free.

On top of the cigarette machine there are other racks, tabletop this time, which offer even more apartment guides and real estate booklets. Sometimes a publisher will have been lucky enough to position his own rack on the front check-in counter or in some other prime location close by. Some of these little magazines are apartment comparison guides, with display ads and line ads detailing the location, amenities, apartment sizes and rental rates for all of the major apartment complexes in the city. If it is a large city there may be two or more of these publications, for when they are successful they are very lucrative. Another rack contains ads for new homes in subdivisions wholly owned by the developers themselves. These publications, too, can be very profitable when market conditions are right. If you do not see a home or apartment guide and you ask the desk clerk for information on apartments for rent or homes for sale, the person you speak to may well reach under the counter and pull out his or her favorite guidebook and hand it to you. After all, handing you a book is far easier than taking the time to tell you what you need to know.

This happens frequently in those motel chains that exclude free circulation publication racks from their lobbies but who nevertheless wish to be helpful to their clients.

At the Airport and in the Mail

When you arrive at your destination airport, you may stop by the traveler's information booth, which is almost always provided by the local Chamber of Commerce, the county economic development office, or some similar agency.

There, too, the real estate guides, including yours when you begin to publish one, will be offered in abundance.

A letter directly to the local Chamber of Commerce or to a leading bank will bring a "newcomer kit" to you by mail. Real estate publications are always an important part of these packets of useful information. Relocation offices of major industries, hospitals, governmental agencies, and others also utilize these pamphlets, booklets, and magazines both in relocation kits and as a convenience for employees seeking a change in housing accommodations.

The cover of the Raleigh edition of the *Apartment Directory* published by my company. We utilized the same design and format for our editions in five other towns, saving greatly on design time and at the same time building company identity in the industry. The publication was later sold to one of our competitors.

Everywhere Else, Too

When you go out to dinner, or simply to a convenience store for a pack of cigarettes or a razor blade, you will also find apartment and real estate publications prominently displayed. They are simply everywhere, a major advertising and promotional tool of the industry. The ads in them are costly, and the percentage of the advertising budget that big management companies devote to buying them is second only to the money spent advertising in daily newspapers.

Most companies with apartments to rent or houses to sell simply cannot afford to lack representation in these guides. The same will be true of your guide, when you publish it, if you take care to do things right.

Money to Be Made

Where there is a great deal of money being spent advertising in any niche market publication, there is also a good deal of it to be made. There is no reason why you, as an entrepreneurial publisher, should not make your share. As with any other business enterprise, however, there is nothing magical about success in apartment and home guide publishing. There are dead ends to be avoided, and certain kinds of competition that you will find it difficult to overcome. The best bantam weight fighter in the world would find it difficult (and extremely foolhardy) to attempt to go fifteen rounds with the reigning heavyweight. As a bantamweight publisher myself, I suffered a rough bout or two before learning to recognize the kinds of competitive struggle I could hope to win and those that, under most circumstances, I had almost no chance of winning. Fortunately, the latter are quite easy to recognize. I'll tell you what I've learned about them as we go along in this chapter.

Surveying the Field

There are three types of publications in the real estate field. Two of them are green pastures in which independent publishers may profitably graze. The third presents those dangers I spoke of and that you would be well-advised to avoid. There are many variations in each category, of course, and even hybrids, as publishers look for a niche that they can profitably fill and that seems right for their own market.

- *Apartment comparison guides.* The large apartment communities always advertise—whenever and wherever they think they can sell leases. There is constant life-or-death competition among management companies in the selling of leases.

  Turnover among tenants is great, as the trend toward permitting six-month (and even three month) leases testifies. In times of low occupancy, some communities will even permit month-to-month tenancy.

  Apartment communities must constantly keep their apartments—and their superior features, if any—in the public eye. They do this in many ways. One of the chief among them is by placing ads in apartment comparison guides that usually show a photograph of the community, give its rental rates and list its advantages in terms of amenities: health clubs, pools, fireplaces, spaciousness, location, etc.

  These advertisements run issue after issue, once they are included in a guide, and they are not reworked frequently. Indeed, in one of my own apartment guides I have run the same ad for as long as four years. It continued to pull clients, year after year, and the advertiser wisely saw no reason to change it. This tendency to stay with what is working increases your profit as it decreases the production and design time it takes to satisfy each of your customers.

- *Publications advertising new homes in wholly-owned subdivisions.* In larger urban communities real estate development companies commonly build entire subdivisions. These new homes are not built all at once. Typically a model home and several others—enough to prime the pump and produce the first line of potential buyers—are built, followed by dozens (or even hundreds) of others as time passes and capital resources are recouped and rolled over into additional homes. Some such projects will go through what the developers term "phases," with phase one concluding one day and phase two beginning the next. Often the buyers themselves do not know the full extent of the developer's contingency planning for piling on the profits, should the project become a great success. This means that though individual homes are built and sold daily, the subdivision itself is continually marketed over many months and even years. Thus, advertising placed for such projects has a much longer life than ads placed for the resale of a single family home. Such ads do not have to change weekly, or even monthly or quarterly. They remain alive as long as they are effective (or until the advertiser tires of them). Furthermore, since such subdivisions are high-dollar projects there is a considerable advertising budget available to support them. It is not a question of whether or not the builders or their agents are going to spend a large sum of money advertising. This is already built into the project budget. It is only a question of where and with whom they are going to spend it.

Publishers, understanding these facts, have brought onto the market booklets (often hundreds of pages long) of full-color ads promoting the character, economic advantages and superior locations of the subdivisions. They find that the development companies can support the premium space rates that they must charge for such ads, so long as the ads are perceived to be effective. These ads are usually, but not always, in full color. Sometimes the advertiser will pay an advertising agency several thousand dollars simply to design the ad, an expense above and beyond what you, as publisher, will charge them to run the ad in your magazine. So long as the ad works, the advertiser will in all likelihood continue to run it issue after issue until the last parcel of property in the subdivision is sold.

- *Publications advertising the sale of existing homes.* Americans move from one home to another, on an average, every seven years. Each time they move, if they are homeowners, there is a house to be sold and another to be bought. That's a lot of housing activity, and it generates a great deal of advertising. Virtually all of these homes are advertised in the real estate sections of daily and weekly newspapers in towns and cities throughout the country.

This active market changes rapidly. Houses are bought and sold every day. What was on the market yesterday is no longer there today. A real estate listing that is alive today may be dead tomorrow. Change is the rule; little is permanent. Prices are reduced; specials are advertised. Since there is usually at least a two-week production schedule for such magazines (as distinct from newspapers, which are routinely laid out and printed in a matter of hours) a real estate magazine which advertises existing homes for resale is often out-of-date almost before it can be printed. For this reason most of the publications advertising existing homes are offshoots or sections of newspapers. A weekly real estate section included in the Wednesday or Thursday issue of a daily newspaper as a tabloid insert is printed in quantities sufficient to distribute as an independent publication for seven full days, until the next weekly real estate insert—with its new listings—is printed and distributed.

Why You Don't Compete with Newspapers in Selling Existing Homes

It should be clear that the subdivision and apartment guides offer more fruitful territory to the home-based publisher than a publication advertising existing homes.

I learned this the hard way. Newspapers have a tremendous advantage in handling the fast turnover of listings in existing homes. Their ad layout departments are richly staffed. Beyond this, their extremely sophisticated photographic and typesetting equipment makes a routine thing out of producing pages containing hundreds of real estate listings, complete with black and white photographs, in a matter of hours. Dozens of very modestly paid advertising salespersons call regularly on each real estate agency, taking changes and new listings. Furthermore, since they own the press and buy paper at wholesale rates, their cost of production is far less than yours will be. Finally, since they already possess a tremendous apparatus of circulation, they can add their real estate tabloid to this system at virtually no additional cost. You can do none of these things. It is possible that you can find a niche in some suburban area or small town that the newspaper is not servicing adequately—or, at least, you think this to be the case. You can try to establish a weekly existing homes tabloid or mini-tabloid publication in this area. But if you do you will soon encounter three hard facts:

- The area will either be so small that it does not return a profit sufficient to pay you for your time (remember, such a publication is time-intensive since it comes out so frequently), or....
- The advertisers, themselves doing business in an out-of-the-way, backwater area, can't afford to pay you the higher rates that would make it profitable, or. . .
- The project will turn out to be fairly profitable, in which case the newspaper, which has been watching your effort with interest, will discover this fact just as fast as you do. They will then send in their own salespeople, fast turnaround times and saturation circulation, thus making it virtually impossible for you to stay in business.

Another Reason to Avoid Existing Home Sales

There is another problem in successfully producing publications which market existing homes. When you call on small-shop (as most of them are) real estate brokers, you will be dealing with individuals who, though personally delightful, are almost wholly inexperienced in advertising. They can be very hard to deal with.

The average real estate agent has little formal training in his or her business beyond the basic course required for obtaining a state salesman's or broker's license. Many work part-time, even when they claim to be working full time.

Often the owner of the agency, who wants his best people out in the field selling homes and getting listings, will have assigned the chore of placing ads to his most inexperienced or ineffective people, or even to an office manager or secretary. These people will have little idea of the difficulties you face as a publisher. Even when they buy space from you they will be late turning in the information you need. Many callbacks will be required to get contracts signed and advertising information complete. Pictures delivered to you will be unusable polaroids.

There will be little professionalism in your relationships with clients. Their attitude will be one of "take it or leave it." They will be only too well aware that they can simply do as they have done in the past and stick with the newspaper, which, they feel, has been serving them well and will continue to do so.

Furthermore, there is a tendency to compare raw costs rather than costs related to benefits. This means that if a quarter page ad in the newspaper costs a certain amount and the same space in your publication twice that amount, your publication will be perceived as being more expensive. No amount of explanation, of pointing out that the newspaper is charging that amount for a single week's exposure, whereas you will keep their ad before the public for two months or more will dent that mindset. It is difficult to explain, but it is a fact. Marketing specialists with apartment management companies or with large development companies may be sophisticated enough to relate costs to exposure obtained, but the usual small real estate agency owner or his office manager will, seemingly, be congenitally unable to do so. Furthermore, it will take many smaller sales in this kind of publication to reach your sales goals.

Why Apartment and Subdivision Guides Work

Apartment and wholly-owned subdivision guides work because these projects are free from all of the negative factors described above and have other positive factors that newspapers cannot easily match. Your only competition will be from those other publishers of such guides who are already in the market and from those who, seeing your own success, will try to come into the market after you to claim a share of it for themselves.

Apartment management companies and large residential development companies have a degree of sophistication in advertising and promotion that is almost entirely lacking in the small residential real estate agency. They desire a mix of advertising, preferring not to trust to any one avenue to bring knowledge of their properties to the public. And they will have no need to revise their ads from day to day. No matter how many apartments are rented or houses are sold, there will always be more where those came from to rent or to sell. Moreover, the kind of publication you will produce and distribute will usually be pocket-sized, with one or, at most, two properties advertised on a single page. It will be a book that not even the biggest newspapers can produce on their presses. Newspaper presses, as enormous and as efficient as they are, are designed and configured solely for the printing of newspapers, tabloids and mini-tabloids on newsprint paper.

Your distribution (discussed fully in a later section) will be difficult for the newspaper to match, since you send your publication to many out-of-town inquirers through every means at your disposal.

Your client-centered service will not be easily matched by any newspaper. It will grow out of a single-minded promotion of a single product. For the newspaper, on the other hand, real estate advertising is fragmented into many different categories and, taken as a whole, is only one part of the mix of advertising that keeps the paper profitable. You can individually answer queries that will come in on your toll-free nationwide 800 number (a quite inexpensive but essential part of the sizzle that you will sell to your advertisers). Then you can furnish the names and addresses of these prospects to those who place ads with you. Newspapers will find it virtually impossible to do this. To cap it all, the profit on the sale of an upscale home or the yearly leasing of two dozen apartments is more than sufficient to pay the asking price for your ads, which will cost as much as $1,000 or $2,000 per page (per issue) in most markets—and sometimes more.

Success Indicators in Areas Where No Apartment or New Homes Guides Currently Exist

Let's say you have understood the profit potential of an apartment or new homes guide, and that you wish to publish one in an area where no such guide presently exists. How can you determine whether or not such a project will work? What signs do you look for? In what kind of town or city are these guides most likely to succeed? I first published my own apartment comparison guides in a cluster of smaller southern cities with populations ranging from 40,000 to 80,000 people in each metropolitan area. Success might be considered unlikely in such small markets, since the number of apartment complexes was limited and I had to sell a fairly large percentage of them to succeed. The guides worked in three of the cities, and continued to be successfully published for five years under my ownership. They continue to be published today after they were sold to others. In two cities the apartment guides never got far beyond break-even, and so were abandoned.

My next two guides were published in major metropolitan areas where populations ranged from 250,000 to almost 500,000. One of these became the biggest money-maker I ever had. The other, while not unprofitable, did not produce an adequate return on the time and energy invested, nor did it compensate me for the risk incurred in bringing out each issue.

My invariable rule for success (and one which I recommend to other home-town publishers) has always been to involve myself in projects that were brains and energy intensive, not dollar intensive. After a two year trial, this second big city apartment guide was abandoned. Time and money might have (probably would have) invigorated it. But I reasoned I was a publisher, not a gambler. There were, it seemed to me, too many sure things in the world on which to risk my hard-earned dollars rather than trying to force success from a recalcitrant and unwilling market.

Here's What Will Work

Today I would not have to go through this trial and error process to find out where apartment guides are likely to work and where they are likely not to. I have learned through experience what to look for to evaluate potential apartment guide markets ahead of time. Here's how I would now evaluate a market, well before bringing our a first edition of a new publication.

- In market research the humble telephone book, as we have seen, can be your best friend. Whatever the size of your trade area, your first move is to study the information contained in the yellow pages. How many apartment complexes are there? You should be able to break even by selling to twenty percent of the total number of apartment communities, and you should begin to make a real profit when you sell to thirty to forty percent of them.
- When you count apartment communities, eliminate all of those that are low rent, subsidized HUD properties. There will be few advertising dollars, if any, to be earned here.
- Next, count the number of management companies. Make some telephone calls. Ask for some brochures. Who are the biggest management players in the market? How many complexes does each handle? It is good to have some management companies that handle substantial numbers of units. Usually they will try one or two apartment complexes in your publications and, if results warrant, increase the number as time goes on.

- Beware of trade areas where one management company has practically cornered the market. This is seldom possible in major, big-city markets, but it does happen in the smaller cities. The danger is that a single "no" from this company can shoot down your entire project. It is always dangerous to get into a situation where success in your project is dependent on getting an advertising commitment from any single individual or company. There's even a proverb that covers the situation: don't put your eggs in one basket. I found myself in just such a situation in one of the small city environments where my apartment guide did not succeed in bringing in enough profit to make it worthwhile to me. There were few enough apartment communities in town to begin with, and all of them were run by a single firm, which, as it happened, did not relish the idea of buying ads in my apartment guide. There was very little I could do to overcome this single negative decision.

- Some smaller cities can be good prospects for modest apartment guide projects, under certain circumstances. These circumstances include the presence of certain factors that produce a more active market for apartment rentals than might otherwise exist in areas of such limited populations. In the case of my own small market apartment guides, the three that flourished were in just such markets. Two of them were in university towns, with the continual influx and outgo of students, professors, etc. There was constant turnover in leases, many of which were very short term. Competition for tenants was fierce. The third of my successful, small market guides was published in a city with a major military base. Like the universities mentioned above, the base created constant turnover in the rental market, making continual advertising a necessity for management companies. The two small market guides that failed were published in cities that had no such institutions. The rental market was not active enough to require advertising in an expensive apartment guide. Competition for leases was limited. People tended to rent apartments and stay in them over relatively long periods of time. Apartment owners and managers concluded, probably rightly, that the cost of advertising outweighed the benefit that could be derived from it.

- In addition, it is always a great plus if there is a cluster of these smaller markets, such that a single salesperson can easily cover two or three of them. In such a case you will have several beneficial factors working in your favor. Your sales commissions can be lower, since it will be easier for a salesperson to make a livable income with lower commissions from three times as many properties. You will get some multiple sales benefits, since some management companies will have properties in two or more of the cities in your cluster. And finally, the actual guidebooks can be produced at the same time by the same printer, resulting in a very substantial savings to you in production costs.

Handling the Competition

There are few major metropolitan areas today that do not have apartment comparison guides already in place and thriving. If you want to get into this lucrative market you will have to go up against these established publications and get your share of the advertising. Can you go head to head with them and succeed?

The answer to this question is yes, if three things happen:

- You carve out a readily identifiable market position for yourself.
- You determine that there are enough potential advertisers for you to break even with an initial 20% market share.
- You present yourself to the market in a highly credible way.

Your research of the yellow pages listings for apartment complexes and management companies will settle the 20% question. You can also survey the ads in the competing publications to see how many of these complexes actually advertise regularly. And you can easily polish your image so that you earn the respect of even the most reluctant management company marketing director. The question of the market position, though, is more difficult. It will require some very careful analysis and your most creative thinking.

Defining Your Market Position

Your market position is your individual niche within the larger niche market of apartment comparison guides. It should be so clearly defined that it will accomplish two essential things:

- Your market position will make it absolutely clear in your own mind— and from your own point of view—precisely what benefits you are selling to your clients, why they cannot get these benefits elsewhere, and the reasons why they should buy them from you.
- Your market position should define your publication clearly in the mind of the potential advertiser. The qualities and benefits that make your publication different must be absolutely clear.

Why Some Customers May Not Be Happy to See You

When I set out to start an apartment guide in a major North Carolina city I was astonished to find that many of the customers that I hoped to sell were not at all happy to see me and my new publication enter the market. They were not just indifferent; they were openly hostile. Why? At first I did not know. After all, wasn't I offering them a new medium to attract the renters that they needed so badly? And they certainly did not have to advertise with me if they chose not to. Right?

Wrong. Maybe they could hold off with their space purchases in the beginning, but to the degree that I succeeded in filling my pages with ads, saturated the marketplace with my magazines and became an important marketing force, they would, in the future, feel virtually forced to advertise with me. They would simply not be able to stay out of one of the most important apartment guides on the racks and in the newcomer kits.

Some marketing managers made no bones about it. They were satisfied with things as they were. There was only one apartment guide in the market, so they had to buy only one ad per issue. They did not want to stretch their advertising budgets. If I succeeded with my new comparison guide they would henceforth have to advertise in two books, thus increasing their advertising expenditures by a considerable sum. I understood then that my market position had to be so attractive that even the hardest and toughest of apartment managers would have to give my guide a try.

Price, Format, Distribution and Service

The four most important factors to consider when you are defining your market position are those of:

- Price
- Quality
- Distribution (circulation)
- Customer service

The last of these is easy. Customer service is something that you know you must do, that you find out how to do, and that you then do. Think creatively about how you are going to provide this service *and be perceived by the customer as providing it.*

Price, quality and distribution also require a good deal of creative thought. On top of that they require careful analysis. You do not have to do something wildly different to carve out a tenable market position for yourself. In the long run, the results that you get for your advertisers will be the basis of profitable, long-term relationships. Getting better results by bringing in more inquirers who go on to sign leases is ultimately the best market position of all; you will be known as the publisher of the apartment guide that works. But first you have to find out precisely what your competitors are doing.

The Intelligence Business: How to Gather Information on Your Competitors

After you have done your initial market analysis, counted the apartment complexes and management companies, and decided that the market can absorb another apartment guide enterprise, focus your attention on the magazines currently in the trade area. You will send out your spies and undercover people (I'm joking, but not by much) to bring in as much information as possible. In your case your core of undercover operatives will consist of yourself, your spouse, one or two of your potential salespersons and an occasional double agent from the competitor's camp. No one is going to simply hand you the information you need. Fortunately, though, it is more accessible than you may think. Here are the steps that you take to get the job done.

- First, gather as many different issues of the publications of your competition as you can. A run of one or two years would be very nice to have, though you can get by with fewer issues, if necessary. You can go by an apartment complex, see the resident manager there, and ask for copies. You can go by the Chamber of Commerce. The publishers of the guide you are investigating will have sent copies to the chamber for distribution in newcomer kits. Ask them for the current copy, then for back issues if they are available. If you still are not able to assemble the booklets you need, visit the bank, especially if the market you are investigating is in the town where you live and you can go to your own bank. Ask to see the newcomer representative. Interview this representative about their total newcomer package. (You might glean other information in the process that you can put to good use.) Ask to see the apartment guide. Ask if there are back issues. And, of course, you can take the direct, but time-consuming, method of simply picking them up at distribution points over a period of time. You should develop a habit of picking up free publications of all kinds whenever you stop over at a motel or visit a restaurant in a new location. You can mine these products for ideas to use in your own publications.
- You will also have to study the media kit of the competing publication. This kit is a collection of information concerning the publication that is sent to advertisers and potential advertisers. It is not secret information, but it is not routinely mailed to competitors. The most important item in the kit is the rate card, which will list the prices that advertisers have to pay for ads of various sizes and frequencies of insertion. It will also contain details of claimed circulation and distribution. It will undoubtedly describe these details in terms deemed to be most flattering to the publication and impressive to the potential advertiser. Bear in mind that the

claims on the rate card may or may not be literally true. Some may be exaggerated. But these facts are the ones that the competitor is giving to customers and you will need to know them. In addition, the media kit will contain other information describing the best selling features of the publication, the features that the publishers think will help them sell advertising in their pages to apartment managers. You can often obtain a media kit by writing to the publication and asking for it. Utilize your laser printer to generate a letterhead that will get results for you. Since I often did advertising design work for a few clients I simply inserted the words "advertising agency" or some equivalent into the letterhead of my business. More often than not the kit was sent soon thereafter. If this does not work for you ask one of the resident managers in an apartment complex to show you a copy. Advertisers will also include major banks, furniture rental firms and other businesses that cater to people who live in apartments. If your bank is among these advertisers, use your contacts there to get a look at a rate card.

- Another technique for gleaning information about your competitors is to undertake a "survey" of apartment marketing techniques and advertising. Prepare a questionnaire. Call on resident managers. When they are not showing apartments they are often a bit bored. They have time on their hands and nothing to do with it. Introduce yourself, or have your representative do so, and give them your card (the one with "ad agency" or "public relations" on it). Pull out your list of questions and fire away. Surveys are common these days, and a goodly number of the managers will go right along with it. Again, realize that you are not asking for secret information of any kind. You are just attempting to find out the going rate for advertising in the marketplace and what your competitor is promising to do for his customers.

- Develop personal contacts in the industry and get information through them. Most people like talking about what they do for a living, and you will have little difficulty finding someone who will enjoy talking to you. The competition, no matter how conscientious, will have made some enemies along the way (a fact that you, when you begin publishing, will do well to keep in mind, since you will inevitably develop your own set of enemies). Such people will be happy to share their gripes with you.

- Advertise for salespeople. Those who respond to your ad can also serve as informants in your search for information. Word your ad to attract people with experience in the apartment industry. You will surely hire some of the applicants once you decide that your project is feasible. Meanwhile, you will have a pool of informed individuals, perhaps former property managers, who will have the information you need at their disposal.

Analyzing the Information You Have Gathered

Once you have gathered the relevant facts about how your competitors are doing business, answer the following questions.

- What is the claimed circulation of your competing publications?
- Exactly how, and through what channels, are they distributed?
- How frequently are they published?
- What are the guaranteed dates of publication?
- What does a page of advertising cost?
- What does a line listing cost?
- Is there a charge for color separations and for advertising layout and design?
- What are the multiple insertion discounts, if any?
- What is the format of the competing publications? What is the trim size of the publication?
- Are the ads all different, or are they formatted and pretty much alike in their appearance? Are most of them in color? Are they all in black and white?
- Do there seem to be seasonal fluctuations in the amount of advertising in the publications?
- Do most advertisers insert their ads issue after issue?
- How many pages of advertising does an average issue contain?
- Multiply the number of pages of advertising by the most favorable (lowest) ad rate for display ads and for line ads. What are the average gross revenues for each issue?
- What is the recent history of the publication? Have rates gone up recently? Has ownership changed? Have there been other changes (in format, way of doing business, etc.) that you can exploit in developing your market position?
- What special features such as maps, postage-paid "bounce-back" cards, how-to information, industry news columns and other devices do these publications include to make them attractive to advertisers as well as to readers?
- What advertising do they contain from non-apartment sources? Add these to your list of prospects.

Mapping Out a Tentative Market Position

Once you have all (or most) of this information and have studied it, you will be in a position to map out a tentative market position for yourself. This is a time for brainstorming. Get out your legal pad. Divide each of four pages into two columns. At the top of these pages write the topic to be covered. The first will be price; the second, format; the third, distribution; the fouth, customer service. Put the name of your competitor at the top of the left hand column on each page and the projected name of your publication at the top of the right hand column. Fill in all the facts that you have been able to discover about your competitor on the left, and on the right put the projected facts about the way you intend to do business. In each case you should try to find a way to give yourself a marketing edge, a benefit that the customer will get if he chooses to do business with you.

Always go as far as you can in increasing customer benefits, but don't cross the line that separates profit from loss. (And always bear in mind that in business, "profit" is defined as the money that remains in the bank after all costs of doing business are paid out, including all overhead and the salary that you pay yourself). Profit is used to build the business, take on new projects, acquire labor-saving machinery, and perhaps make an investment or two. The salary you pay yourself pays the mortgage and puts groceries on the table. Profit builds your net worth. Notice, too, that the heading at the top of this section talks about a tentative market position. Don't worry too much about the details as you brainstorm the problem. Just get all the ideas down on paper. Later, you'll go back and decide what is feasible and what is not.

Your Format

Format comes first, because what you have to charge your customers for their ads will depend to a considerable degree on the cost of producing your publication in the format you choose. By format I mean:

- The trim size of the publication
- The amount of color it contains
- The way ads and line advertising listings are displayed, etc.

Every change you make in the format may well force changes in price. Selecting prices that you consider competitive may, in turn, affect the format. This is because your greatest single cost will be that of printing your publication, and the format you choose largely determines what this cost will be. In Chapter 19, "How to Save Money on Printing," I will help you understand printing cost factors and keep them in mind as you go forward with your planning.

There are a limited number of options:

- If you are using the popular booklet-style format, your publication must fit into a pocket or a purse with ease.
- Your trim size should be a standard size, so as to utilize printing paper in the most economical way possible.
- If you are going to opt for a saturation circulation publication printed on

newsprint, your page size must be one of those standard to tabloids. Check with the printer who is going to do the work for you.

Format Options

Within those limits you do have some choices:

- *5.5 by 8.5 inches.* This standard size (known as the "digest" size) is close to that of many paperback books. With a color cover it can be very attractive. The very successful *Apartment Finder* publications utilize this format very effectively. If you want to vary this slightly, consult your printer for cost-effective options. I have seen a wholly-owned subdivision guide in Atlanta that is somewhat smaller and more square looking. Aesthetically, it is very appealing. Some publications go slightly larger, to 6 by 9 inches, another standard size.

- *3 by 8.5 inches.* This size varies enough from those discussed above to be immediately recognizable in the marketplace as an alternative. This format is widely utilized throughout the country by the Haas Publishing Co. for its successful *Apartment Guide* publications. The unique size brings very powerful market visibility to the Haas product.

- *Tabloid and mini-tab.* The two formats described above are more typical than tabloid formats. The products in those sizes are more permanent and give off the feeling of stability and permanence. They are less likely to be discarded immediately. A person who picks one up is likely to take it home and keep in on the shelf for a while. It does not tear or wrinkle nor get spread out on the floor to sop up the water overflow from the ceramic containers that hold the office's potted plants. Mindful that in the long run advertising results—leases signed as a result of ads—are what build success, some entrepreneurs in the apartment and homes guide field are beginning to publish massive circulation tabloids as a substitute for the more expensive, elaborate and time-consuming full-color publications we have described. The strength of the tabloid is the rock bottom cost of production. Turnaround time on the printing is reduced, too. The weakness here is that the shelf-life of a tabloid is very short. After a tabloid has been on the rack for a few days or weeks it will look, feel and actually smell old and out-of-date. This means that you will have to publish tabloids more frequently. You also risk attracting the envy and ire of the newspapers in town, who can easily smother you in the tabloid field should they desire to do so. Still, there may well be competitive situations in which the tabloid is the way to go. The format you ultimately choose will be the one that gives you the most favorable market position.

- *Color.* You can be quite successful with color and without color. The

Apartment Finder publications, for instance, contain mostly full-color advertising, although advertisers have an option to choose black and white. Haas Publishing Company's *Apartment Directory* publications are largely black and white. Color has its obvious appeal. In a publication that contains mostly full-color ads the pressure is on every advertiser to select higher-priced color advertising as well. The cost of color separations, typically anywhere from $100 to $200 a page above and beyond advertising costs, are passed on to the advertiser by the publishers. This is a one-time-only charge, but it is still substantial. For the publisher, color advertisements are more time-consuming to produce and run up printing costs. A color publication is usually printed on more expensive stock (paper) to show off the quality of the color itself. You want the color to snap off the page. Color printed on cheap paper does not snap. It lies there and whimpers. Many, but by no means all, of your production costs for individual ads can be passed on to the advertiser. But even if all of them were passed on, there would remain the disadvantage to the publisher of the time factor, considerably more of which is required both in the preparation of the ad in the first place and in readying it for the printer.

• *Black and white.* Other publications choose a format that is predominantly black and white. Color on the inside is the exception rather than the rule. The cover will be in full color, front and back, both outside and inside. These pages and a limited number of additional pages can be made available to apartments and other advertisers who insist on color, but this is not encouraged. More than a limited number of color pages would force a change in the entire production process and in the amount of time allotted to it. A black and white publication is much cheaper to produce. Preparation time is drastically reduced. There are no color separations to buy. The printer has to shoot only one set of negatives for the body of the book rather than four. Press time is much reduced as are problems of quality control. More books can be printed for a lower price, and this can be done more frequently with the same number of people (or even fewer) working on the book in the publisher's office. If there is already a color publication in the market, you may well position yourself as the black-and-white, lower cost (but higher circulation and therefore more effective) alternative. If a black and white publication is established in the market, you may find that you can position yourself as the sensibly-priced color alternative. Often you can reduce costs enough through production and printing knowhow to lower your advertising rates appreciably without adversely affecting profits. If there are both black and white and color publications in the market your positioning job will be harder, but not impossible. There will be, for instance, the question of the use of formatted or unformatted advertising inside the magazine. In the formatted ad the arrangement of the advertising elements is always identical. No variation is possible. Typically there will be a picture of the property at the top of the page. Beneath the picture there will be a description of the property—including location—rental rates and summaries of the amenities that the apartments offer. Often these property descriptions are preceded by a strong headline—or, if they are not, they ought to be. Examples of formatted ads are shown in this chapter. Unformatted ads are custom-designed, and each is different from the others. Many of these will have been prepared by advertising agencies. Unformatted ads will be far more time consuming to prepare than formatted ads. Often this "design time" can be passed on to the advertiser on an hourly or flat fee basis.

- *Flex format.* In my own apartment guides we successfully used what I call a "flex format." Our guide featured full color ads. We accepted ads from agencies who had prepared them on behalf of clients or we would custom design them ourselves. Our ads were often quite imaginative. One ad in an early issue—which literally made our reputation in the market—was the work of a part-time designer who was an art student in a local college and worked for me in the evening. This was a full-color pop-up (children's books style) in the center of our book. Nevertheless, since we were a small company, we did not have the space or the people to spend this kind of time on everyone. As an alternative we developed what we called our "*format book*." In the book were ten basic ad designs, each different, some with one photograph, some with two or more. But all were easily manageable. It was a matter of an hour to drop in the particular message and photographs that specific clients wanted. To encourage them to use our format book and thus save us valuable time, we did not charge back any design time for these ads. The formats were "free." We continued to charge, however, for the color separations themselves. The format book worked very well indeed. There were enough formats that, leafing through our guide, the casual apartment shopper would not ever have been aware that the ads were formatted at all. The format book was unique to my company, and it became an important part of my market position. I hereby bequeath the idea to you.

- *"Listing" formats.* The so-called listings (line ads which appear in geographical and alphabetical order in the body of many apartment and homes guides) repeat much of the information that is presented in the display ads but in handier, easier to use, form. These listings are the reference part of the guide. In the listings all apartment sizes and square footage are given, along with costs. Discounts are listed one by one. These listings are completely formatted. No one of them looks different from the others. There is usually a flat fee for listings and a limitation as to the number of lines of space each can occupy. Had I continued in the guide business I would have offered some options, such as certain words in bold or specials overprinted in a 20% screen to call attention to special incentives in force at the time of publication. Each of these options would have added, say fifty dollars to the cost of the listing. Since these special effects would not have cost me anything at all, and there are many listings in the typical guide, these small charges could add several thousand dollars of pure profit to each issue, just as a $1.50 glass of iced tea or soda adds tremendously to the profitability of any restaurant that markets its basic blue plate special at rock bottom prices.

Setting Ad Prices

This is a thorny question, and I will tell you from the start that there is no way to know ahead of time that you are absolutely correct in your judgment on what you should charge your advertisers for space in your book. What is certain is that you want to charge as much as you can and still sell ads. You also want to create a strong market position, such that clients will feel that they are getting more for their money when they advertise with you than when they advertise with competing publications.

Here's what you do to come up with your asking price:

- In the beginning you may have to settle for a little less than you would like to get. To make yourself feel better, though, you can go ahead and forecast (to yourself) a gradual series of rate increases as you strengthen your market position through the results you obtain.
- You must resist any pressure—whether brought to bear by yourself or by advisors—to begin to sell ads at an artificially low rate. You can't, as the old business saying goes, lose money on each ad you produce and make up that loss by selling a great many of them. There is a base below which you cannot go, and that base is the amount of money that pays your expenses, your salary, and provides a modest margin of profit for growth and expansion as well as a nest-egg to see you through market fluctuations and the occasional recession.
- In thinking about what you are going to charge, you have learned, from your espionage activities, what at least one other company in the business (your competitor) thinks it has to charge to be profitable. This price is your point of departure. If you can't meet it or better it you may have to abandon your idea, unless you can add significant benefits to go along with your higher price, benefits such as full color or vastly increased circulation. Even then, you will be in difficult straits. If your price is higher, it will usually be perceived as high and less advantageous, regardless of

the added benefits you offer. Perceived value is more important than real value when you are entering the marketplace. You are the new kid on the block, the one with everything to prove.

- To increase your profitability, utilize add-on pricing. Keep your base space rate as low as you can, but then develop a menu of "extras" that you can charge for, such as the boldface words and phantoms in the line-ad listings, special typographic effects, special position, etc.

- Find ways that will enable you to print more magazines at a lower cost. You might do this, for instance, by printing more magazines less frequently. It is far cheaper to print 50,000 magazines twice yearly than to print 25,000 magazines four times a year. This is because much of the printing cost is incurred before the presses begin to run. These are pre-press and press setup costs. The more you print in a single run the cheaper each magazine is to produce.

- Look for ways to cut printing costs. Incorporate as many of them as possible in your plans when you ask for quotes on printing. I refer you again to Chapter 19, "How to Save Money on Printing."

- Put pen to paper and develop specifications on a color guide, a black and white guide, and, if you wish, on a tabloid guide. Get firm quotes on these publications and find out precisely how much it will cost you to produce each of them.

- Add up the costs of getting the magazine out, including office expense, auto expense, sales commissions, ad design, printing and circulation, and any salaries and commissions, including your own. Don't fudge on any of the costs, but don't exaggerate any of them, either. One of the things you have going for you in the beginning is the fact that, since you are home-based, your overhead is lower. Since you will be doing much of the work yourself in your area of expertise, either your sales expense, your production expense, or both, will be lower.

- Divide the total cost by the number of full-page equivalent ads you expect to be able to sell. The figure you get from this arithmetic is your break-even advertising page cost for the first issue. Is it a competitive advertising rate? If, selling at the same cost, you can increase the number of ad pages you sell in following issues, will you be sufficiently in the black to make the project worthwhile? Now you've got a preliminary figure to play with, but you are still not through. What you have come up with is the actual, profitable full page rate. This is what most clients will look at when they make their first, superficial comparison of costs. At this stage you have already covered your costs and provided for a modest profit. Every extra dollar you get now is pure profit. Let's say, for ease of calculation, that you've come up with an advertising rate of $1,000 per page. This is for your top-of-the-line ad. Now, some will want a three-quarter page ad. You discourage this, but they insist. The cost of the three-quarter page ad will be $850, not 75% of $1,000. More likely is that some will want a half-page ad. These will go for, say, $695. Thus your per page revenues will, on the average, amount to considerably more than the $1,000 basic rate.

- You make a final adjustment when you look at your projected revenues per issue. If they are inadequate, you will have to find a way to increase them. Study all the samples of guides from all of the markets that you've ever passed through. Try to ferret out techniques that you can use to produce more revenue. If, after doing this, you still can't get your income figures up high enough, you may have a problem on your hands. There just may not be an adequate profit potential to justify your effort. But before you make that depressing decision, take one more step. Work carefully and thoroughly through the areas of distribution and customer service. There may be enough new that you can offer in these areas to justify the slightly higher advertising rates that you feel are necessary.

- A happier circumstance—one that actually happened to me—comes about when you calculate the bottom line on your projected advertising page rates and discover that you are far below the rates of the competition. You estimate that you can raise your prices by ten or twenty percent and still remain quite competitive. Go ahead and do it if the market will permit you to. You won't have a second chance.

Circulation and Distribution

I use both these terms because there are two sides to this all-important part of your business. The first term, circulation, refers to the number of guidebooks you print and send out. This is your circulation. The second term refers to the way in which you get these guidebooks into the hands of potential apartment leasers or home buyers. This is your distribution. For the people who buy your ads, both of these are very important, of course. In terms of getting results, of actually getting clients to come in with their checkbooks and sign leases, the quality of distribution is the absolutely essential factor. You may print 100,000 books, but if you put them in places where potential apartment renters are not likely to go, your results will be poor. On the other hand you can print 25,000 books, place them in exactly the right locations, and get far better results. What you want to do, then, is to develop a system that has the circulation numbers and the distribution. You want to get lots of guidebooks into the hands of as many as possible of those individuals who are looking for apartments at any given time. Here is how to do it:

- Contact major employers in your trade area. Lists of these businesses will be available from the local chamber of commerce or from the county economic development office. Make some telephone calls and get the name of the human resources (personnel) officer. Write a letter to this person. Offer copies of your apartment guide as an aid for relocating personnel. Along with your letter, enclose a request form on which this officer can indicate how many copies he or she will need, and how often; accompany this form with a self-addressed, stamped envelope. As an alternative, print your request form on the back of a self-addressed, stamped postal card. Also include your telephone number for faster response. Design this letter or card as carefully as you would any other direct mail solicitation.

- Make a list of those who do not return the card. Call these people personally. In this way you can convert many of these to "yes" responses. While you are on the phone, do a little marketing research. Ask the human resources director what features would make the apartment guides even more useful to their incoming personnel.
- Contact hospitals and other large semi-public organizations.
- Contact college and university housing offices.
- Contact the post housing offices of military bases.
- You have been in touch with the Chamber of Commerce and the city/county economic development office to get lists of major employers. Now contact them again and make sure that your publication is included in their newcomer information kits. Place a flyer in each magazine that you send to the Chamber and the development office inviting those who get the kits to write or call. Tell them you will gladly send them a supply of guides for them to distribute to relocating personnel.
- Contact every bank in town, and get your magazine into their newcomer kits.
- Set up racks at airports.
- If your market area is served by a commuter airline, try to get your guides on that airline. Advertisers will love it.
- Place your magazines in convenience stores. If you meet any resistance, offer to trade out a full-page ad in return for the right (exclusive right, if possible) to place your ads in the stores.
- Place your magazine in the reception area of every hotel and motel in your trade area.
- Place your magazine in the waiting area of all restaurants.
- Place your magazine racks in shopping centers, outside post offices and other major distribution points.
- Plough early profits back into the purchase of racks which will hold your publications. These will vary from the weatherproof, enclosed racks to wrought-iron-looking indoor floor and desk racks. The weatherproof ones are expensive. Ask for the prices on reconditioned ones. You will not

need the coin rack, so this will make your rack much more affordable.
- Get proof of circulation. When someone requests books by telephone, send them out, but also ask for written confirmation of the request. Call later and ask how they liked the books. Better yet, send an evaluation sheet with a large space for "comments." Some of the letters will bring in blurbs that you can use to sell with.

Conspicuous Circulation

Circulating your magazines is not enough. You must also be *perceived to be circulating them.*

Keep them on the shelves, counters, and racks near the locations of all major advertisers. Service racks regularly to keep supplies on hand. Exploit every high-visibility location you can find. You may consider some of these locations inferior to others in their capacity to produce actual leases. But your advertisers need to see your publication everywhere they go. Make sure that all your racks, whether wire or cardboard, counter-top or freestanding, weatherproof or indoor, are emblazoned with the name of your publication.

If you have a pickup truck or van, print the name of your magazine on the side of it as you service your racks. If you use the family car, have three of the magnetic signs made, one for each side and one for the rear. It is amazing how frequently these delivery vehicles will be seen by your advertisers. This reassures them.

Never forget that in magazine circulation, seeing is believing. It's not enough to tell your advertiser what you are doing for them. They want to see for themselves what you are doing for them. In fact, they insist on it.

Your "Credibility Brochure"

When I went into my first big city market, head to head with established competition, I furnished my sales rep with an eight-page, slick paper capabilities brochure. Sporting a good deal of color (it appeared to have more that it actually did) the brochure told the reader about our company: what it had done, what it could do, what it was doing, and for whom.

- We featured our expertise in coming up with advertising that gets results. We listed the major clients we had designed advertising for. We told about our other publications and their successes. We told about our knowhow in the broadest possible range of print-media promotion.
- We included photographs of publications we had worked on, worked for, been published in, or had published ourselves.
- We included testimonial blurbs from clients, critics and others who had kind things to say about our work.

- We included a paragraph on our CEO (namely, me) and listed his credits. You will do the same. We listed the credits of free-lancers and others who had expressed an interest in taking on assignments for our publications. We listed the credits of the graphic designers who would work for us, either as salaried employees or as independent contractors and free-lancers.
- We included, in a separate folder, mock-ups of our projected publication, including sample covers, page layouts, sample advertisements, and sample line listings.

You will be surprised to discover how many good things you can find to say about yourself and about those who work for you when you put your mind to it. Don't limit yourself to accomplishments in your present business. Look back over the years. A prize-wining artist or writer is a prizewinner no matter when the good work was done.

If, in spite of your best efforts to ferret out every past accomplishment that can lend credibility to you and your company, you still feel that you are coming up a bit short, incorporate the sample pages and covers we discussed above into your main capabilities brochure.

Your capabilities brochure is the first item your sales rep will hand to a potential client. It is the piece that the client will, in turn, present to his or her boss or management team. You have a lot riding on its quality. Don't skimp. Do the very best job you can with the resources available.

This piece has to be first rate. If you think you can't afford it, perhaps you can do as I did. I found a printer who was willing to trade out the printing against future advertising in my publications. If you can find a printer whose shop is working at about half-speed for one reason or another, he or she may very well be interested in taking on the project if you make the prospect of advertising in your publication sound exciting enough and profitable enough.

If you have difficulty closing such a trade-out deal, you may suggest that you will pay for all out-of-pocket costs of paper, ink and color separations and trade out the rest. Further, make it clear that you will do the typesetting in your own office and furnish him with camera ready copy.

Your Media Kit

They call it a media kit, but it has a far wider range of use than that. In fact, after the first promotional efforts your media kit will seldom, if ever, be sent to the media again. It will, instead, be given to clients along with, or even prior to, an initial sales call. It is simply an information pack, containing everything good you can think of to say about yourself, including the credibility brochure that we described in the last section.

A media kit is usually tucked into the pockets of a presentation folder. One of these pockets will be die-cut to hold your business card or the business card of the salesperson whose responsibility it is to sell the client your own circulation efforts.

The more flexible your media kit is, the more use it will be to you. There are a number of companies that specialize in printing the presentation covers, and their products are very slick indeed. One of these is Admore. As with the other printed products you use, you can save yourself at least 40% by buying directly from the wholesale supplier. All it takes is a letter on your company stationery to set yourself up as an Admore dealer. You will never have to order any more from them than the few products you will need for your own purposes, but you will get a 40% discount from the price your local printer will charge. He orders from Admore, too, and marks the cost up to his customers.

Following is a list of items that your media kit should contain:

- *Your capabilities brochure.*
- *A sheet describing your demographics.* Who does your publication reach? How old is the typical reader, the range of readers? How much money do they make? How many times a year do they move? Remember that you will be selling ads to banks and other firms as well as to apartment complexes. Banks, which make money by selling loans and bank accounts, will want as much financial information as possible: credit card use, plans to buy an automobile, etc. In the beginning there is necessarily some guesswork in coming up with a demographic profile. You can glean some information from the demographic information furnished by similar publications in the same trade area, from the census records and from your own circulation efforts. At this stage you say that you are "targeting" a certain cross-section of the population. After you've gotten a few issues out you can do your own survey of your readers and furnish hard numbers (always in terms of percentages, of course).
- *Copies of testimonial letters from satisfied customers.* Some of these will come in unbidden by you. Others may come as a result of subtle nudging and suggestion by you. Some will result from outright requests. Once someone says "OK, I'll write a letter," ask if they would like you to prepare one for them on their letterhead. Some will readily agree to this. You do, of course, let them know in general what you're going to say. I once designed a membership directory and magazine for an international trade organization. The president of the organization was so pleased that he sent me a letter in which he said that the new directory "exceeded [his] fondest expectations" and that it had "raised the organization to a new level of professionalism." Naturally a copy of this letter went into my media kit.

- *Your rate card.* Your rate card is the key item. It contains all the information your salesperson and your client will need to make a deal. The rate card is most often a two- or threefold piece printed on heavy stock with an enameled (glossy) finish. It contains the costs of advertising in any size and for any number of insertions. It will also include clear information about ad sizes, requirements for photographs, color, etc. It will include closing date, that is, the latest date on which you can accept advertising for a given issue. It will also contain, in a sentence or two, the essence of your demographics, circulation, features and benefits, etc. It should be so complete that a salesperson, with the rate card alone, would have all the information necessary to close a sale.
- *Your contract.* When the media kit is used on a sales call, it should contain a contract.

Making Your Pitch to the Right Person

The organization of management firms and real estate marketing companies can be more complex than you may think. In the apartment business there are at least four management levels in most big companies. At the top sits the overall company sales manager who oversees the whole marketing and advertising process. A step down on the scale comes the property manager. Each of these experienced people may have two, three or even more apartment complexes under their supervision. Finally, in the apartment business, there is the level of the resident manager. A resident manager resides in each complex, selling leases and overseeing operations.

These levels of management can be quite confusing, although in the largest companies the functions of each are fairly well defined. The overall manager makes deals involving the total advertising budget. If you sell an annual package of ads to the entire company, he or she is the person to talk to. But even if you don't sell an overall package, the property managers often have some discretionary advertising funds available and may elect to place a trial page in your magazine for one of their properties. In the largest companies, the resident managers seldom have the authority to sign advertising contracts.

Be on your best public relations behavior with individuals at all three levels, but make your presentations only to the one who can buy. There is no greater waste of time than to make a sales presentation to someone who cannot make a decision and sign a contract. It may take some doing to find your way around in this maze of divided responsibilities, but you must do so. In smaller companies there may be only two levels, those of the property manager and the resident manager. In the smallest companies, the resident manager often does the buying, although the owner of the property may get involved as well. Keep this important fact about resident managers in mind:

although they most often cannot say yes to your advertising sales presentation, they can send negative vibes all the way back up the ladder and make real trouble for you. Time spent cultivating the good feelings of resident managers pays off in the long run.

Your Production Schedule

As crucial as it is, selling the ads is just the beginning of getting your publication out. You will still have to design, typeset and lay out the ads, get them back to the advertisers for approval, make requested changes and get them approved all over again. You will have to photograph some of the properties. You will have to gather all the line ads listing facts and figures, typeset them and get them out for approval. You will have to make the maps, directories, tables and other materials and get them ready for printing. You will have to do all this and still get your camera-ready book to the printer on time so that it can be printed and on the racks on time.

All of this will require a carefully planned and ironclad production schedule. There will often be a great temptation to put this chore or that one off until tomorrow. But when you do so the whole production process is thrown off balance, a balance that you may never again achieve.

How to Make a Production Schedule That Works

In making your production schedule for any publication, work backwards. First, set the date that you will be out for distribution. Then ask yourself the following questions and come up with precise answers.

- To get your book out on time, when do you have to get to the printer?
- To get to the printer on time, when do you have to have your ads complete and approved?
- To meet this deadline, when do you have to send them out for the advertiser's approval?
- To meet that deadline, when do you have to have all the advertising information in and complete for your art department to work with?
- To meet that deadline, when do you have to close sales?
- Review all of these dates. Where do you have to tighten up? How will you do it?

Work the hours necessary to meet each of these deadlines. It may be difficult, and you may want to just go home and forget about it for a while. But you can't do it. Putting things off just makes everything else more difficult. When you miss a publication date you lose enormous credibility. There are always others out there who will say, "Hey, Mr. Advertiser. Those guys may be pretty good, but you can't count on them to get their magazine out when they say they will. We're the ones you can rely on. Try us next time." Be late time after time and you create an irresistible "on-time" market niche for the hungry competition.

Customer Service

In publishing your guides, as in publishing any other project in this book, the care and feeding of customers quickly becomes one of your most important jobs. Neglect customers, or treat them with anything less than the courtesy and consideration that they expect, and they become very vulnerable to the sales solicitations of competing salespersons who promise not to neglect them. Think of every executive associated with the running of a client company as your personal customer, not just the ones who actually buy ads and sign contracts. Whenever your name, the name of your publication or the name of any of your salespersons comes up for comment, you want someone there to tell a pleasant story of how you helped out at the last association fund raising, helped solve a problem, provided a lucrative lead (these must be equally circulated among all your customers), kept the latest issue of your magazine in good supply at the rental office, took them out for lunch or otherwise made it clear that you cared, personally, about their work and their success.

Do not neglect to stop in to say hello, write letters of thanks after sales calls, take someone to lunch from time to time, write or telephone when some item of information of use to the recipient crosses your desk. Never repeat industry or personal gossip, however. Gossip always backfires, often at great cost to you.

Frequency of Contact

Frequency of contact is important. Your publication schedule may require a sales call just two, three, or—at most—four times a year. Over the months between publication dates, however, people can forget what a nice person you are and how much they enjoy buying ads from you. You can be certain that your competition will be dropping by.

You stay in touch. Make sure that your salespeople stay in touch. Make sure that even the person who drives your company station wagon or truck gives a personal greeting, by name, to resident managers and property managers when delivering magazines. I once had a winner in this category. I hired a retired newspaper circulation manager who loved to get out and drive and who loved to get to know the people that he dealt with. He was a demon of efficiency, and brought in many a fond mention of that "nice little man" who delivered our apartment guides.

Send Christmas cards, Hanukkah cards, Easter cards, Birthday cards. Trade

Production Schedule Dates to Live By

Your completed production schedule will consist of these dates:

1. Close of sales by _____.

2. All ad materials in by _____.

3. All ads designed by _____.

4. Ad approvals sent out by _____.

5. Ad approvals in by _____.

6. Page layout completed by _____.

7. Date of delivery to the printer _____.

8. Date of publication (new magazines on the stands and racks _____.

If you set these dates realistically, and if you live by them and have everyone who works for you live by them, you can avoid one of the major errors made by beginning publishers: not getting the product out on time.

out vacation weekends with resort owners and draw names for free weekends.

Two or three sales calls by the competition, with no appearance by you or someone on your staff to reassure your customers that they are already buying the best advertising available, can easily result in someone's agreeing to "just try" dropping out of your guide for an issue or two and "testing the response" from another one. Do not let this happen for lack of thought or effort on your part. A customer once lost is very difficult to regain.

Joining Up

In a town of any size, there is usually an apartment or home builders' association. These professional associations work to enhance the professional image and skills of those working in the field. They give seminars leading to such certifications as the CAM (Certified Apartment Manager) and others. They sponsor trade shows once or twice a year at which suppliers rent booths and display their wares to the apartment professionals.

You will want to join and become very active in these associations. Seek out a leadership role; volunteer for association activities; help produce association newsletters, insofar as your time and facilities permit. It is possible, as you learn more and more about the advertising business, that you can give seminars on how to sign more leases, close more sales presentations, design better ads or any number of other topics.

Never miss a trade show. Rent your booth early so that you can choose the best possible location. Try to design an eye-catching booth that adds life to the event. The sponsors will appreciate this. Offer door prizes from your backroom barrel of trade-out goodies.

Sometimes the trade shows are organized around "fun" themes designed to increase attendance by the membership at large. If it is "Monte Carlo Night," for instance, really get into the spirit of the affair. Dress like Riviera croupiers. Set up a roulette wheel or a blackjack table where participants play for prizes that you have brought along.

Tracking Results

Your customers will want to know whether they are spending all those advertising dollars wisely or not. To find out, almost all of them do some kind of customer tracking. These tracking efforts will vary from the reasonably professional to the amateurish and, finally, to the downright incompetent. But whatever the method your customers use, you will need to understand it, prepare for it and see that you and your publication are not shortchanged by it.

How is this tracking done? In the larger management companies there may be a central office that will tally results from the call-in inquiries resulting from ads placed in your magazine. They will also count the business reply cards that may have been bound into your publication, torn out and returned by readers.

The resident managers, too, will be counting inquirers. When a potential customer comes into the apartment office the resident manager will ask them, "Where did you hear about us?" They will then fill out a form and credit the inquiry to one of the advertising outlets that the company uses.

This all sounds simple and straightforward, but it really isn't. The trouble is that clients often don't remember which book they looked at to gather information about homes or apartments. When asked the tracking question, they may reply, "In the little apartment guide." Now they may in reality have used your book. But if your book is called "Apartment Directory" and the competitor is called "Apartment Guide," then the competitor gets the credit. The resident managers are interested in selling their product, not in badgering their clients until they are absolutely sure that the answer they get is correct. Some resident managers just don't care about the accuracy, not understanding its importance. Still others may have become close friends with competing salespersons and simply fudge the report by routinely assigning credits to that friend's publication. While you can never be absolutely certain that the tracking done by others is accurate, you can take steps to make sure that it is as accurate as possible. When tracking results come out in your favor time after time, there is nothing for you to do, of course. If it's not broken, don't fix it. If you think you aren't getting your due, you must find ways to help your advertisers come up with more accurate figures. Much of this is done on a case-by-case basis, and you will use your ingenuity to come up with remedies. Here are a few techniques that have worked for me.

- Prepare a stand-up easel-type board displaying the cover of your magazine and a copy of the ad that the customer is running. You can print the backboards on inexpensive index stock, in one color, with reverse borders and the legend, "As Seen in XXXX Apartment Directory." Affix your cover and the ad with spray adhesive and take it down to a copy shop to be laminated. After lamination, glue a cardboard easel stand to the back, take it by your advertiser's sales office and place it prominently on a desk. Ask that the salesperson, when asking tracking questions, point to your display and ask, "Is this the ad you saw?"
- If you suspect some chicanery or some sloppy procedure on the part of your customer's sales and tracking personnel, send a secret shopper by. This will be an unknown person who will pose as a legitimate shopper and watch the tracking procedure firsthand. Analyze the feedback you get and come up with strategies to improve these procedures in your favor.
- The "secret shopper" technique can become a special promotion. Advertise the fact that you will be sending around a "secret shopper" in your

own magazine. The names of all those who ask the shopper if he or she saw the ad specifically in your book will be put into a hat for a drawing every two months. The winner will get a free weekend vacation or some other prize. Always publish the winner's picture in your magazine. Send a certificate suitable for framing. Make announcements of the winners at association meetings.

- You can furnish free tracking forms to your clients and potential clients. These will consist of a simple checklist, but you will have phrased the questions so that objective, careful responses are encouraged. There are scores of ways to protect yourself from tracking errors, and much depends on your ability to do so.

10

How to Publish Weekly Newspapers, Niche-Market Tabloids, and Shoppers

A weekly newspaper can be a very attractive business enterprise. Such a publication has a lot going for it. It easily meets our three criteria for success in regional and local publishing: it has a clearly defined and limited trade area; it targets a finite list of advertising prospects, all of whom are easily reached; and, because it is free to the consumer and cheap to produce, it easily achieves saturation circulation.

There are some modest start-up costs, mainly for office space and initial supplies. You can avoid the space cost if you have a large basement or double garage that could be converted to use for your business. Most needed equipment, chiefly your desktop publishing computer and laser printer and an enlarging/reducing copy machine, can be leased by paying a couple of monthly installments up front. Production tables, files, and other paraphernalia are generally very simple to design and can be homemade.

These virtually negligible up-front costs are more than balanced by the short weekly billing cycle you will be working on. By the time your next month's lease payments come due you will already have four or five (yes, some months will have five Wednesdays in them!) week's accounts receivable to pay them. If, in the beginning, you do not need to draw out great amounts of cash for your own living expenses, it really is quite possible to start a newspaper of your own and pay for it as you go, wholly out of current revenues. This is precisely what I did with the *Mecklenburg Gazette*, a weekly newspaper that I owned in Davidson, North Carolina. When I got hold of the newspaper it was literally a week away from bankruptcy. I had no cash to speak of—just a few thousand dollars in savings to live on until advertising revenues started coming in.

Types of Newspaper Publications

Local circulation newspapers, tabloids, and shoppers fall into six categories: the traditional community weekly; the modified community weekly; the niche market newspaper; the editorially-supported shopper; the outright shopper, which has no editorial matter at all; and the all-classified outright shopper. Which is right for you? The answer depends in part on your own personality and career goals and in part on the niche markets that you find open to you.

I

The Full-fledged Community (Weekly) Newspaper

Community newspapers flourish in small and medium-sized towns all across the county, and they constitute the bedrock of the newspaper trade. Many reporters get their start in weeklies. In fact, many newspapers that are currently dailies also got their start as weeklies and simply grew with their towns. As the towns became cities, the weeklies became dailies.

The community weekly is a real newspaper. As such, its job is to report all the news and to tell what happened last week in the town it serves. There are many good reasons for starting a full-fledged weekly newspaper, but they are almost all of a personal, and not a business, nature. The kind of person who edits and publishes a successful weekly is a person who really cares about his or her community, the things that happen there and the people who live there. One of the best books on publishing weekly newspapers is Bruce Kennedy's *Community Journalism: A Way of Life*.

The subtitle of Kennedy's book—"A Way of Life"—is revealing, for the publication of a true weekly newspaper is indeed a way of life for the person who undertakes it. A good weekly newspaper soon becomes an integral part of life of the community, a community asset. People in town soon began to think of it as "our paper." When, in conversation, they use the expression "I see by the paper...," it is the paper you publish that they are referring to. Technically it may be your paper and you alone enjoy its profits and are responsible for its debts, but in reality it is "their paper." When you hear people start referring to it in that way, you know you are on the right track.

The weekly does everything. It publishes all the hard news of the week, gleaned from police reports, fire reports, city council meetings. It publishes church news, scouting news, civic club news. It publishes social news, especially the weddings that the big dailies no longer cover, complete with full descriptions of the bridal gown, bridesmaids gowns, family attire, reception news, and every other fact of interest that can be gleaned from whatever source is available. Prior to that, news of the engagement will have been published.

There will be a sports page, with school athletic news and features and news of the children's baseball, softball, soccer and basketball teams. There will be an arts and entertainment section. There will be an editorial page and an op-ed page. There will be a page of legal ads and, of course, a well-developed classified page. All of this takes a great deal of work—often sixty or seventy hours a week of it.

The full-fledged weekly option works best for individuals who are as interested in the publication itself as in the financial rewards it can bring. Writers and editors who hire salespeople to help them with that part of the job will have a head start, and are the ones most likely to choose this option. Publishing entrepreneurs who are not primarily writers often find the niche market publications listed below a more attractive business option — just as profitable, far less time consuming and much easier to publish. Those who come to publishing from a background in sales, for instance, may or may not have a sense of what constitutes good writing, and of what readers want to read and what they do not want to read.

Fewer Slots Available

Niche market opportunities abound, but opportunities for publishing full-fledged weeklies are more limited. You should look for two things when testing the market for a full-fledged weekly:

- *A growing community with no weekly and no small-town daily.* Such communities most often result from the development of new areas that attract large numbers of new, reasonably affluent residents. I lived for a time in the town of Washington, NC, on the north bank of the Pamlico River. Across the river on the south bank, eight or ten miles away, was the hamlet of Chocowinity. In the last five years the south bank has been the scene of intense real estate development by the Weyerheauser Corporation, which for years had bought waterfront timber acreage in the area. Chocowinity now has 1800 residents. It has no newspaper. I believe that a weekly would survive and thrive there. And since it is clearly a growth area, the paper would grow with it. The population of the town where I published my own community weekly was only 2800 and, as a matter of fact, there was only one discount drug store, and not a very big one at that. There was also a big city daily competing for market share (the Charlotte *Observer*, published just eighteen miles away) as well as a free circulation shopper. Yet my paper was successful, and my family of five derived a comfortable income from it.
- *An advertising base of businesses adequate to support your paper.* The population of Chocowinity and its environs now has the population and purchasing power to make a real weekly newspaper possible. There are local grocery stores that would certainly advertise on a weekly basis, and the larger ones across the river would probably advertise as well.

Secrets of Newspaper Success

How do you evaluate the chances for success? Mainly by studying the base of ready and willing advertisers. I once gave a talk on community newspapering to a class of journalism students at a nearby university. "What is the secret of success?" one young woman asked me. "What makes one weekly paper do well when another might fail?"

Now, I am sure she wanted me to talk about fine writing, investigative reporting, and an editorial page that gets nominated for a Pulitzer Prize. My answer was in a quite different vein. "Success in the weekly newspaper business require six things," I replied. "Four grocery stores, a K-Mart, and at least one large discount drugstore." The point, of course, is that if the advertising base is not there will be no paper to publish all that fine reporting.

Success is a word that has different meanings for different people. One publisher may be content with a newspaper which provides thirty-five or forty thousand dollars a year in take-home compensation while another wants much more. Forty thousand is not much in Washington, New York, or San Francisco, but it can be a living wage in many other regions of the country. Especially for those happy souls who, like Epicurus, understand that happiness lies, after all, in the limitation of desire.

Pluses of the Full-fledged Weekly

Let's say you do find just such a community. What are the good things about running a weekly? This turns out to be a personal as well as a business question. Here is a quick survey of the way I would answer it:

- The personal satisfaction factor can be quite high. As editor of a weekly newspaper you will take your place among the leaders of your community. The town doctor, the bank president, the head of the local industry and the newspaper editor are all up there together in public esteem. There will be many opportunities for public service: boards and commissions to serve on, civic clubs to join and be active in, churches to go to regularly, etc. If you are a good candidate for running a full-fledged weekly you will be, by temperament, very content to do these things.

- While running such a paper is clearly not a get rich quick scheme, you will be able to pay yourself a very livable, "executive-level" salary by the standards of the place where you live.

- The long-term value of your newspaper is likely to be very substantial. If your paper has been solidly established over a number of years, and if it has won community acceptance both as an editorial voice and as a vehicle for advertising, it will be a sought-after property. When the time comes to sell the business to someone else and retire, you should be able to realize a handsome profit and so repay yourself for all those long days and weeks you spent getting the paper out issue after issue, well-written, well-designed, and chock-full of advertising. The full-fledged weekly may command a higher price—often two to three times its annual gross—than any of its easier-to-manage periodical cousins.

Disadvantages of This Kind of Weekly

How about the downside? It, too, is both personal and financial.

- The ratio of time spent to profit earned will not normally be as favorable to you as with the other publication types described below. You can often make more money, with less effort, publishing niche market tabloids.

- Although you will be taking home a good salary, it is often difficult during the first few years to afford to hire a managing editor to take some of the load off your shoulders and reduce the number of hours you have to spend at the office. You can pay salespeople on commission and many writers by the word, if necessary, but a middle manager will require a livable salary.

- If you are really not the kind of person who enjoys the kind of life that the weekly editor lives, you will be miserable in the job.

• You can easily duplicate many niche market publications. If they work in one community, you can also publish them in another. A chain of them can be established and run by a single individual. A traditional weekly, on the other hand, is rooted so deeply in the character of a single town that it is not possible to duplicate it elsewhere.

One Very Risky Reason for Starting a Weekly

It sometimes happens that some members of a community may become disgruntled with the editorial stands their community paper takes or with its coverage of social events, sports, or any category of news. When this happens one inevitably hears grumblings that the community "needs another newspaper." Maybe the editor of the paper in place is a liberal Democrat and the complainers are conservative Republicans—or vice-versa. And people keep telling you that they would "like to see" a competing newspaper and encourage you to start one. This happens more frequently than you might imagine.

Just remember, though, that it is advertisers who will make your publishing business successful. It is the advertisers who spend the money to buy your ads, and money—as I have said elsewhere—is definitely not sentimental. The question you must ask yourself is not "Does the community need another paper" but "will the businesses in this community advertise in this paper?" Money does not take sides. It seeks only to multiply itself and make a profit.

You may not want to consider these hard and even unpleasant truths, but there they are. Advertisers spend money to increase sales, not to "support" one side of an argument over another. When you make a presentation to a major food store chain, their questions will always center on circulation and the cost of space, not whether your editorial page is liberal or conservative in the stands it takes on the issues.

II

The Modified (or Modular) Community Weekly

If there is no market opportunity for a true weekly newspaper in your area, or if you just don't think you would enjoy owning and editing one, consider the modified community weekly.

The modified weekly represents the best of both worlds. It does not attempt to "cover all the news" as the traditional weekly does, but it does print feature articles about local people and places. These articles can be quite popular and often build a faithful readership. Such a weekly is much easier to produce, and can easily be run, if necessary, by its owner and one other person during a start-up phase. The modified weekly is particularly appropriate where a small town daily already exists. (See my account of the unlikely and almost accidental success, *The Scoop*, a modified weekly, in the chapter on niche markets.)

Editorial Content of the Modified Weekly

The modified weekly gives the feeling of covering local happenings far more fully than it actually does, and it does develop a community identity. In this format you establish up front certain news categories. You will generate a fixed number of editorial modules or slots each week. This becomes the editorial format of your paper. There is no need to rethink it from week to week. Just fill in the blanks. Leave fast-breaking news up to others (TV, dailies, etc.) to cover. You do feature stories only, people-centered whenever possible. Use as much photography as possible. Establish a few regular columns by well-known local personalities, editing or rewriting these as necessary.

There will be a great many local writers eager to get their work into print who will contribute many of the articles you need. Local authors will enhance the reader interest of your paper, so you will use them whenever possible. There may be a great cook who wants to do a recipe column or a local historian—every town has at least one—who will do an ever-popular weekly article on local history. When you can't find a local author to handle a subject, you can write the articles yourself or buy them from syndicates.

One warning here: when a writer comes to you with a column idea, and you like it, ask to see ten sample columns. There are many short-winded writers who take on long-winded commitments, and the mix is disastrous. These writers lack follow-through, and you can't afford to deal with them. Just when they are beginning to develop a following, they fail to send in next month's piece. Readers like to see the same columns in the same place, issue after issue, right where they are supposed to be. They look forward to their favorites and are disappointed when they are not there. They like predictability and permanence. If you have doubts about the long-range commitment of the author of a column, don't begin publishing the item. If you are a good writer with wide-ranging interests you can always write several articles per issue, under various pseudonyms. Here are some of the subject article types from which you can choose your editorial content:

- *A profile of some interesting person,* with generous use of pictures: an award-winning gardener, the volunteer of the week at the local hospital, a civic leader, a church leader, an artist—anyone at all who stands out from the ordinary in some special way.
- *A profile of a new business start-up: the idea, the people involved, ob-*

stacles overcome, prospects, etc. Such stories not only give much needed and deserved recognition to individuals who are putting themselves on the line to make an idea into a reality but, in the long run, create a loyal base of advertisers for you. Your local daily probably has a policy against doing such stories and often even charges businesses for running the standard ribbon-cutting photo with its brief cutline. But your own weekly newspaper will never forget that behind every business start-up there is a strong human interest story that you can print.

- *A local history column* written by the established (there is always at least one) specialist in the history of your town. Old photos, maps, etc., will do much to heighten reader interest. Such a column is a real winner and will help to establish a loyal readership.

- *All You Ever Wanted to Know About.* . . . These background articles on items high on the local political agenda will attract readership. Are there environmental questions? Decisions concerning annexation and expansion? Complaints about utility rates? Just gather and publish all available facts without taking sides. This feature could be called the "Citizen's Notebook," or something similar.

- *If local sports is an important subject, publish a column by the high school football coach or basketball coach.* You can't cover the weekend games; these would be old news by the time you got to them nearly a week later. But the coach's reflections will draw strong reader interest. A column on golfing by the local pro could be a strong feature.

- *Community information,* such as school lunches, school schedules, etc.— anything furnished to you in news release format by community organizations.

- *The list.* Ten most powerful storms; Ten most beautiful women; Ten best cruise buys, etc.

- *Tests and Quizzes.* How do you rate as a lover? Can you take these deductions? Ten questions on good nutrition, etc.

- *How to Do It.* As a sidebar to an article on sex in marriage, "Ten Ways You Can Be a Better Lover."

- *Information Sources.*

- *Maps, graphs, graphics.*

- *Flesh these regular features out with columns purchased from the syndicates* (more about these later) on how-to subjects of wide reader interest: How to Supply Your Own Vegetables from a Backyard Garden; Treasures in the Attic: A Guide to Antique Hunting; Saving Money with Coupons; Furniture Refinishing; How to Write a Family History; Cash in with Free Government Publications; How to Start Your Own Business; How to Supplement Your Income with Your Own Home Business, etc.

III

The Niche Market News Tabloid: Weekly or Monthly

The niche market news tabloid publishes news articles and features of interest to its target readership and derives its revenues from advertisers interested in reaching that target readership. Examples include arts and entertainment tabloids, business weeklies, professional specialties (*Hospital Management News*) and many others. Examples of niche market news tabloids are extensively discussed in Chapter 5. These tabloids also develop a fixed editorial format but target all its articles toward its special readership. News releases and new product information releases provide a rich source of publishable material. Successful niche market news tabloids can easily be duplicated in nearby towns and cities, or in nearby neighborhoods and suburbs of major metropolitan areas.

IV

The Editorially Supported Shopper's Guide

An editorially supported shopper's guide also has some editorial matter to support the advertising it carries, but this editorial matter is not local in its appeal. It has none of the local personality of either the traditional or modified weekly but relies on canned articles purchased from syndicates. My own shoppers—*Dollarsworth* and *Bucksworth*—were of this kind. I did not take time to write any of the articles and columns I printed. I bought them from news and feature syndicates, which sell professionally written articles and features prepared at very low prices. All of the reading matter in my shoppers was chosen to appeal to the natural readership of the shopper. None of it was locally written. All of it is purchased from syndicates.

These shoppers are even easier to move from neighborhood to neighborhood or from town to town, since even the articles they contain, being generic in content, can be moved right along with it. What kinds of article are best? I recommend articles on such high reader interest subjects as the following:

- Furniture refinishing.
- How to spot real buys in used furniture stores and auctions.
- "Gold in the attic" type articles on book collecting, stamp collecting, and similar subjects.
- Many how-to pieces on doing it better and cheaper yourself.
- Herbal medicine and home remedies, etc.
- Saving money with your own home garden.

- Crossword puzzles and games.
- The editorial mix is sometimes spiced up by surefire crowd pleasers like articles on ghosts, UFO's, strange phenomena, and similar pieces.

Such articles all come ready-made each week in packets mailed directly to you from the syndicates, sometimes in hard copy and sometimes on disk. Your goal in using them is to build readership loyalty, to create talk and discussion, and to give the shopper a shelf-life of at least a few days—all, of course, with a view toward increasing results for your advertisers.

Editorial material such as this can also serve to create a market position and a distinct identity for your shopper. It gives your sales rep an easily understood talking point and should sway some advertisers in your favor.

V

The Outright Shopper (No Editorial Copy at All)

Some successful weekly shoppers are published with no editorial copy at all. These will use design principles to hype the money-saving, bargain-hunting aspect of the advertising.

The outright shopper's guide contains ads and nothing but ads and makes no bones about it. Its pages are crammed as full of advertisements as possible. Layout is secondary. Aesthetics of design are seldom a concern. The shopper promotes sales, bargain hunting, and discounts. It is filled with as many clip-out, money-saving coupons as possible (the only place where I really recommend coupons).

The success of these publications is due to the universal desire to buy goods at bargain-basement prices. The ads in such publications proclaim end-of-the-week sales, discounted cars, factory outlets, clearance and close-out sales. All of this is beefed up by scores of classifieds, which always have high reader interest. Typically, classified ads of a certain size will be given free to readers (not to businesses) for the advertisement of personal items for sale, trade, garage sales, etc. This insures a good flow of these reader-pulling miniatures. Businesses have to pay the going rate. Success factors for an outright shoppers' guide include the following:

- *A sufficient advertising base* of businesses that feature frequent sales. Image-enhancement ads for institutions like banks will not appear in these publications. The appeal is strictly to the pocketbook.
- *An identifiable market position* for your paper that makes it a desirable advertising medium for your customers.

- *A readership large enough to justify reasonably high ad rates.*
- *Saturation circulation of your market area.* Shoppers are often mailed, but this is can be expensive and not every market area will require it. A split circulation pattern may be possible, with post office delivery to rural routes and carrier delivery to in-town addresses.

VI

The All-Classified Version of the Outright Shopper

The outright shopper also exists in an all-classified version. These papers are often in a quarter-fold format, half as large as a tabloid, magazine-sized but still printed on newsprint. Inside you will find only classified line ads and classified display ads. One such shopper—the *Flyer*—comes to me in the mail twice monthly. It is printed on the lightest and cheapest newsprint available. I often throw it away unread, but wherever I am in the market for a kitchen appliance, car, or some piece of used office equipment or furniture I always read through it.

The often-seen "car trader," "boat trader," or "truck trader" publications are examples of all-classified shoppers.

Your Readership: Does It Have Purchasing Power?

It is always surprising how often publishing entrepreneurs focus so exclusively on their readership that they overlook the absolute necessity that readership possess purchasing power. In one of my seminars a participant—believe it or not—suggested to the group that a tabloid intended for food stamp recipients and poverty-level families might be a good idea. This person was focused entirely on her own interests and not at all on the marketability of her interests. Even when others in the group asked who the natural advertisers might be in such a publication and found no answer forthcoming, she clung stubbornly to her idea.

11

Niche Markets: What They Are and How to Find Them

Successful newspaper, shopper and tabloid publishers exploit niche markets. This is the key to their success. Niche markets exist everywhere and on every level in the publishing business. On a national scale, *Writer's Digest* magazine, for instance, is a niche market publication. Advertisers buy space in it because they want to reach the niche market of beginning writers who constitute its readership. *PC World* is a mega-niche market, but a niche market nevertheless. The *Wall Street Journal* targets a niche market of business people and investors.

Niche market activity is even greater on the local level, and well within the reach of any publishing entrepreneur. As I walked into my favorite bookstore a few days ago, I passed a rack holding more than a dozen free circulation newspapers and shoppers, all targeting niche markets. One of them was the *Jewish Journal*, targeting the very large Jewish population in Dade and Broward counties. This is a 56-page tabloid, with an advertising-to-editorial ratio of 70 percent.

Although specialty tabloids like this one rarely get ads from major grocery chains, the *Jewish Journal* carries several two-third page ads from deli's and grocery stores that feature kosher foods. Founded as an independent tabloid, the *Jewish Journal* duplicated its success by expanding into several area-specific editions. Turning to the masthead on page six, I note that it is now owned by the *Sun-Sentinel*, Broward County's major daily. On the day when the *Sun-Sentinel* came around to buy, the founders of the *Jewish Journal* scored a great financial coup. (The big dailies will let the small fry sink or swim. But when they start to swim too well, the big boys will step in to buy out the competition.) Next, I picked up a monthly tabloid called *South Florida Internet Weekly*. Advertising fills only five of its 16 pages, so it is marginal at best. Still, it has been around for 33 monthly issues, according to the masthead. A niche like this one could only exist in a major metropolitan area. Only such a rich business environment could furnish the necessary advertising base for the publication. If this publication does not succeed in the long run, it may be because even the rich Miami-Ft. Lauderdale metroplex is not adequate to support it. I noted also that the design of the publication as a whole and of the advertising it contained was not as effective as it could be. (Note that in my chapter on advertising design I emphasize that your ads should be as appealing and as high in reader interest as you can possibly make them.)

The tabloid *Business to Business* was also there. In its fourth year of publication, *Business to Business* is published by a Fort Lauderdale firm called Business to Business Newspapers, Inc. The masthead does not provide any information on any other publications by this same group of entrepreneurs. This monthly filled 16 of its 28 pages with advertising, for a ratio of nearly 60 percent. Advertising included two pages of the very profitable "nested" ads which always indicate a faithful and continuing advertising base. Prediction: continued success until the day when the *Sun-Sentinel* comes knocking and offers the big payoff.

In addition I found a 36-page tab called *Senior News: for the Fifties Plus*. *Senior News*, in its fifth year of publication, carried 22 pages of advertising, for a healthy 61 percent ratio. Next was *New Times*, the very successful "alternative" weekly featuring a spicy mixture of Generation X culture, political muckraking, and entertainment news. In addition to its two South Florida editions, *New Times* now has sister publications in several cities across the country. It is a major success story. When and if this company sells out to a bigger one, the price will undoubtedly be well up in the seven to eight figure range. Rounding out my collection were the *Entertainment News and Views*, *Florida Baby*, and two all-classified publications offering used cars for sale. And this was all gleaned from a single location.

Three Characteristics of a Niche Market

So niche market publications can pay off big time. But what is a niche market? How do you recognize one? How do you estimate its potential for profit? When scouring your town, city, or county for niche market opportunities, there are three things to look for:

- A large group of individuals or businesses that share interests and needs.

- A large group of individuals or businesses in a limited geographical area, and so easily targeted and reached.

- Intensive sales possibilities due to broad base of other individuals and businesses ready and willing to buy advertising space in order to reach your niche readership.

An Example of a Recent Niche Market Start-Up

At a luncheon given for the media by a local university, I met a young man who had just cranked up a very successful tabloid called *Hospital Business*

News. He publishes this bi-weekly in the Miami-Fort Lauderdale area, a massive metropolitan market. He had identified this niche himself and had noted that he had virtually no competition in it. He also recognized immediately that he could target both readers and advertisers with great precision. Furthermore, the potential advertisers he had in mind (medical equipment and supply companies) all had a great deal of money budgeted for the purchase of advertising space. This publisher had discovered a niche market that met each of the success criteria described above and is well on his way to establishing a successful publishing business.

The Importance of Specialization

The more specialized your niche market the better off you are, so long as the market is large enough to generate the volume of advertising sales that you need. A specialized market can be more easily mastered by a small organization. Every nook and cranny of it can be plowed and farmed, like a small, fertile plot of land.

I developed a successful niche when I first ventured into the publication of real estate guides. The field of real estate publications is a broad one. Further specialization is needed—a niche within a niche.

The niche I chose was that of apartment comparison guides. Even in a large market like the state capital of a major southern state (where I brought out such a guide), the number of apartment management companies handling apartment complexes was limited. There were some 350 apartment complexes, but fewer than 20 major management companies. Some of these handled as many as 30 or 40 different complexes. Now, this was a true niche. It offered intensive sales in a limited geographical area and to a highly targeted clientele. I could call on this number of clients myself, if need be, and in the beginning I did just that. Because we published semi-annually I was also able to handle all photography, ad design, production and distribution, with a minimum of free-lance help. The apartment guides themselves were easy to produce, and each of them contained up to $100,000 in advertising.

Niche Markets Are Manageable for Independent Publishers

A niche market is important because it is manageable: you can easily get your mind around it, your pocketbook around it, and your hands around it. It is also much easier to create the necessary visibility for your own company within a limited segment of the business community. After I had made a preliminary call on the most important management companies and generated a few news articles in the business pages of the daily newspapers, I was pretty much known and talked about among those who would be interested in advertising in my pages. All that remained was for me to position myself in the market by prov-

A South Florida Niche

When I moved to South Florida several years ago I began searching for a niche market publication that would be likely to succeed.

I had bought a small cabin cruiser — my first big boat — and got to know the marine business, which is very, very big down here. Two publications in particular were of interest to me, the *Waterfront News* and the *Intracoastal Times*. Both of these were well edited, regularly appearing niche market periodicals.

Was there another niche in this market? My 34-foot Mainship trawler was something of a classic, but it was in need of renovation, a task that I tackled with enthusiasm. Then I realized that I had found my niche: a publication devoted to yacht renovation and repair. There were literally thousands of potential readers between Palm Beach and Key West who had boats and the money to maintain and operate them. There were hundreds of marinas, suppliers and specialty marine businesses eager to reach these readers. And they could afford to buy advertising.

It was a classic niche. It offered the possibility of intensive sales, in a limited and manageable geographical area, to a readily identifiable clientele of readers and advertisers. Furthermore, it was easily expandable to other areas.

I did all the preparation for my new tab, which I christened *Shipshape: The Magazine of Yacht Renovation and Repair*. At about the same time a couple of the books I had written began to take off in sales, and I decided to devote my time to those projects instead.

If you look hard enough and long enough, you will discover niche markets of your own, in your own neck of the woods, that can return profits to you.

ing to potential advertisers that my magazine was more affordable, more widely distributed, better designed, and therefore more effective than the publications of my competitors.

From the very first issue my apartment comparison guides showed a profit. This profit continued to grow issue by issue until I sold the business some five years later.

Some Other Niche Successes

You can measure the viability of virtually any publication idea when you understand the three success factors: intensive sales, a targeted pool of advertisers, and a limited geographical area.

Here are two examples: *The Independent*, an excellent arts and entertainment tabloid published in the university town of Durham, North Carolina, is a niche market publication. It targets young, well-educated, liberal men and women in a limited geographical area. It then sells advertising to people who want to reach precisely this segment of the population. *The Independent* operates out of an old house in a less-than-thriving part of town. It owns little equipment and has virtually no overhead beyond personnel and printing costs. Start-up costs for a tabloid like *The Independent* can be quite small.

The *South Florida Business Journal*, a tabloid published in Dade County, Florida (Miami), and targeted toward the business community, is a niche market publication. It started out with just a few thousand subscribers. It still claims fewer than 20,000 paid subscribers, but it is nevertheless a very successful business publication. It was recently bought out by a national chain of business publications.

The Market Always Comes First

Some eager publishers get things backward. They have an idea for a publication that excites them. And it may indeed be a very good publication. But the question such a person must ask is, "Will it excite potential advertisers as well? Will anyone buy the advertising space? If so, who? Why? Is there a market for the idea?"

It is axiomatic in publishing (and in any other business) that market always precedes product. When you forget this fact you can get into trouble. A case in point is the recent history of the failed *Southern Magazine*. The initial edition was published with high hopes. Yet the gloomy future could have been predicted. Was there a market need for this magazine? No. Were advertisers crying out for another channel to reach this group of readers? The answer was no again. Was the readership highly targeted? Not at all.

What there was, was a group of young editors and writers who simply wanted this magazine to become a reality. A business plan was developed;

meetings were held with potential investors. Eventually the project was capitalized at a reported (according to a conversation I had with the first editor) five million dollars. Two or three years later this entire sum (and more) had been spent and the magazine collapsed. It changed its name and tried again, but still with little success.

The creators of this publication started with an idea and then tried to make the market like that idea. The successful entrepreneur analyzes the market first, decides what it needs and what it will accept, then creates a specific niche-market magazine or book that will satisfy a specific niche market need.

Is There a Niche for You?

Even quite small towns offer great opportunities. Can you identify a well-defined group of readers in your town or area that advertisers want to reach? Can you devise a publication that will appeal both to these readers and to your base of potential advertisers? If so, you may have discovered the opportunity you are looking for. Now you have to commit yourself to running a tightly organized, reader-friendly, and customer-oriented publication that takes account of the realities of the marketplace.

A Small Town Success Story

A new tabloid that will print features and stories about the local scene with its characters and goings-on—just like they used to do in the old days—can do very well. It will be eagerly read, building a contented circulation base issue after issue. Many merchants will advertise in it just because they like it. The nice thing is that you can leave all the investigative journalism—the bad news—up to those aggressive young reporters on the daily. Let them be the "Bad News Newspaper." You can become the "Good News Newspaper," an enviable role and a very desirable, marketable and readily identifiable market position.

Here is a true success story based on this "Good News" modified weekly scenario. It took place just a few years ago in the town where I was then living and publishing magazines, a small city in eastern North Carolina. The population base was 14,000. The local newspaper, prior to World War II, had been a weekly. In the 1950s it grew into a full-fledged daily, and in the 60s and 70s began to focus more and more on regional and national news.

A friend of mine stumbled into this wonderful market niche virtually by accident. At that time John Thompson, as we will call him, had a small business selling specialty advertising to drugstores throughout the South. He had an office in his home, and he had the computers and other equipment he needed. He also had three small children.

As a way of teaching his kids something about the publishing and advertising business—and about business in general—John Thompson decided to start a small tabloid, which he called *The Scoop*. It would be written by children, the ads would be sold by children and it would be distributed by children. It would be published on no particular schedule, but come out whenever the articles were written and the ads were sold.

And a funny thing happened. People actually liked *The Scoop*. They read it and talked about it. The young writers naturally focused on local stories, since that was all they knew about. Thompson, acting as editor, put their work into more or less acceptable form, and many of the articles were quite readable.

Over the next few issues, more people—including some adults—began to contribute editorial matter. John himself began to write some features. Within a few months he realized that he had a viable, going business on his hands. He and his wife began to sell ads themselves and plan an editorial and production calendar. The paper came out more regularly. The children, though no longer the only or even the chief sources of articles, remained active in the enterprise.

One morning John Thompson woke up to the realization that he was actually earning a considerable portion of his income from his little tabloid. Readers were hungry for the local slant; they wanted happy, upbeat stories about things that concerned them and people that they knew. *The Scoop* became the talk of the town, and advertisers began to include it in their budgets, not simply as an enterprise that they wanted to "support," but because it offered effective advertising at a reasonable price.

Other Niches You Can Exploit

Once you begin to think in terms of niche markets you will discover them everywhere. When you let your imagination run free, when you become aware of the many niche market publications already working in your city and in other cities, you will come up with idea after idea. You will only have to do the necessary market analysis and choose the one most likely to bring you the success you are seeking. Here are some likely prospects:

- *Create a niche market publication in a neighborhood or suburb.* In larger metropolitan areas there are opportunities in neighborhood tabloids. A year or two ago I worked in Raleigh, NC for a short time. One success story in publishing during that time was that of a tabloid called *North Raleigh*. This part of town had a character of its own. As would be the case for any discrete part of the city, only the most unusual or dramatic stories concerning the area found their way into the pages of the metropolitan *Raleigh News and Observer*. So a couple of publishing entrepreneurs had the idea of publishing a weekly newspaper for

Niche Market Checklist

- Is the niche manageable in size and extent?

- Is the readership targeted so that you can reach it easily with your publication?

- Is the advertising base large enough that you can turn a profit from the very beginning?

- Can you easily reach the advertising base with your sales personnel?

- Can you sell your ads issue after issue at a price that will be profitable to you?

- Can you position yourself to stand out from and above any competitors?

that area of town. I do not know what has happened since, but while I was there the idea of the paper seemed to have a lot going for it. The essential ingredients for success were present. There was a ready readership and an adequate supply of merchants, professionals and other businesses who found it advantageous to buy advertising to reach that readership.

There are no fewer than three such ventures in the Fort Lauderdale suburb of Coral Springs, where my home is. The mail regularly brings in the Coral Springs *Town News*, the Coral Springs *Forum*, and the *Coral Springs Newspaper*, as well as several all-classified shoppers. There is good, strong motivation for advertising in a neighborhood tabloid: it is cheaper by far than the daily newspaper, whose rate per column inch can reach $120 or more. Many businesses draw their clientele entirely or predominantly from one part of a large city. These businesses are very ready and willing to pay lower rates to sell to their own target prospects, so long as you can show them that you actually reach these prospects. The results they get will, in the long run, let them know if the money they are spending in your paper is producing business for them.

These neighborhood tabloids will work when you combine an identifiable readership with an adequate advertising base and bring these two elements together through the medium of a strong, reader-pulling editorial product.

• *Create a niche market publication for an ethnic segment of the community*. An ethnic segment of the community is readily identifiable because of its shared history and culture. There will be many of these to choose among, but I remind you that economic success for your publication requires two things: that this ethnic segment have a community of interests that you can address editorially and that it constitute a pool of potential customers sufficient to convince advertisers that they should place ads in it. You must also be able to get your paper into the hands of potential readers. Among the ethnic segments that could possibly form the base for a profitable publication are the following (and there are many others).

1. *African-Americans*. If the town or city where you live doesn't already have a weekly paper for African-Americans, or if it has a poorly run and edited one, a publication for this segment of the community could be a very profitable one.

2. *Religious groups*. In South Florida there are several successful weekly tabloids slanted toward the Jewish community, which is very strong here. This community furnishes a very viable circulation base. Since its discretionary income level is considerably above

Some Niche Markets I Can See from Here

Niche makets exist everywhere. I have mentioned the ShipShape tabloid. Just looking casually around in my own backyard, I note the possibility of bringing out a series of advertising-intensive "walking tours." South Beach and Key West are prime prospects. This could be a monthly or even a quarterly. Moreover, I can duplicate it in many other locations.

Another niche is a "South Florida Bride" publication.

Then, there is an opening for a "Home Business Weekly," possibly a lucrative niche.

I could also start a series of "newcomer guides" for each of a dozen suburban communities: Coral Springs, Plantation, Davie. This would also work in Boca Raton, Delray Beach and other nearby locales.

There are student survival guide opportunities at five or more universities and two large community college systems.

The opportunities are there. There is literally no end to them.

the average, it is also a very viable advertising base. There is also a state-wide tabloid called *Florida Catholic*.

3. *Persons of shared national origin*. Many large cities have sizable populations of Vietnamese, Cuban, Italian, Greek or other national peoples. Tabloids directed toward these markets, sometimes even in the language of the national homeland, are successfully published in many cities.

4. *Focus on persons with shared interests*. There are often sizable market segments made up of people who share similar interests, and each of these groups offers the opportunity for a potentially viable publication. In Fort Lauderdale many people own boats of every conceivable size, shape and mode of propulsion. The monthly tabloid *Waterfront News* is widely read and full of advertising. This is a special interest publication.

• *Develop specialty, once-a-year tabloids*. Alongside these regularly appearing tabloids are some specialty tabs that you can publish more randomly and quite successfully. Most of these are related to special circumstances in the town or city where you live. Let me give you just one example: the *Student's Survival Guide*.

I have almost always lived in university towns. In such places merchants derive an enormous percentage of their annual gross income from money spent by students. Such merchants are interested in reaching students early in the year when they are forming their spending habits and deciding on favorite restaurants, clothing stores, and night clubs. They are also renting apartments, choosing a bank for all those part-time pay checks and checks from home and making a variety of other decisions that can bring prosperity to local businesses.

This is a wonderful opportunity for the small publisher. I did a tabloid format student survival guide almost as an afterthought one year in Greenville, NC, home of East Carolina University. We found ourselves with some time on our hands late one Spring. We had a very good salesperson whom we wanted to keep busy so that she would continue to sell for us. We noticed that, in the past, the Chamber of Commerce had published a student guide to Greenville. It was not very well done, but it was successful enough that no one felt like going up against it. But this year, we discovered, the Chamber was not going to do this publication. We jumped into the market niche that was suddenly open to us. We designed a tabloid, complete with feature and department ideas calculated to interest the student reader. We christened our tab *Student's Survival Guide to Greenville*. We told our advertisers that it would be distributed to students within hours of their arrival on campus. We won permission from the university to distribute it on university property and even in the dormitories. We also distributed our publication to the community college campuses and even to the high schools. The ads practically sold themselves. We filled the *Survival Guide* with dollars-off coupons and promoted these on the front page, above the flag. This alone was enough to insure heavy use of the *Guide* by student-readers.

Success was due to three factors:

1. *We began selling our ads in the spring,* before anyone else had gotten into the market.
2. *Our distribution was at near-saturation levels.*
3. *Our editorial matter and coupons were powerful enough to draw a very large readership to our Survival Guide.* Most of those who saw the guide picked it up and read it—ads and all. The advertisers got generally good results. We worked on it for a month and cleared about $12,000 beyond ad sales, commissions and printing expense.

Duplication: Doorway to the "Big Time"

An advantage of all of these tabloids is that, if you so desire, you can do a similar publication in any nearby town, piggy-backing additional publications onto the planning and many of the feature articles already written for the first one. A whole business can be built on this kind of publication.

Other annual tabloids can be planned to coincide with the seasons (Gardening, travel, vacations), trade shows, special events, and civic festivals. Any happening that will provide both the readership and the advertising base can provide the foundation of a successful, yearly publication.

By now you will understand that we are just scratching the surface in this list of niche market possibilities. Opportunities are everywhere. Find them and act on them.

12

Publication Design Tips and Techniques

Ninety percent of the weekly newspapers and tabloids that I look at fall short of acceptable standards in either the quality of editorial content or in overall publication design. Yet these are two of the easiest things about your paper to get right. Selling the advertising is the hard part. If you will take care to publish good, readable articles in a cleanly designed and easy to read publication, you will immediately place yourself in the top ten percent of the market and go a long way toward creating a strong market position and immediately recognizable identity for yourself. When the reader's eye scans the newsracks, you want your paper to stand out as clearly as a well-groomed man at a biker's convention—clearly the best of the lot.

But how do you do this when you have never done it before? In this chapter I will take you through the basic elements of newspaper and shopper design and recommend sources of further information. Pay attention to these sources. They are culled from dozens upon dozens of books out there and are the best of the lot. No need for you to go through the whole sorting out process again. The combination of the information in this chapter and your study of the books that I recommend will provide all the know-how you need to get up and running.

Troll for Ideas

In addition to utilizing these how-to sources, look at the existing publications themselves. Assemble as many different weeklies of all sizes and shapes as you can. Study them carefully. Look at front page design, the flag, the masthead, headings for nested ads, regular column heads, the way photos are handled, etc. When you see something you like, clip it out. Make a file of these clippings. In this way you will get a good idea of design possibilities. You can adapt the best of these for your own use.

You may also be surprised how often you leaf through one of the papers you have collected and do not find a single element worth cutting out and saving—which will give you a good idea just how easily you can build a strong market presence for your own product by creating a handsome physical format.

While you're at it, take the time to clip ads that seem particularly attractive. In the chapter on ad design I point out that good-looking ads have as much reader interest as other graphic elements. You might as well start your collection of ad ideas while you've got the scissors out.

Your Goals: Personality, Character, and Unity

As you gather these materials and study them, keep in mind that you want to design a publication with its own, unique personality and character, and one that has an inner coherence and unity holding it together. The reader should feel comfortable holding your paper in his hands. He should find it well-ordered, thoughtful and pleasant to browse through.

Here are four important points to remember about publication design:

- Your publication should be recognizable at a glance. Even when spread on a freebie rack with dozens of other publications, yours must stand out from the pack so that the reader will reach for it without hesitation.
- Its design should mirror content, trade area, readership. Publications have character. Consider the *New York Times*, *USA Today*, and the *Wall Street Journal*. Each of these is immediately recognizable: the design of the ultraconservative WSJ would be right at home among dailies of the nineteenth century; the *New York Times*, is more contemporary, yet still not nearly so much so as the colorful *USA Today*. Who are your readers? What is the nature of your market? What is the nature of your niche? Each of these things can have an effect on overall design decisions. A tabloid targeting yacht owners—such as the *Waterfront News* here in Fort Lauderdale—will have (or should have) a different look and feel from a tabloid targeting returning university students or the entertainment and tourism industry of South Beach. You will be amazed how few publishers seem to give the personality and character of their publications the thought and attention they deserve.
- Your publication must maintain consistent appearance throughout. Do not switch from style to style at random. A clean and consistent unity of design is very pleasing to the reader.
- Plan for the long haul. You are going to have to stick with it.

Choice of Format

There are three basic newspaper formats to choose among: the tabloid (more like a magazine and the size of *The Christian Science Monitor* or the *National Enquirer*), the broadsheet (standard, full-sized newspaper) and, in a few instances, the mini-tab (magazine-sized, and often used for all classified publications). Which should you choose? Almost all weekly newspapers, both free circulation and paid, are designed in a tabloid format. If I had to summarize some of the most viable reasons for choosing this format I would start with two points:

- Tabloids are easier to hold and read. They are more like magazines, and readers like them.
- Tabloids are very versatile in design, permitting you to easily match the look of your paper to your subject matter, readership demographic, and the nature of your advertising base.

There is at least one very good reason for going broadsheet, however, when publishing a full-fledged weekly. A broadsheet page, because it is twice as large as a tabloid page, contains twice the space and carries twice the advertising cost. (See the earlier discussion of the full-fledged weekly newspaper.) This fact can have important consequences for your bottom line. Full-fledged, community weeklies usually carry grocery and department store advertising on a weekly basis. This advertising provides the indispensable core of their advertising revenues. Grocery stores and many large chain stores typically think in terms of buying full pages, two-thirds pages or, rarely, half pages. Such businesses, as a part of their marketing strategy, want to dominate their space. They especially do not want to take the chance that competitors will advertise on the same page with them. They are not thinking of the cost so much as the proportional space on the page, which they want to dominate. My newspaper, the *Mecklenburg Gazette*, was losing money in a tabloid format. When I converted it into a broadsheet paper, my income from my grocery store advertisers virtually doubled overnight and put the paper once and for all on a sound economic basis. However, if you are not publishing a full-fledged weekly, the tabloid is likely to be your format of choice.

The mini-tab is useful for some specialty products. Newsprint TV guides —the kind that come as weekly inserts in your daily newspaper—are usually mini-tabs. So all-classified publications and coupon book-type publications may also find a mini-tab niche. I know of at least one mini-tab niche market publication that has succeeded over the years. This is the *Intracoastal Times*, published in Broward and Dade counties, in South Florida. It is a handsome little mini-tab magazine, very well edited, and fun to read. It is self-sustaining, but, perhaps due in part to its small size, does not produce tons of ad revenues.

Typography

In designing your publication you will choose a type style (or "font") for your headlines and one for your body copy, and you will assemble a variety of fonts for advertising design. Choose a clean and readable font. The type style you choose should also contribute to personality, character, and unity of your publication. Your word processing and page layout programs will come with a variety of fonts available for use, and others can be purchased very cheaply or even downloaded for free from the World Wide Web.

Two Basic Styles

There are two basic type styles, *serif* and *sans serif*. A serif typeface has the little curlicues on the tips of the letters and in the corners, such as where the top bar is connected to the stem of the letter "t." The text you are now reading is typeset in a serif style called Times Roman. This sentence, on the other hand, is printed in a typeface called Arial, a sans serif (without serif) typeface.

Choose a serif font for the text of your articles, and a contrasting sans-serif font for the headlines. (If you prefer a more traditional, decidedly conservative look, you can set your headlines in serif type as well. The *Wall Street Journal* and the *New York Times* both do this, while most other metropolitan dailies use sans serif fonts for heads.) The glossary in the back of this book gives some further details and examples of basic type faces.

Make a "Style Sheet"

Begin by drawing up a *style sheet* for your publication. This sheet will specify type style, sizes and leading (the space between the lines of type) for body copy and for headlines. Generally, it will list only two type "families," one for text and one for headlines. The use of more than two type families for editorial matter and news headlines is likely to create a cluttered appearance and detract from the unity of design that you want to develop.

Though you will use only two families, you will find that you can vary these quite extensively. Let's say you choose Times Roman, a readily available and quite suitable font—it was originally designed for newspaper use—for body copy. You will also have at your disposal Times Italic, Times Roman Bold, Times Bold Italic—the other members of the basic family.

If you choose a basic sans serif font like Helvetica or Arial (another name for the same font) for headline type, you will also have available Helvetica Bold, Helvetica Italic, Helvetica Bold Italic and in this case, a variety of other variations: Helvetica Narrow, Helvetica Extra Bold, Helvetica Expanded, Helvetica Black, etc. You can also expand and contract any of these fonts virtually at will by utilizing the typographic control tools built into your page layout program. So, in limiting yourself to two basic families, you still have considerable freedom in the choice of type. And, needless to say, in advertising design anything goes. You can use any font that gets the job done.

Type Size and Leading

After you have chosen the font you want to use for your editorial matter, you still have two decisions to make: how big will your type be, and how much space (leading) will you leave between the lines. Both of these decisions will affect the readability of your publications. Type size and leading are measured in "points." There are 72 points in an inch.

A fairly standard choice would be ten point type, plus two points of leading. This arrangement would be referred to as ten on twelve (the point size plus the two points of lead). You can vary it any way you want, of course. Your goal is a clean appearance and a very readable product.

Fonts differ in their density and in their width. You can get more characters of ten point Times Roman in a column inch of space than, say, Century Schoolbook. This is an advantage in a narrow, newspaper column format, since it leads to less unsightly white space between words and fewer hyphenations. Which font is best for you? Trial and error is the best way to make a choice. Take a random paragraph of copy, define your column width, and drop the typeset copy into the column in point sizes from nine to twelve, with variations in the leading as well. Then choose the one that pleases and that is most suitable to your readership. If you were publishing a *Condominium News*, slanted toward a niche of elderly and retired persons on Fort Lauderdale Beach, you might choose a point size on the larger end of the scale to enhance ease of readability for elderly eyes.

Headlines

Your use of headlines can convey a nice feeling of orderliness and competent design to your publication when you take care to set up and implement a simple headline schedule. This schedule tells you the type size and leading which you will *always* use in identical situations: one column heads, two column heads, three column heads, etc. In the absence of such a schedule the layout person (or persons)—who may or may not have significant publication experience—will be tempted to use whatever size seems to fit best. The way it should be done, however, is to rewrite the headline until you can make it consistent with the headline schedule.

- *In addition to the main headline is the "deck"*—a kind of subhead that amplifies the headline itself. In the old days of newspapering, decks were common. The main headline would say something like: "Titanic Strikes Iceberg, Sinks!" The deck would say, in smaller type, "Thousands Feared Drowned." Your headline schedule will include type sizes and leading for decks, if you intend to use them. It's best to

Ears	FLAG	Ears

This page illustrates a six-column broadsheet format. The dotted line shows the fold. On the right are two tabloids—one four column and one five column—showing the tab's relationship to the broadsheet. The dotted box on the lower tabloid shows the relative size of the mini-tab.

21.5 inches

15 inches

FLAG

15 inches

10. inches

FLAG

FLAG

10. inches

7.5 inches

15 inches

go ahead and include the parameters of decks, even though you may make rare use of them.

- *Headlines may be set "upstyle" or "downstyle."* In the upstyle, all words are uppercase, with the exception of articles and propositions. In downstyle headlines only the first word is uppercase. Upstyle is considered more traditional; downstyle more contemporary. But it is really a matter of taste. Chose the style most pleasing to you—then stick to it.

The Number of Columns

A broadsheet (full-size) weekly newspaper will normally have a six column format. In a tabloid, you will choose a four column or a five column format. Four columns is most often chosen because it is easier to lay out and permits modular ad sales: full page, half page, quarter page, etc. If you are going to sell ads by the column inch, then you may want to choose a five column format. A tabloid in a four column format will have approximately 60 column inches on a page, while a five column tab will have 75 column inches on a page. Thus your "column inch rate" for the five column format will *seem* less expensive that for the four column format.

Your classified page will have seven or eight narrow columns in a tabloid and as many as twelve columns in a broadsheet format. Typeset the classifieds in seven or eight point type.

This page is always sold on a column inch basis, no matter how the rest of the paper is sold. Thus, on a tabloid classified page you may have as many as 105 or 120 column inches to sell. A classified page filled with paying advertisers is a major profit center for your publication.

Some Constant Elements

After you have settled on the number of columns you will have on a page, turn your attention to the design of the various constant elements that will remain the same issue after issue.

- *Flag.* The flag (also called the "nameplate") is the name of your paper as it appears on the front page. The flag should be carefully designed to be as attractive and distinctive as possible. Try several different typefaces, and kern (adjust the space between individual letters) carefully. The flag can be accompanied by a company logo, if you have a suitable one. Although the flag normally stretches across the top of the front page in a broadsheet paper and in many tabloids, some designers opt for a "floating flag," which appears elsewhere on the front page, often enclosed in a "cartouche," or box.

- *Masthead.* The masthead lists the publisher, editor(s), staff members, and advertising personnel of your publication. This important element also gives contact information: street address, editorial and advertising phone numbers, email addresses and web site URL's. The masthead should be easy to find. In daily newspapers and full-fledged weeklies, it traditionally appears in the upper left-hand corner of the editorial page. In publications that have no editorial page—specialty tabloids, magazines, etc. —the masthead should be placed on one of the first four or five inside pages. It is annoying to pick up a publication, look for the masthead so that you can get advertising or editorial information, and be unable to find it. To hide your masthead from the reader is a serious error in design. It surprises me that it is so often done.

- *"In this issue."* It is important to let the reader know what goodies are awaiting him inside. This is the function of an "In This Issue..." box on the front page. This box lists the major articles and gives a one or two line teaser for each of them. In a shopper, this box can also highlight bargains on the inside, *i.e.*, "See Page 12 for Money Saving Coupons."

- *Specialty page heads.* Your tabloid or newspaper will have a number of special pages devoted to particular interests. In a daily newspaper you have the lifestyle page, the sports page, the business page, etc. In a niche market tabloid devoted to yachting you will have "Marinas and Harbors," "In the Galley," "Cruising Destinations." A niche market tabloid devoted to hospitals and health care will have special pages titled something like "New Products," "Staff News," etc. The important thing is that you use a consistent design for each of them. This, again, reinforces the unity of your publication, its businesslike appearance and, ultimately, the comfort level of your advertisers.

- *Column heads.* You will soon develop a group of columnists whose work you publish issue after issue. Give these columns catch names to heighten reader interest and design them with similar formats. If you use a photo of your writer, incorporate it in an interesting way, extending beyond the frame of the column heading for a three-dimensional effect. Another device that works well is to use one of the special computer programs that converts photos to line drawings. I have one of myself done this way, and I much prefer the computer-generated drawing to the photograph I took it from. Above all, avoid the deadly dull straight-at-the-camera mug shot that looks more like a passport photograph than anything else. Such bland photos fairly scream out an unintended message: "I am a dull person, with nothing interesting to say." This is the opposite of the effect you want your column heads to accomplish.

- *Nested ad heads.* In the chapter on advertising sales I mentioned "nested

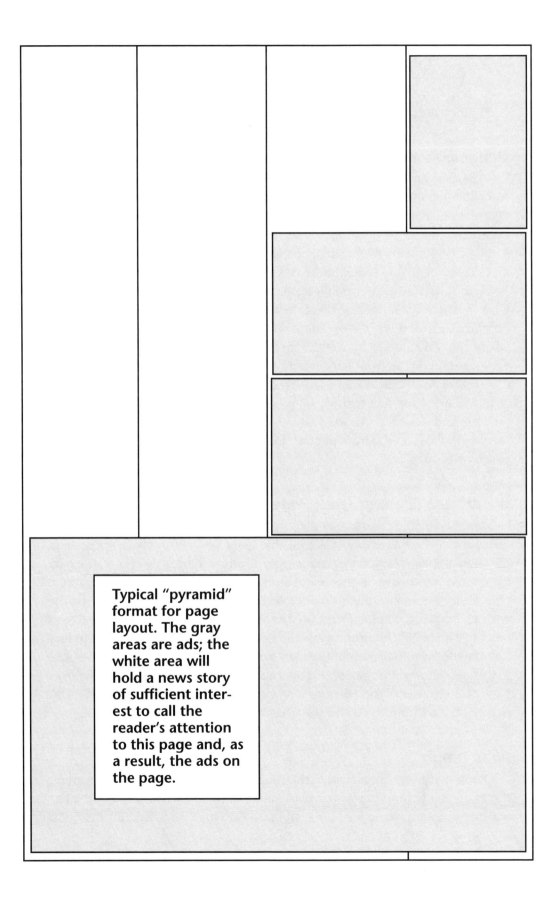

Typical "pyramid" format for page layout. The gray areas are ads; the white area will hold a news story of sufficient interest to call the reader's attention to this page and, as a result, the ads on the page.

ads" and pointed out that these would be a constant and important source of revenue. Each of these (*Who Can Do It*, *Fine Dining*, *Play Schools and Kindergartens*, etc.) needs its own head, again following the guidelines already established for other special pages and sections.

Designing the Front Page

Traditionally, the flag is placed at the top of the page. A story is sometimes placed above the flag to add emphasis and create immediate pulling power. On each side of the flag you can place "ears," (little nuggets , often boxed in, of information likely to heighten reader interest). A floating flag can be placed almost anywhere on the top half of the page that is consistent with good design. This will give you even more flexibility in highlighting your top stories.

The front page of your publication must entice the potential reader to pick it up, look it over, and decide that it is worth his time to browse through it. To accomplish this, there are several strategies you can employ. I have already talked about the importance of the "In this issue..." feature. Place it in a prominent position on the front page where it will not be missed, perhaps in one of the ears. This is especially important if the publication will be distributed folded, so that only the top half of the front pages is visible at first. Place the headlines for your lead stories above the fold as well, with secondary stories below. Get as many of these on the front page as possible, continuing ("jumping") them to pages two and three.

A Full-page Photo as Front Page

Another strategy that works very well, and that more and more tabloids are using, consists in filling almost all available space on the front page with a huge photograph that is linked to a major story. There will be little else on the page except the photo, the "In this issue" lines and, perhaps, the first paragraph or two of the lead story. There is no denying that a tabloid can be very attractive with such a photograph on the cover to draw the reader in. A success story of recent years in North Carolina was the development from simple idea to multimillion dollar publication of the *Carolina Farmer*, a tabloid distributed free to the agricultural community throughout North and South Carolina. The front page of each issue of the *Farmer* is devoted to a oversized photograph of the person about whom the cover story has been written.

Photographs

Photographs are important to the success of most publications. In general, the more good photographs you use—and I stress the word "good"—the better. This rule holds true for all the publication types discussed in this book, with the exception of the all-advertising shopper. Here are some tips on the effective use of photographs:

- *Your photos must be dynamic, not static.* A boring photo is no better than boring writing. The old standby of the business owner at his or her desk, phone in one hand and a note pad in the other is duller than dirt. Make sure that you do everything possible to publish photos that are *active*. Photos should show people in action: craftspersons plying their trade, shop owners showing goods to customers, the winning shot at the soccer match.

- *Your photos must be high in human interest.* Make sure that the photos you publish are rich in human interest, showing events, people or scenes that will evoke an emotional response on the part of your readers: joy, pleasure, happiness, awe, fascination and, above all, ego-satisfaction.

- *Your photos should show as many people as possible from your trade area.* Charity balls, meetings, community barbecues, graduating classes, marching band concerts, scouting jamborees. . . . All of these and scores of other events will provide a great source of reader-pleasing photos for your paper. Below the photograph you will carefully list the name of each individual shown wherever it is possible to do so.

- *Advertising-related photos.* Photographs can give you a powerful means of promoting your paper in the eyes of advertisers. Any new business that opens in your trade area qualifies for a brief article and a photograph. The expansion of an existing business provides another opportunity. Promotions, new hires and other activities can also lead to goodwill photographs. Even in photos of this kind, remember to keep your images dynamic and high in human interest.

- *Cutlines, catchlines, and credits.* The two most frequently read items in your paper will be the classified pages and the cutlines underneath your photographs. Cutlines should always be written as fully as possible, with all details. Even if many of the details are given in a related story, give them again in the cutline, where most readers will see them. The catchline is like a little mini-headline, attracting attention to the cutline. The credit tells who took the photo.

- *PR use of photos.* Photos published in your paper make great promotional items. Cut them out, laminate them and send them to the persons shown, along with any accompanying news story, if there is one. You can adhere the more important ones to a piece of card stock, laminate it and affix it to an easel stand, with the legend "As

There's more in there than golf balls! —————— **Catchline**

Bass fisherman Ron Gallo, of Coral Springs, holds a twelve pound largemouth bass caught last Saturday at the Lake Landing Country Club pond. The three acre pond, located just off the fairway of the club golf course was stocked three years ago with a population of —— **Cutline** bass. Fishermen like Ron are now reaping the rewards. Ron used a black plastic worm to land his catch. (Photo by Jane Doe)

A human interest photo with both catchline and cutline. Note the richness of detail in the cutline.

Photo credit. Be sure to mention the name of the person who took the shot.

seen in Neighborhood News..." printed across the top.

- *Where to get photos.* You will be very busy getting your publication out, especially in the beginning. So where do you get all these great photos? Here are a few ideas that have worked for me:

  1. *Sponsor photo contests.* Give something free to the winners in sports, nature, people, and kids categories each week. Also publish the honorable mention photos. This does not have to cost you a cent out of pocket. You can work a deal with a restaurant (or other business) to give away a pizza or a gift certificate to the winner in return for promotional space in your paper.
  2. *Encourage the writers who submit columns* and articles for publication to include photographs.
  3. *Seek out (through an article in your paper) historical photographs* of "The Way We Used to Be...." Such photos are sure reader pleasers.
  4. *Keep a digital camera with you at all times.* Photo opportunities can't always be planned.
  5. *Attend Fourth of July picnics and other such occasions.* Publish full-page photo spreads on them, complete with names and rich, readable cutlines.

- Editing by design. Study manuals like Jan V. White's *Editing by Design* for ideas on the layout and use of photographs in page enhancing ways. There are more possibilities that you ever dreamed of, and you should regularly use as many of them as possible.

Other Graphic Elements

There are many other graphic elements that can give life to your pages. Remember, anything that heightens reader interest will increase the positive response that your advertisers will get. Spread these elements throughout the paper so that every two page spread has at least one of them. Here are some of the basic graphic elements:

- *Maps (how to get there from here).* Maps are the most useful of these additional graphic elements. They do not have to be elaborate. A simple grid showing major intersections, with a star to mark the targeted location is adequate, although anything you can do to dress these up will work wonders. In many areas, maps are a virtual necessity. Nationwide, one-fifth of the population changes address each and every year, and in the suburbs—such as Coral Springs, Florida, where I now live—that number can rise to forty or fifty percent. In such locations, a mini-map in the corner of an advertisement can be a strong reader service device and a strong selling tool as well. Larger maps can show the locations of all your advertisers' places of business, public institutions. libraries, civic centers, etc.

- *Other graphic elements include drawings, cartoons and crossword puzzles*, etc., which can be purchased from the news syndicates. In my weekly newspaper I published the *New York Times* crossword and an array of old-time comic strips that suited my targeted readership.

Layout Strategies: Where the Ads Go

There are two kinds of advertisement, special position and ROP (run of the paper).

- *Special position ads* include the center spread, front page, back page, classified page, restaurant and entertainment page, and so on. Often these special positions carry an increased ad rate.
- *Most ads, however, are not special position ads, but are "ROP."* These ads can be placed anywhere that space permits. Try to avoid promising special position to what are essentially rop ads. ROP ads are generally laid out on the page in a "pyramid" format, with the larger ads at the bottom of the page and the smaller ads slanting up toward the outside of the page.

Getting Printed

With your paper all laid out—either digitally or in hard copy—you will take it to press. You will already have gotten some preliminary quotes to determine your production costs when you did your market analysis. Now shop around for prices until you find the best one. Here are some things that will be important to you:

- *At the top of the list is cost*—printing, halftones, color, etc.
- *Availability of a variety of newsprint stocks* so that you can choose the one most consistent with your market position.
- *Turnaround.* You want to be able to get printed on a same day basis or, at most, next day delivery.
- *Color.* You want to be able to use spot color and process color, as needed, and at a reasonable price. You will also do well to check your printer to make sure that their equipment can handle digital presentation of publications, especially if you are going to use process color. Create needed color separations yourself on your page layout program

- *Cost of delivery to your warehouse.*
- *Mailing.* It is more convenient if your printer can handle mailing chores for you. If he is able to do this, what is the cost?

13

Designing and Pricing Your Advertising

Weekly newspapers and free circulation shoppers are advertising-driven publications. In doing your market analysis you identified the potential customers in your trade area. Now you are going to have to sell advertising space to as many of them as you can. If you have chosen to do a newspaper which included editorial matter, you must still fill 65 to 75 percent of your available space (or more) with ads.

Others do this, so you can too, especially if you have carefully designed your product to take advantage of your competitors' weaknesses and to highlight your own strengths. But it does take careful planning, a well-trained sales force, and an understanding of the basics of advertising. What makes a good ad? What kind of ad will work? How do you design and present a spec ad to a prospective customer?

Reader Appeal of Advertising

Whatever format you choose for your paper, you can go a long way to making it a solid hit with readers as well as advertisers when you go the extra mile in producing first-class advertising design and copywriting.

Here are two facts that you never want to lose sight of: from the point of view of the average reader, the advertising has very high reader interest. People who pick up your paper want to read the advertisements; they want to know where the bargains are. Anyone who watches much television will quickly notice that commercials are often more entertaining and more professionally produced than are the programs on which they appear. You should work hard to see that your newspaper ads have this same exceptional quality.

People love to browse through advertisements looking for that special bargain, that nugget of consumer information that will save them big bucks on some purchase they are planning to make during the weekend. When my wife's copy of *Better Homes and Gardens* comes in each month, she immediately turns to the small twelfth and eighth-page ads in the back of the book, looking for new products, bargains, or sources for unusual items. I do the same with the trade publications that come to me. Each issue has an article or two that catches my attention and that I may or may not read through. But I scan every page looking for new product information or product offerings that will make my business more efficient, more profitable, more fun—or all of these.

When ads are well-designed and interesting to the eye, readers will pore over every column inch of them looking for what they need. The point I am making—and it is often misunderstood by newcomers to the business—is that the quality of your advertising has as much to do with the readability of your newspaper as the stories themselves. The same care should be taken with ad design as with the writing of a front page story.

Elements of An Effective Ad

Entire books have been written on the techniques of effective advertising design. The following tips are distilled from the best of them and verified by my own experience. Any good newspaper advertisement has a definite structure. Each of its concrete, definable elements does an important job, and it is important that you understand them. Use them and you will get results for any advertiser who has a desirable product or useful service to sell. Here is what you need to know to get started:

- *Headline.* The headline is the single most important element in an ad. The headline attracts attention and entices the reader to browse down through the details which the ad offers. Here are some rules of thumb for writing good headlines:

    1. The key to selling any product is to identify the benefit that it will bring to the customer and to convey that benefit in a dramatic way to the customer. For that reason, your headline must state as clearly and forcefully as possible the benefit to be found in the ad. Say that your advertiser is a chiropractor. A headline like "Chiropractic Cures!" is much too general. "End Back Pain Now!" gets right to the heart of the benefit. If your client is a bank, "100 Years Serving South Florida" says nothing about a benefit. "Save $500 a Year with Free Checking!" does. If your client is a shoe store, the headline "Sale on Famous Designer Shoes" is not as benefit oriented as it could be. "Save 50% on Designer Shoes" is better. "Save Up to $50 a Pair on Designer Shoes" is even better, because it is even more detailed, mentioning a specific sum of money to be saved.
    2. Avoid humor in headlines. This sometimes works, but can be dangerous. Not everyone will share your sense of humor.
    3. Avoid any headline that is unclear or confusing.
    4. One warning: your clients may suggest headlines that you know

are not likely to work. In such a case suggest headlines of your own that make a stronger pitch. Remember that if an ad doesn't work, the advertiser will blame you and your paper and not the headline he himself came up with.

- *The subhead* is also known as the "deck." It may introduce more details of the benefit. If your client is a television repair service, the headline might be something like "TV Problems? Call Us for A Free Estimate." The subhead might be "Free pick up and delivery." In the case of the chiropractor, your subhead could state, "A simple ten-minute spinal adjustment and that nagging pain is gone."
- *Body of the Ad*. The body of the ad gives more extensive details of the offer, if any, and develops further benefits. The TV repair service ad might include body copy listing the models the company services: "Any make or model, new or old, large or small."
- *Too Many Words?* Some people maintain that too many words will produce a no-sell ad. Experience does not bear this out. It is true that merely wordy ads may turn the reader off, but ads in which the body copy is carefully prepared to give hard information about benefits to the reader often yield very good results. You will often see ads in magazines, for instance, that have a full page of copy and almost no graphics. You see these ads month after month for one reason only: they get results. They get results because they are directly keyed to reader benefits and give concrete information as to how the reader can easily reap those benefits if he will only respond to the ad.
- *Testimonials*. Testimonials are first person accounts of individuals endorsing the services or goods that the advertiser is offering. Testimonials are very strong selling tools, and they should be a part of every ad where they are appropriate and available. Always remember to ask the advertiser if he has any such testimonials available. You must have permission to use a real name, but you can substitute initials if necessary. A TV repair service might have the following testimonial: "Middle City TV lived up to its promises in every way. Delivery was free, service was effective and affordable. Best of all I had my TV back in just two days." Mary Doe, Coral Springs.
- *Graphics*. The graphic elements in ads are referred to as "art." All ads benefit from the addition of clip art showing the services and products or satisfied customers using the product or service. You will obtain clip art from newspaper service bureaus and ad service bureaus. (See the Contacts and Sources appendix for details and contact information.) You can also pick up art elements from other ads, catalogs, flyers and brochures that the customer distributes. The logo of the advertiser is also

used. If the customer—a new business, for instance—has no logo, you can offer to design one for him for a modest additional fee.

- *Call for action*. Always include some element that will ask readers interested in the product or service advertised to *take action now*. "Sale ends midnight Saturday!", "Call today for a 10% discount!", and "Why suffer with back pain one more day? Call for your appointment now" are examples.

- *Guarantee*. Always include a guarantee when you can. A chiropractor cannot guarantee relief, but a TV repair service can guarantee that the new parts that it installs will not fail for, say, 30, 60 or 90 days.

- *Address, telephone and other contact information*. At the bottom of the ad be sure to include your advertiser's street address, telephone number (both toll and toll-free), email address, if any, and a web site URL, if the customer has one. *Double check these items very carefully. The single most frequent cause of advertisers asking for refunds or credits for their ads is typographical errors in telephone numbers or addresses.*

- *Mine other ads*. You will now read newspapers and magazines with a different eye. Analyze and mine all ads for ideas that will help you do a better job in your own ad design or help you sell ads to your customers. Keep a notebook for the specific purpose of noting down these ideas. Clip out the best ads and keep them in an ad idea scrapbook. This technique is especially useful during the first months of operation.

- *The recognition factor*. Profit comes through repeat business. One way to insure this repeat business is to design an ad format for your customer that has an unmistakable and immediately recognizable "look" identifying the design with the advertiser from week to week.

- *Typography*. You will find a great many typefaces available on your computer, and you will probably buy more. However, be economical in using them. Here are some rules of thumb you would do well to observe:

  1. Never forget that the first rule of typography is legibility. Avoid fancy typefaces (the so-called Old English, for example, and most scripts) that are difficult to read. An important rule: if you can't read an ad immediately and easily, scrap it.
  2. Never use more than two typefaces in a single ad. To do so creates a cluttered, unpleasant look.
  3. Use a background screen to highlight text blocks or coupons.

- *Coupons*. Stay away from coupons whenever you can. They can be a trap for you. Advertisers sometimes want to insert them to "check the response" from their ads. But if the coupon is too small, or doesn't offer significant value, it won't work. Neither will it work if the product or

All I Know about Advertising

Advertising is the business, or the art, if you please, of telling someone something that should be important to him. It is a substitute for talking to someone.

It is the primary requirement of advertising to be clear, clear as to exactly what the proposition is. If it isn't clear, and clear at a glance or a whisper, very few people will take the time or the effort to try to figure it out.

The second essential of advertising is that what must be clear must also be important. The proposition must have value.

Third, the proposition (the promise) that is both clear and important must also have a personal appeal. It should be beamed at its logical prospects; no one else matters.

Fourth, the distinction in good advertising is that it expresses the personality of the advertisers; a promise is only as good as its maker. Finally, a good advertisement demands action. It asks for an order. It exacts a mental pledge.

Altogether these things define a desirable advertisement as one that will command attention, but never be offensive. It will be reasonable, but never dull. It will be original, but never selfconscious. . . . And, because of what it is and what it is not, a properly prepared advertisement will always be convincing, and it will make people act.

This, incidentally, is all that I know about advertising.

—Fairfax Cone
Foote, Cone & Gelding Agency

service is not one that most people want most of the time. A coupon for $25 off on a new refrigerator, for instance, will not pull dozens of responses. Compared to the price of the appliance the 25 bucks is insignificant. But even if the coupon offered a $100 price reduction, it still might not pull up to the advertisers expectations. After all, how many people in a given trade area are in need of a new refrigerator in any given week? If you are publishing a weekly newspaper with circulation of 5,000, there may be only two such readers among your subscribers. Even if the advertiser got 100% of those who actually needed his product, he might still conclude that the "ad didn't pull." He got all the business that was out there, but it did not meet his expectations. An exception to this rule is made when you publish a shopper made entirely of coupons and achieve saturation circulation with it. Then it will be picked up and scoured for every available bargain. Still, the refrigerator ad would have the same problems. If your customer insists on a coupon, here are two rules to follow.

1. The coupon should be as large as a $1 bill.
2. The value has to be worth at least one-fifth of the total purchase price, or an equivalent value.

You should also point out to your advertisers a real downside to coupon use. Some people, aware of the coupon, will not come in to purchase an item if they do not have the coupon with them. They will feel that they are being gouged. This problem is avoided when you tell the customer to "present this coupon *or* mention this ad."

Nested Ads

Nested ads are groups of small ads offering similar products or services. This technique draws attention to the whole group and increases the pulling power of the ads themselves, which would be lost when scattered at random throughout the paper. Moreover, such ads are quite profitable when repeated week after week. (They are usually sold on a monthly or even an annual contract.) On a per-inch basis they are more expensive than much larger ads (see the discussion on pricing your ads later in this chapter). They increase reader interest and make your paper a resource similar to the yellow pages.

Nested ads have another, very distinct, advantage. As your paper becomes more and more successful, more and more potential advertisers will decide that they simply can't afford *not* to be included in your nested ad sections.

Examples of nested ads include a *Who Can Do It* section for the service trades; *Fine Dining* for restaurants; *Kindergartens, Day Care and Nurseries;*

Your Guide to Churches and Places of Worship, and countless others. Train your salespeople to sell larger ads if they can, but, failing this and before leaving the prospect's place of business, always go to the fallback position and make a strong pitch placing a small ad in one of the special sections.

Classifieds

Readers dearly love the classifieds. Research shows that more people read the classifieds than read the editorial page, the sports pages, or even the comics. Yet there is not a single news story to be found in this section of the paper.

A problem is that in your first few issues, you will not have as much classified advertising as you would like. You will have to prod things along a bit. Here are some things you can do to generate classifieds:

- Furnish free personal (as distinct from business) classifieds, at least in the beginning.
- Put up posters offering free classifieds in grocery stores, meeting places, anywhere that you can.
- Attach a tear-off pad to your posters with your phone number and address on it and space for the classified wordage. If you have a postal service business reply permit, these can be free postage cards. Otherwise, leave space for a stamp. Also include email and fax instructions.
- Develop a "Yard Sale Headquarters" section of classifieds.
- Offer free yard sale signs.
- Offer to publish free photos of used cars, trucks or boats. Also include email and fax instructions. Call merchants advertising in other papers and offer them a free month of classifieds in your paper. Don't neglect the classified columns in the big daily whose trade area includes yours. Your classifieds will seem dirt cheap by comparison.
- You might even try placing classifieds in other papers, offering free classifieds in your own paper. Sneaky, but legal.

Classified pages include both line ads (words and nothing more) and display ads (small ads with some graphic or logo included). Classified display ads sell for a premium price.

Store Ads on Your Computer

Create a formatted file for your classifieds that you can update and print out as each new issue is published. You must also be careful to save the display ads that you develop for all your other clients. You should have a zip disk or similar storage device for every regular customer. This disk will contain every ad in every issue that you have published for them. You will use these advertis-

Ten Ways to Please Your Advertisers

1. Be aware of the things they are trying to do in their stores. Compliment them when some change of display seems especially well done and effective.

2. Send birthday and other greetings regularly and on time.

3. Clip articles about your client or about his or her business from your own and other publications. Laminate these clippings and enclose them in some kind of presentation folder. Hand this folder to your client when you call or mail it just before you call.

4. Prepare rectangles of art board in convenient sizes. Across the top, have the words "As Seen in Your Publication" printed. Affix your client's most impressive ads or news write-ups to this board. Laminate it and place a cardboard easel stand behind it so that it will stand up beside the cash register or at some other prominent point.

5. Photograph your client in his or her place of business; photograph the facade of the store, shop or office and present these photos to your client for advertising use.

6. Refer friends to your client's place of business.

7. Do business with them yourself. It's a two-way street.

8. Read the trade papers. Be up on the news. . . not gossip, but news. Share this information with your clients.

9. Always show up with a marketing idea or two to discuss, and always show up with spec ads in hand. Your client should think of you as a colleague, a person who has his or her best interest at heart and not as someone solely interested in making a sale and getting out as quickly as possible.

10. Feed legitimate stories about their business to your editors. You ask: "Anything going on around here that we should know about?" If you hear something that is newsworthy, let your editor know. If you are also the editor, write it up yourself.

ing files over and over, combining elements, lifting art and logos, and utilizing the stored files in many other timesaving ways. In the beginning, every ad will be created from scratch. You will find your work immensely simplified through the use of these resource disks.

Pick-Up Ads

From time to time a customer will ask you to "pick up" an ad that he has published in another paper, perhaps a competing one. Many papers operating in the same market recognize that to maintain a positive relationship with their customers they must agree to allow pickup usage and have a liberal policy concerning it. You should, too.

When you face such a request, call the paper in question, tell them that their customer has requested that you pick up their ad, and let them know that you will return the favor when the time comes for them to pick up an ad that you have designed. Failing this, the customer himself will have to request permission for the pickup. If he has trouble getting it, reassure him. Tell him that you can design a very similar but even better ad for him, and that your policy, unlike that of your unfriendly competitor, will allow him to use the ad whenever and wherever he desires.

Setting Ad Prices

How much will you charge for your space? This is a thorny question, especially when you are just starting out. I will admit from the start that there is no way to know ahead of time that you are absolutely correct in your judgment. What is certain is that you want to charge as much as you can and still sell ads. But you also want to create a strong market position, such that clients will feel that they are getting more for their money when they advertise with you than when they advertise with competing publications.

Here are some things to consider as you build your space rate schedule:

- In the beginning you may have to settle for a little less than you would like to get. To make yourself feel better, though, you can go ahead and forecast (to yourself) a gradual series of rate increases (which you will call "rate card adjustments") as you strengthen your market position through the results you obtain.
- Even so, you must resist any pressure—whether brought to bear by yourself or by advisors—to begin to sell ads at an artificially low rate. You can't, as the old business saying goes, lose money on each ad you produce and make up that loss by selling a great many of them. There is a base below which you cannot go, and that base is the amount of money that pays your expenses, your salary and provides a modest margin of

profit for growth and expansion as well as a nest-egg to see you through market fluctuations and the occasional recession.

- In thinking about what you are going to charge, you will have learned from your espionage activities (see "Scoping Out the Competition" in Chapter 4) what at least one other company in the same business in your area thinks it has to charge to be profitable. This price is your point of departure. You will have to meet it or undersell it *unless you can add significant benefits to go along with your higher price, benefits such as vastly increased circulation.* Even then, you may be in difficult straits. If your price is higher, it will usually be perceived as too expensive, regardless of the added benefits you offer. Perceived value is more important than real value when you are entering the marketplace. Remember that you are the new kid on the block, the one with everything to prove.

- To increase your profitability utilize add-on pricing. Keep your base space rate as low as you can, but then develop a menu of "extras" that you can charge for, such as the boldface words and background screens in your classifieds, special typographic effects, special position, etc.

- Look for ways to cut printing costs. Incorporate as many of them as possible in your plans when you ask for quotes on printing. Ask your printer to suggest ways to lower the cost of production.

When you begin your actual calculations, get out a work sheet and perform the following operations:

- Add up the costs of getting your paper out, including office expense, auto expense, sales commissions, ad design, printing and circulation, and any salaries and commissions, including your own. Don't fudge on any of the costs, but don't exaggerate any of them, either. One of the things you have going for you in the beginning is the fact that, since you are home-based or small-office-based, your overhead is lower. Since you will be doing much of the work yourself in your area of expertise, either your sales expense, your production expense, or both, will be lower than those of your competition.

- Divide the total cost of getting your publications out by the number of full-page equivalent ads you expect to be able to sell. The figure you get from this arithmetic is your break-even advertising page cost for the first issue. Is it a competitive advertising rate? If you continue to sell at the same cost but increase the number of ad pages in following issues, will you be sufficiently in the black to make the project worthwhile?

- At this point you've got a preliminary figure to play with, but you are still not through. What you have come up with is the actual, profitable full page rate. This is what most clients will look at when they make their first, superficial comparison of costs. At this stage you have already covered your costs and provided for a modest profit. Every extra dollar you get now is pure profit. Let's say, for ease of calculation, that you've come up with an advertising rate of $500 per page. This is for your top-of-the-line ad. Now, some advertisers will want a three-quarter page ad. You discourage this, but they insist. The cost of the three-quarter page ad will be $225, not 75% of $500. More likely is that some will want a half-page ad. These will go for, say, $300. Thus your per page revenues will amount to considerably more than the $500 basic rate.

- You make a final adjustment when you look at your projected revenues per issue. If they are inadequate, you will have to find a way to increase them. Study all of the papers and shoppers that you can get your hands on. Ferret out techniques that you can use to produce more revenue. If, after doing this, you still can't get your income figures up high enough, you may have a problem on your hands. There just may not be an adequate profit potential to justify your effort. But before you make that depressing decision, take one more step. Work carefully and thoroughly through the areas of distribution and customer service. There may be enough that you can offer in these areas to justify the advertising rates that you feel are necessary.

- A happier circumstance—one that has actually happened to me—comes about when you calculate the bottom line on your projected advertising page rates and discover that you are far below the rates of the competition. You estimate that you can raise your prices by ten or twenty percent and still remain quite competitive. Go ahead and do it if the market will permit you to. You won't have a second chance.

Pricing Strategies

People, being human, do make comparisons—and not always in the most intelligent and analytical way. In pricing your advertising you can take advantage of the less than logical way in which some of your clients think. Some tabloid newspapers, for instance, employ a four column format and some a five column format. Each column in a tabloid is approximately 15 inches high. When you multiply the number of inches in each column by the number of columns you discover that the four column format contains 60 inches per page while the five column format contains 75 inches. (Some tabloid classified pages have a seven or eight column format, with even more inches per page.) Broadsheet pages are usually 21.5 inches high. The same math applies.

If two competing newspapers had exactly the same full page rate—say

An Ad Rate Worksheet

Throughout this book we have talked about setting profitable, competitive rates. There is a good deal of intuition in this—good old seat-of-the-pants flying. Yet there are some facts to take into account. This worksheet will help you define them.

If you get results you don't like—if your prices are too high or your profits too low—you will have to reduce your sales and production costs or find some value-added features to justify your necessarily higher prices.

Itemization of Costs per Issue	Price
Prorated rent and utilities	
Writer's fees per issue	
Printing per issue	
Distribution per issue	
Layout and design per issue	
Ad sales commissions	
Miscellaneous	
TOTAL COST PER ISSUE	

CALCULATIONS

$$\frac{\text{Total Cost per Issue}}{\text{Number of ad pages sold}} = \text{BREAK EVEN COST PER PAGE}$$

$$\frac{\text{Cost per issue plus desired profit}}{\text{Number of ad pages sold}} = \text{RETAIL COST PER PAGE}$$

$500—the column inch rate for the four column tabloid would be $500 divided by 60 inches: roughly $8.33 per column inch. The five column paper would divide $500 by 75 to fix its inch rate at roughly $6.66 per column inch. The second paper appears to be cheaper to the person buying by the inch, but, in fact, its rates are exactly the same. As a matter of fact, it could charge $7.00 per column inch, be more expensive while still appearing to be less expensive to many advertisers.

Modular Ads

For this and other reasons, many publishers today prefer modular ads. They do not divide their pages into column inches but into percentages of a page.

Modular design requires a four column format so that ads can be easily divided into full page ads, half page ads, quarter page ads, eighth page ads, sixteenth page ads and so on. The number of column inches is not mentioned. Thus, when an advertiser compares the cost of a "full page" in your newspaper, a tabloid, with that of a full page in the competing broadsheet, you can appear to be less expensive though, on a strict space basis, you will be more expensive. "A full page in the *Daily Blah* costs $1000," your ad rep can say. "In our paper it is only $500." What he fails to mention is that there is twice as much real space on the broadsheet full page. For some reason, this mode of reasoning is perfectly acceptable to many merchants.

A nice thing about the modular sales approach is that your modular ads facilitate page layout and eliminate many pesky problems brought on by running ads of many irregular column inch sizes.

"Earned" Rates

While the larger dailies will usually peg ad rates to annual contract commitments from their clients, smaller publications will generally employ "earned rates" to reward frequent, large advertisers. When dealing with earned rates, advertisers will commit themselves to placing a given amount of advertising in your publication. The rate paid by your advertiser will be pegged to the amount of space he has agreed to purchase. On a column inch basis, for instance, the "open" (or non-discount) rate may be set at $10.00.

Modular reductions work in the same way. If an open rate full page is $1000, then the customer who buys three full page equivalents during the month will get a 10% reduction in his total charge. More space will give a greater reduction; less space will get a smaller reduction. If the advertiser fails to keep his commitment, then the advertising he has already placed will be rebilled at the "short," or non-discount rate.

Your Ads Should Have Reader-Pulling Appeal

When ads are well-designed and interesting to the eye, readers will study every column inch of them with much the same spirit that a grizzled prospector might have pored over an ancient map purporting to show the best spots to dig for that long sought-after treasure. The point I am making, and it is often misunderstood by beginners, is that the quality of your advertising has as much to do with the readability of your newspaper as the stories themselves. The same care should be taken with ad design as with the writing of a front page story. Both have powerful appeal for the reader.

14

How to Sell Advertising in Your Newspaper

Once you have assembled your sales force (see Chapter 18, "How to Hire the People You Need at a Price You Can Afford to Pay"), move on the tasks of organization and training that are essential to your success. The first step is to prepare a prospect list of your trade area. Your best resource is a simple but extremely valuable one: the Yellow Pages in your local telephone book. Leaf through these pages one by one. You will find not only names, addresses and telephone numbers for all the businesses that readily spring to mind as potential advertisers, but of others that perhaps might not have come to mind so easily: day care centers, churches, printers, tree surgeons.....The list is a long one.

Next, research any competing publications. Who advertises in them? What kinds of ads do they run? What size? What do they pay for these ads? Can you come up with any strategies to give a value-added dimension to the advertising of these businesses in your own paper?

Check the membership listings of the Chamber of Commerce, as well as the advertising in the chamber's own publications. Check the big daily newspapers for business and service establishments from your trade area that are advertising in them. You can offer these customers saturation circulation in the area from which they are likely to draw their customers at much lower rates.

Your list of prospects will include retail business, service business, institutional business, professional businesses, physicians and hospitals, chiropractors, industrial concerns that may take community-interest sponsorship ads, and others.

You will list every possible advertising prospect. At this stage, don't eliminate anybody, but place everyone in one or more of the categories given above. Later, you can prioritize them as to their likelihood to buy and their importance to the financial health of your publication. Be sure to get the names of contact persons whenever you can.

Make a Call Schedule

Take your priority list and divide them into five groups, one for each day of the week. List these prospects by name. Remember that you are going to try to call on the same client at the same time of the same day each and every week (or month, if you are doing a monthly). These columns represent your master call schedule.

Next, divide this master list into smaller lists, one for each salesperson in the field. Since you will be using many part-time people, you will gear these individual lists to the amount of time that each salesperson has agreed to work. When you hand an individual list to a salesperson, go over it carefully. Suggest any ideas you may have for presentations. Make sure that the salesperson understands that coverage of this list constitutes his or her commitment to the publication.

This system gives you an easy way to keep a constant check of sales activity. If, after a day or two, you find that one of your people is not doing the job, look into it. If the neophyte sales person is suffering from a real case of call reluctance, you will want to replace that person quickly.

The Ad Sales Process

Secrets of successful ad sales? There are many, and you will have your own long list before you have been in business for more than a few weeks. But to get things under way, here is a starter kit of bedrock basics. Every item in it is derived from hands-on, first-person experience. I learned the hard way. When I began to publish the *Mecklenburg Gazette*, I had never worked for a newspaper, never sold a newspaper ad, and never written a newspaper story. Yet I closed the deal one Thursday afternoon and brought out my first issue the following Tuesday—right on schedule. It wasn't the most beautiful paper in the world, but it was mine, it was on time, and it contained enough advertising to break even.

What I didn't know about ad sales would have filled a book much longer than this one. I set about learning all I could. I went to newspaper management and ad sales seminars whenever and wherever I could afford it. I never came away from any of these without an idea or two that I was able to turn into real profits as I began to build my paper.

I went to the director of advertising of a very successful weekly in a nearby town. He agreed, for a modest fee, to come down and give us a day's training in sales-building methods. I took his very helpful tips and tried to put them into practice, winning a few and losing a few. You will go through the same trial and error learning process. It is inevitable, since no two trade areas or advertising clients are identical. Still, there are some fundamentals which, when implemented, will give you a leg up:

- Retail merchants and other businesses are going to advertise somewhere. They have to if they want to make money. It is not a question of whether to advertise or not, but of where to place their ads and how big to make them. The important thing, therefore, is to develop a long-term relationship with each client based on professionalism, customer service and delivering on your promises. As you learn more you can become an unpaid (except for the price of the ad) consultant to the small businessperson. Analyzing results week after week, you will soon develop a pretty accurate feel for what works and what does not. Relate success stories to your clients. Make recommendations. Research out-of-town papers for advertising ideas that are likely to bring customers in the front door for businesses that advertise with you. Become a storehouse of information and a source of positive, business-building ideas. Show your customer, week after week and issue after issue, that you have his best interests at heart.

- Make your calls on individual businesses at the same time of the day on the same day of the week for each issue. If you call on a client at 10 A.M. on Thursday this week, you should be back in his shop at 10 A.M. on Thursday of the next week. And the week after that. You or your sales rep should show up as regularly as clockwork. You will be expected. If you are consistently well prepared, if you are upbeat and positive, and if you have advertising ideas in mind to suggest to your client (preferably in graphic form), your visit will be profitable.

- When dealing with key accounts, find out when the salesperson for any competing publication comes to call. Make sure that you get to the customer first.

- Reduce this schedule of client calls to written form. Make it into a weekly checklist with every actual and potential client represented on the appropriate day at the appropriate time. Check each of them off as the call is made. If you supervise the work of other salespeople, prepare this list for them and require them to check off the calls as they are made.

- Always have something in your hands to show the prospect. Sales increase measurably (some consultants estimate by as much as 25%) when you have an advertising idea sketched out and in hand to show the client. This technique enables you to control the sales call and to begin right away to discuss the strengths and benefits of the idea you have presented. You listen carefully, of course, and begin to make changes and adjustments as your client suggests them. Note that you are now discussing the details of the advertisement that will run and how to design it for maximum effect. You are not asking the more basic question of whether or not the client will run an ad at all. At a minimum you need last week's ad neatly cut out and affixed to an art board. A lift cover of tracing paper dresses this up and reinforces the professional effect you want to get. Along with—or in place of—last week's advertisement, you may show an ad pulled from another source, but with the customer's name and logo pasted in. Your ad service (see the Contacts and Sources appendix) will be a good source for such materials.

Finding the Person Who Can Buy

There is no greater waste of time than to make a sales presentation to someone who cannot make a decision and sign a contract. A presentation made to the wrong person may be worse than no presentation at all. When this happens, the person upon whom you have been lavishing your best sales spiel looks at you with innocent blue eyes and says something like, "Oh, you know, I don't buy the advertising, but I'll tell the boss about it when she comes in." Later, when the boss comes in, the clerk looks up from her work and says, "Some guy came by selling advertising. You want any?" This is hardly a presentation designed to get results, so the immediate answer of the cash-poor boss is a firm "No." And once you've gotten a "no" it is all that more difficult to convert it to a "yes" later on. You would have been better off not to make any presentation at all. Sometimes, in spite of all your effort to avoid it, you will make a presentation to the wrong person. But don't let it happen twice. As soon as you know the name of the real advertising buyer make sure to enter it in your records. Be sure that all your sales reps do the same.

Product Knowledge Sells

Salespeople who have knowledge of their own product and of their customers' products and services sell more advertising. And the more product knowledge they have, the more advertising they sell.

There are two kinds of product knowledge—knowledge of your own product (advertising that works) and of your customers' products and services.

- The salesperson's own product—his stock in trade—is skillfully conceived and designed advertising that works. Spend the time necessary to study every book you can get your hands on about the design of effective advertising. Know this material. Reduce it to its essentials and teach it to your salespeople at training sessions. Read *The Wall Street Journal* and *Adweek*. Read *Editor & Publisher*. Read *Free Newspaper Publisher*. Memorize relevant statistics and increase your store of them week by week. Look for and talk about success stories involving advertising that seemed to do a super job. Reproduce copies of key information and hand these copies out to your salespeople. Pass around copies of the few great books that you know about on advertising design. Since some of these people won't be big readers, mark the most important pages so that they can turn right to them. This kind of information and training will give the good salespeople the information they need to become even better at their jobs and the marginal ones the confidence they need to become good producers. Absolutely essential are two resources I have already mentioned: John Caples, *Tested Advertising Methods*, available in paperback, and the hard, practical information on creating successful print media advertising in David Ogilvy's *Ogilvy on Advertising*. Ogilvy is talking about the rarefied atmosphere of national, big-money campaigns, but the lessons he teaches will bear rich dividends across the board— even at the relatively unglamorous level of the local weekly. The other books that I will recommend later also contain chapters on advertising design. Study all of these; make the information your own. Teach it again and again to everyone who works for you. Your customer expects you to know what you are doing. He is trusting you with his money and the future of his business. You want him to consider you or your representative the most knowledgeable source of advertising ideas, strategies, and information available in the market. In the beginning you will be walking a thin line, especially if you come from an editorial background, as I did. Those who come from a sales background will be better prepared, but still have much to learn about print media advertising. You will know a lot more just a few short weeks later. In spite of this, use the things you have learned with confidence and authority.

- Knowledge of the customer's product. This kind of knowledge is gained by carefully studying the customer's store or place of business, noting what he is most interested in selling, and coming up with suggestions for him to consider. Talk to your customers, but above all, listen. Given half a chance, each of them will share with you their sales goals, sales concerns and problem areas. When you help them solve their problems, they will become faithful customers.

Don't Forget "Little" Ads

What about all those individuals and businesses who would like to advertise with you but can't afford the big bucks for the larger ads. Do you just write them off as bad advertising bets? Not at all. In fact some of the most lucrative page rates that you have will come from the special advertising sections that you develop for just such clients.

Examples? Open *Better Homes and Gardens, Entrepreneur* and many other magazines. The back pages are chock full of tiny ads, each containing an amazing amount of copy and graphics advertising fascinating and useful products and services. These ads constitute a buyer's paradise. As a matter of fact, I bought the Apple computer on which I am presently writing this chapter

Important: Meet Those Deadlines!

Newspapers, all of them, work on rigid deadline schedules. Yours will be no exception.

Space should be reserved by 10 am Monday. All copy should be in by Monday noon, with the exception of camera-ready copy, which you can allow to come in up to a few hours before press time. You will work as late as necessary on Monday to paste up ads and paste up pages.

On Tuesday morning you will drop in the camera-ready ads from your larger clients. You will set aside two hours for careful proofing of the ads you have typeset and designed yourself. At the appointed hour you will put your pages together and deliver them to the facility that will print them.

An hour or two later you load up your freshly printed papers and set the distribution process in motion. You have told your advertisers when you expect to be on the street. Be there, rain or shine, holiday or no, whatever the circumstances. The professionalism and credibility of your enterprise are on the line.

from one of the small ads in the bargain basement section at the back of *MacWorld* magazine. So interesting are these ads that many readers habitually open the magazines from the back cover and read through from back to front. A glorious extra is that, because they get results and because they are so afford-able, these ads are easy to renew. After a few issues some advertisers will sim-ply tell you to keep them in the magazine until they give you the word to pull them out.

There may be several of these nested ad sections. One might be for spe-cialty retailers; another will be for hotels, motels, and accommodations; a third may be for schools, colleges, and specialty educational opportunities ("Double Your Income! Become a Dental Technician!"); a final section will contain ads for restaurants, along with restaurant reviews. Each section will have its own, easily identifiable heading: *Bed and Board, Who Can Do It,* etc. In addition to the advertisers to whom they are ideally suited, these back-of-the-book sec-tions are your fall-back ads for virtually everybody. When a larger firm can't take out a big ad don't fold up your tent and stop selling. Instead, extol the wonders that the $190 mighty miniature ad will work for them. Often they will be so relieved not to have to spend $1000 that they will say "yes" out of sheer gratitude. There are no limits to the business you can do with these special sections.

"Plus Lineage"

I learned about plus lineage in one of the earliest seminars I attended after starting my weekly newspaper. It was a profitable lesson indeed. In newspaper jargon, plus lineage refers to advertising space bought by the customer above and beyond what that customer would ordinarily buy on a weekly basis. Here are some tried and true ways of generating plus lineage.

- *The holidays and special occasions* that you are accustomed to may appear to be scattered randomly through the year. When you look more closely, you discover that they are spaced rather evenly through the cal-endar and that they are merchandising tools. In recent years we have seen National Secretaries' Day, National Grandparents' Day, and even Na-tional Bosses' Day — all sponsored by the American Florists' Association, much to the profit and benefit of its membership.
- *Special supplements.* At regular intervals you will want to distribute, along with your weekly paper, special sections relevant to the time of year. In March, for instance, there will be a lawn, yard, and garden supple-ment; in April, a bridal and wedding supplement; in the summer, a home improvement and an outdoor fun supplement. August brings the back to school supplement and November the gift ideas supplement. These supplements usually have a magazine feel to them. They are typically

A Tip on Ad Sales for Any Publication

Here's a tip on ad sales in general. In large corporations with huge advertising budgets the person who buys the ads is not spending his or her own money. The dollars are not real to the person buying the ads in the same way that the far lesser sums in their personal bank accounts are real. This fact simplifies the salesperson's job and paves the way to closing deals.

It is always far more difficult to sell a $200 ad to a small business person who is spending his own money than a $2000 ad to the corporate executive who is spending someone else's money. To the owner of his own small business the dollars are real. He fished them out of his own back pocket. Every ad purchase represents a decrease in the dollars available for him to take home at the end of the month or the year. He thinks very carefully indeed before he spends his hard-earned money on them.

designed in tabloid format and include articles appropriate to the special subject matter that they focus on. These articles are furnished by the advertising services such as Metro. Often your ad service will send you a completely designed and laid out publication with only the ad spaces to fill in.

- *Sell supplements far in advance.* Remember, you haven't gained anything if your advertisers simply shift their ads from the regular sections into the special supplement. The technique is to sell the supplement six to eight weeks in advance. Then, the week before it appears, you can still make a call for your regular pages. So, when the supplement appears the client will have ads in two places, in the regular pages and in the supplement. Plus linage can, however, result when advertising is shifted over, as long as the supplement itself is a strong enough sell to encourage larger placements.

RECOMMENDED RESOURCE! A good source of clip art and ready-made ads is the Dynamic Graphics Co. They send their subscribers a monthly collection of advertising and clip art keyed to holidays and seasonal advertising needs of weeklies and magazines. If you're just starting up and can afford it, go ahead and buy the previous 6 or 12 months worth of art. You can reach Dynamic Graphics at (800) 227-7048.

- *Sponsorship of special features.* Plus linage also results from the sponsorship of special features, especially in community newspapers. Such special features will vary from section to section of the country. A favorite in the southern town where I once lived was the illustrated Bible story. This is done quite well in comic book style in a space covering the greater part of a page. At the bottom of the story there appears the list of the names of the firms "sponsoring"—that is, paying for at normal advertising rates—the Bible lesson. Many of these firms, such as industrial or service concerns, would not normally be prospects for the usual advertising sales. The Bible story appeared every week, as did the names of the sponsoring firms. The result: an additional page of paid space in each issue of your paper. Variations on this theme include special pages for the United Way solicitation, the American Cancer Society solicitations, Back to School safety campaigns, and many others. Most small newspapers utilize these special promotions, though they are rarely seen in big city dailies. Other plus linage strategies that work include ads designed like Christmas greeting cards in sizes ranging from twelve to twenty-four column inches. These are an easy sell around Christmas. Business is good, and merchants wish to thank their faithful clients. As services also furnish books of advertising layouts and ideas, often complete except for prices and logos, and keyed to the month and season. A good ad service is very valuable to you and quite affordable. It would be almost unthinkable to attempt to publish a newspaper without one.

Dealing with Ad Agencies

From time to time you will get insertion orders from advertising agencies, along with a slick (a printed version of the ad ready for inclusion in the paper). This ad may or may not be sized to fit the format of your tabloid or broadsheet. Hopefully, the agency will have asked in advance for your "mechanical specifications," that is your column size or modular ad size. But often the ad will have originally been designed for another publication with different specifications and you will have to adapt it to make it fit. Always call the agency, tell them what you are going to do and why, and get approval from them. You will bill the agency for these ads and not the advertiser. Advertising agencies normally qualify for a 15% discount on the advertising they place. From your point of view they earn this discount by designing the ads, saving you the chore of doing the work yourself. Cultivate your relationships with advertising agencies. Make sure that they always have a complete media kit on hand.

Compensating Salespeople

Pay your salespeople on a straight commission basis, with no advance against commissions and no weekly or monthly draw against commissions. (Draws and advances can be costly and nonproductive. You can string along an ineffectual salesperson, hoping for better, for several weeks or months. If this person is drawing $150 a week against commissions—a modest enough figure—you will still be out a thousand or more dollars before the relationship ends. I have always been able to find very good people without having to pay a draw.) I generally set the sales commission at 20% of the gross sale amount for new business, with a lesser percentage for renewal of old business, say 15%. I set the commission level high enough so that I do not have to pay expenses, except for out-of-town travel that I have pre-approved. This relatively liberal commission rate also helps make up for the delayed payschedule. Until you develop a dependable cash flow, the sales commission is *always* paid only when the money actually comes in. After you become relatively prosperous, you can use this pay-on-receipt plan only for new salespeople.

An occasional bonus offer is a powerful incentive to sales. The allure of an extra end-of-the-week check can work wonders on sales enthusiasm. In slow times, offer $50 in cash to anyone who breaks a certain level in ad sales—say the $2000 or $3000 mark—for the week. When this happens make it a point to write the bonus check then and there.

Ad Sales Schedule				
Monday	Tuesday	Wednesday	Thursday	Friday

An ad sales schedule like this one should be put into the hands of each salesperson as the sales period begins. The salesperson will fill in the new business section as opportunities arise, but will always be careful not to call on any customer whose name is on another salesperson's card.

Sales Manual and Sales Control Forms

One sure fact of life in the independent publishing business is that you will be hiring salespersons more frequently that you might wish to. You can count on yourself and on one or two other people — probably part-time and for one reason or another less mobile than the others — to hang around and continue working. But most of your salespeople will come and go. Some will join your staff, fail to sell enough to meet their financial needs or expectations, and wander off to other, in their eyes less chancy, jobs. Others will do very well indeed with you, but then be attracted to much higher paying sales jobs with larger companies that have generous expense accounts and loads of benefits and perks—companies that you cannot compete with. An unfortunate few will sit at their desks, stare at the telephone, and never call a prospect at all.

So, for whatever reason, you will be constantly hiring and training salespeople. Although you will train these people personally to the degree that time allows, there will be a need for a simple sales manual that you will put into their hands. You will want this manual to do a number of jobs:

- Give the salesperson some information about the background of the company.
- Give the salesperson clear instructions on procedures and policies, though not repeating the details of the operations manual.
- Summarize the tried and true sales techniques that you know will work, if intelligently and assiduously applied.
- Tell the salesperson in clear, unequivocal terms just how you expect the work to be done.

Just remember that you are not writing a treatise on the art of selling. Your sales manual should be brief and to the point.

Appendix One reproduces a brief sales manual I developed for one of my earliest publications and which I used continually, for publications large and small, thereafter. With this little manual in hand to reinforce a day-long sales training session that I had given them, an enthusiastic crew of five part-time and totally inexperienced salespeople went out into a town of 14,000 inhabitants to establish a city magazine. They succeeded, and the magazine was published regularly until I sold the business five years later. Will this kind of manual work for you? I believe that it will. Details will vary, of course, as the particular publishing project at hand varies. But the heart of the message will remain unchanged. I have used this manual again and again over the years, with just slight variations.

15

Eight Specialty Book Projects
for the Periodical Publisher

Like most writers, I wanted to publish a book long before I actually managed to do so. I wanted the sense of accomplishment that book publication would bring; I wanted the prestige and recognition of being the author of a published book; and, of course, I wanted the money that I thought I could earn in that way.

The Three-Way Test Again

But what books would I publish? Applying the rules that I had developed for gauging the success potential of periodicals—and checking down a list of successful titles that others had published before me—I decided that books are almost always publishable and profitable when they:

- Have the potential for intensive sales
- In a limited geographical area
- Or to a well-defined, clearly targeted readership.

Moving Out

In four years I published four successful books. Each title in this series was slanted toward the regional market and each was self-published. Gradually, I developed a profitable book publishing business, eventually bringing out some books by other writers as well as my own. I define book-publishing success as publishing books that get good reviews, sell to the targeted readership, and make money. Here are eight proven ideas that will get you started. These books often have tie-in's and sponsorship opportunities that can guarantee profitability. Each is planned to take much of the risk out of book publishing.

Book Idea Number One:
How to Write and Publish a Picture History of Your Town

Such a book was my own introduction to the world of regional book publishing. It started like this. One night I read an article in our town's newspaper about an upcoming bicentennial celebration of the founding of the city of Greenville, NC. It suddenly occurred to me that the time was surely right for a pictorial history of the town. If the book were well-designed and well-written, I knew it would sell very well. As I saw it, the project had five things going for it:

- It had a ready-made market. The two-hundredth anniversary of the town's founding was coming up. People would be ready to buy such a book, and they would pay premium prices for it. Even those who were not normally book buyers would want a souvenir copy. (Intensive sales— remember the three criteria?)
- I could easily reach this market. The buyers of the book were all local, living within a fifty mile radius of my office. No extensive sales trips would be necessary. I would not have to go to the expense of a national marketing campaign. I would have intensive sales in a limited geographical area, one of the key requirements for successful self-publishing in the local and regional market.
- The book would be easy to write. No original research would be required. A modest narrative thread to hold the book together and give it unity was all that was required. This, I felt, would amount to as little as eight to ten thousand words, the length of two or three longish magazine articles. Other than that, most of the historical information would be communicated through the cut lines accompanying each of the old photographs I would gather. Few people like to read long historical texts, but everyone likes to look at pictures and read the cutlines, especially when the pictures deal directly with their homes and their history.
- There was no such book already on the market. I knew my book would sell.
- I could possibly get a corporate or civic sponsor. More about this later.

There were two problems. The first was that it was May. The celebration was scheduled for September. That gave me three months to write, design and print my book. Could I do it? "Sure," I answered myself. "You can do it."

I was too inexperienced to know that this schedule was virtually impossible to keep. I got myself into gear, acted as though it were impossible to fail, and met the challenge. One day before the festivities began I had my book in hand. On opening day I was behind my table at bicentennial headquarters, happily autographing books for the considerable number of my fellow citizens who came to buy them.

I made a schedule: thirty days for gathering material, thirty days for writing, and thirty for typesetting and printing. The miracle is that once I had set these goals I managed to reach each of them. You can accomplish more than you ever thought possible when you put the full force of your mind to it. As my old buddy Napoleon Hill taught me, "Whatever the mind of man can conceive and believe, the mind of man can achieve!" I had never really believed him before. I mention this frantic schedule to prove to you that nothing is impossible. I do not necessarily recommend it, and I have not tested myself in such a way again.

I Published It Myself

The second problem was that I would have to publish the book myself. There was simply no time to find another publisher. If I found one, they would not get the book out on my almost impossibly tight schedule. I know now, of course, that I would never have found anyone willing to take on such a book for one single city market.

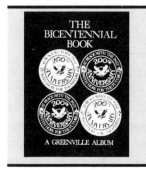

To the left is the cover of my first book project, the Greenville, NC, Bicentennial book. This illustrated city history gave me my first experience of the power of the "three way test" for project viability. I used this invaluable insight again and again throughout my publishing career.

I was totally without experience in book design and production. However, I liked books; I knew books. I figured I could get hold of a similar book that I thought was handsomely designed, take it to the typesetter and printer and say, "Make my book look like this one." This is precisely what I did, and it worked just fine. To this day I recommend this simple, copycat technique to others starting out in self-publication. I don't think it can be improved on.

A Boost from the Media

I let the daily paper and the local television stations know of my project. A couple of articles appeared a few days later, and that got the ball rolling. I appeared on local TV talk shows and spoke to historical societies. Word of my book project quickly got around and generated considerable interest. I enlisted the aid of each and every well-wisher in my search for old photographs, maps, and other reproducible documents of interest. I got hold of the one available history of the town and county, and I interviewed a couple of dozen old-timers. This gave me the necessary materials I needed to write the narrative thread that wound through the book and held it together.

The publicity worked. When I knocked on doors of likely prospects to ask if they had old photos of Greenville in albums or attic trunks, I was usually welcomed in. These people had heard of me, I found, through the news stories and TV spots. I was not a stranger, banging on doors unannounced and unsolicited. The little PR I did had legitimized my project.

Make Them Feel Comfortable

One of the few difficulties you will have will be prying people loose from cherished old photographs. You will have to convince them that you are businesslike and that you respect their property.

To allay all fears, have some large envelopes printed up (or use a specially designed rubber stamp on standard ones) to hold each picture separately. The label should include space to enter the owner's name, address, and telephone number along with a complete description of the place or persons pictured.

You should also have some simple, printed receipt forms and leave a signed copy with each contributor. They will find this quite reassuring.

Careful Cataloguing

Once the photos started coming in, things began to move swiftly. I was always careful to catalogue each of these meticulously, and I interviewed the owners of the photographs extensively. As a result, I was almost always able to write the accurate, informative and sometimes lengthy captions that please readers and sell books.

As easy as it was to do, my Bicentennial Book became a valuable resource for local historians. These photographs might have simply disappeared as their owners passed away and estates were dispersed. Now, thanks to my little project, they were preserved for future generations.

In order to meet my schedule, I called on some others whom I knew to contribute chapters to my book. The archaeologist David Phelps, a friend of mine, wrote a fascinating chapter on the Indian past of Greenville. Stan Riggs, a well-known geologist, wrote a chapter on the prehistory of the area and Claire Pittman contributed chapters on social life in old Greenville and on the great fire that once destroyed the clapboard business district, as has happened at one time or another in most 19th century clapboard downtowns.

2,500 Books to Sell

With these chapters, the photographs and my own narrative in hand, I was ready to begin designing my book. As self-publisher I was in charge of every detail, and I thoroughly enjoyed the work. I decided on a large page format (magazine size) to show off the pictures better. The page was based on a two column format to facilitate ease of reading. I designed a cover and sent the whole thing off to the printer. Three weeks later I was wondering what to do with the 2,000 paperback copies and 500 hard cover copies that Estes Van Lines dropped off at my front door. I did not wonder long. The book did very well. Every one of those 2,500 was sold. I made money. I gained recognition. And I contributed to the cultural enrichment of my town.

A Big Bonus

Once you have done a book like this you will have earned a tremendous bonus. Everything you have learned is transferable. You can apply them to similar projects elsewhere. You have worked out the method. You have created a design that works. You know how to price for profit. You know how to do the writing and collecting. Now you can apply all this, with the greatest of ease, to a nearby town or city. And then to another. And another.... Successful writing and publication of pictorial histories need stop only when you grow tired of the whole idea and decide to move on to something else.

Secondary Profit Centers

Publishing a pictorial history opens the way for a good deal of extra profit. You may, for instance, get a major bank, S & L or industry to sponsor your book, buying the entire first edition—or at least a major portion of it. If you do get a sponsor, here's what you do. Print a first edition with, perhaps, a foreword by the president of the institution or industry, which then disposes of the edition as a premium. The fee paid to you is sufficient to pay for research, writing, printing and a very generous fee to you as publisher. You can bring out any second edition on your own, *sans* the paid-for introduction.

I did this with one of my self-published books, *Tales of the Tobacco Country*. A leading PR firm in our state bought the first edition for their client, the president of Phillip Morris, to give away as an executive Christmas gift. I have been selling subsequent editions on my own for years now. You can also sell one-page family histories to notable families or institutional histories to businesses. You can also simply sell full page advertising on the back pages and flyleaves to those with the money to pay for them.

Book Idea Number Two:
The Institutional History

Is there a church, college or similar institution near you? Is there a bank or an industry about to celebrate an important anniversary? If so, there is a ready market for an institutional history. Churches and colleges develop strong, emotional loyalties among their congregations and alumni. A history of one of these institutions cannot help but be successful when well written and marketed. Banks and industries are just as proud of their pasts. Some may do a book in honor of a retiring founder. Others will do this simply to let the community know that the company is a solid, public-minded entity and therefore deserving of patronage and support in their endeavors.

What? A problem? You say that you are not a historian? Don't let that word scare you off. You don't have to be a professional in the field to get the job done. In fact it is probably better that you are not. You won't get bogged down in detail to the extent that you never get the job done or produce a manuscript that is as unreadable as it is historically exhaustive. We're describing forests here, not counting trees. If you go overboard on any aspect of the project, do it gathering photographs, not digging out obscure facts.

Likely Prospects

Here are your likeliest prospects for an institutional history:

- Colleges and universities
- Banks, especially local banks or regional banks with their headquarters nearby.
- Savings and Loan Associations, assuming that you can find one that is still solvent. Even the solvent ones have tremendous PR problems today. They need to reassure the public that they are solid, prosperous, trustworthy, and an integral part of the community. An institutional history will help them do this.
- Industries, especially those that have been around for a while and have their corporate headquarters in your town or in a nearby town.
- Large commercial enterprises with local headquarters.

Beware of the PR People

One serious obstacle to your getting an agreement to do an institutional history can come from the PR departments of the industries themselves or from their ad agencies. You've got to stroke these people if you want the assignment. Since most PR people have broad job descriptions they are almost never writers of books or even primarily writers at all. Even if they were, their job duties would not allow them time to carry out the assignment. They need you to do the work for them. Nevertheless, they want to be included. They must not feel that they are losing any face by letting you write the book rather than doing it themselves. Perhaps you could suggest that you list them on the title page as consulting editors or otherwise credit them.

Ad Agencies

Many of the larger firms will have ad agencies. Almost always these agencies will be somewhat jealous of your project on two grounds. First, they want to protect their turf. Second, they earn a living by getting commissions when they spend their client's advertising money. They don't want to see you take a big bite out of the ad budget without getting their share.

If your client never mentions his ad agency and you can get the assignment without getting them involved, so much the better. But if you have to meet with the agency account executive, assure him or her that the book is commissionable to the agency—that is, that you will pay them a percentage of the overall fee for services. This fee, ranging from five to fifteen percent, can then be negotiated. Your own fee—the one that you charge to your customer—will simply be increased by a like amount. It may seem strange, but this is the way that business is done in the world of advertising.

Only a Writer Can Do the Job

In an institutional history you are mainly telling a story, the story of real people who make things happen and of institutions that affect the lives of those who are associated with them. And story telling is the province of the writer, which is exactly what you are. Research will be quite limited. Simply utilize sources already printed in newsletters, magazines, newspaper articles and previously written pamphlets. You will supplement these sources with a great many interviews. These interviews will do more to give you a real feel for the subject you are writing about than any abstract research could ever do. Such an approach has other strong points, too. Every person interviewed and quoted is another person with a vested interest in the success of your project, another person who is likely to sign up for the "signed and numbered" pre-publication sale of "heirloom" copies of your book.

Fewer Words, More Pictures

What is required is not a historian but a writer who will simply tell the story of the institution in a highly readable, interest-packed way. In doing so, pictures will be of immense importance, just as they were in the picture history of your town. If I were doing such a book and had to decide whether to spend more time researching the text or searching for pictures, I'd go for the pictures every time. Not that you neglect the text or do a sloppy job of writing. You certainly can't afford that. But when you've got a story of this kind to tell, pictures do it best. There's a hard fact that you, as a writer, have to accept and live with: most people don't read books, but everybody likes to look at pictures, especially their own pictures. Pictures sell books.

How Many Readers?

If you are publishing your institutional history on your own, without an institutional sponsor, you must carefully analyze your readership potential. The number of readers who buy books does not have to be enormous for you to make money. This kind of book can be printed in an edition of 300 to 500, for instance, and sold at a premium price as a special, limited edition. But calculate closely the number of copies you will need and do not print any more than you think you can sell within a one-year period. You should do an advance sales campaign to generate orders for enough copies to pay costs for the entire first edition, if possible. With this kind of project such up-front sales are not at all unlikely.

An Institutional Sponsor

You may easily find an institutional sponsor to support your project financially. A wealthy alumnus may be interested in underwriting a history of a university, for instance. You will make your profit on the advance money thus generated. In return for the monies advanced to you by your sponsor you agree to pay a royalty into the alumni foundation fund, the scholarship fund, or any other fund that might support some special academic interest of your benefactor.

Let Them Pay the Bill

An industry or financial institution will always be happy to have you present your proposal to them for an institutional history. It's the kind of thing they will understand and will invest in. In general, you will make a deal in which you will simply write, design, and publish this kind of book for a generous fee, with all expenses paid by the sponsoring institution. Be sure to approach them at least one year or possibly two in advance. You do this to insure that you will have time to complete your project, to insure that no one else beat you to it, and, above all, to get into the budget.

A book like this can be done over a 90-day period if you work hard enough and long enough at it. But there's no hurry. You can devote whatever time to it that you desire so long as you get it out on time.

And You Can Do Others!

Like the pictorial history of a town, the institutional history also has that important by-product of transferability. Everything you learn while doing your first one can be applied to another, either in your own town or in other towns. Writers have built very profitable careers for themselves doing this kind of project. Some quite successful publishing houses specialize in them. Once you've done one and have it in hand to show to others as a sample of your wares, you're up and running. You've been through the routine involved. You know the ins-and-outs. It gets easier every time you do one.

Book Idea Number Three:
Historical Documents and Narratives

There are only modest profits to be made here, but the project itself is one that will interest many periodical publishers.

Journals of explorers and early settlers make interesting and popular books. I used to live in North Carolina. In that state, as in most states, there is a rich literature dealing with the discovery and exploration of the area, much of it quite dramatic. In those days, coming to the new world was as strange and exotic an experience as going to the Moon or Mars is in ours. Everyone who made the trip, and could write, composed memoirs, journals and letters in which they vividly recorded their experiences for the folks back home. Such accounts can form the nucleus of your next book.

But haven't they all been collected and published by now? Not at all. There is undoubtedly a good deal of material out there just waiting for your fine touch. As writer you contribute an introduction, any explanatory notes you may wish to add and possibly a good deal more.

As settlers moved westward, a continuing stream of these first-person narratives was produced. Every great historical period has generated men and women who possessed "the gift of the pen", as one of them called it, and who bore witness to it.

The letters and diaries of such times—written with no thought of publication, and therefore with great directness and frankness—are especially valuable and revealing documents.

Much Is Still Out of Print

Many of these papers never found their way into print, and so remain inaccessible to the general public. But they can be published now, and you can be the one who publishes them. In my part of the country a writer-publisher named F. Roy Johnson, a citizen of the small town of Ahoskie, NC, brought out an impressive series of such books. He wrote and edited many of his books, liberally paraphrasing traditional stories. He printed, bound and sold all of them. His titles figured prominently among local history selections in every bookstore in the region.

A Book of Civil War Letters

I recently published a book by Elizabeth Whitley Roberson called *Weep Not for Me, Dear Mother*. This book is based on a collection of letters written by a young Confederate soldier, Eli Landers of Gwinnett County, Georgia, to his mother. Eli was a member of the Flint Hill Grays during many of the great battles of the Civil War.

North Carolina historian Elizabeth Roberson came by a rich collection of civil war letters almost by accident. Her book based on these letters, *Weep Not for Me Dear Mother,* is shown on the left. Weep Not went through three printings with my company, Venture Press, and was eventually placed with Pelican Books. Ten years later the books is still a strong seller on the Pelican backlist.

Elizabeth Roberson had never written a book before, although she had written articles for various magazines that I had published. She was a teacher of history in a small town high school, and she was a Civil War buff. Inspired by her materials, she wrote a 30,000 word narrative into which she embedded the text of the letters themselves, all of which had great human interest. Elizabeth got hold of the letters by chance. They had been retrieved from an Atlanta landfill in the early 1960s by the merest stroke of luck. Subsequently they found their way to Raleigh, NC and finally to the small town of Williamston, where they were shown to Roberson. She immediately recognized their value and set about writing the book that would become *Weep Not for Me, Dear Mother.* Advance sales were strong enough to pay for the entire first printing.

I tell this story to illustrate the point that there are many unpublished papers of great historical interest, often lying quite neglected in some manuscript collection or even totally unknown in someone's attic. If you set about it with determination and look long and hard enough, you may strike historical gold yourself.

How to Find Documents to Publish

Unpublished papers that may form the basis for a book fall into three categories:

- Diaries.
- Letters.
- Unpublished historical accounts from earlier times written by a well-known person about whom we wish to know more; a little-known person who lived through historically important events and wrote about it; or, a person who wrote so well that his or her materials are of true literary merit. Often when you uncover such a nest of papers there will be other documents of interest along with them, such as maps, drawings, or photographs. The more of these you find, the better.

How to Go About Your Search

There will undoubtedly be some sheer luck at work in your search. After all, the letters of Eli Landers came to Elizabeth Roberson by accident. A neighbor had them lying in a dust-covered attic and casually asked if Elizabeth would be interested in seeing them.

On the other hand, it was Elizabeth's widely-known interest in historical research and writing that prompted the neighbor's suggestion. So while luck plays a part, we all tend to make our own share of it.

If you are looking for historical documents to write about and to publish, here's how to get started:

- *Place an advertisement for yourself.* If you are a member of a state historical society or some similar group or association, publish a note in the organizational newsletter announcing that you wish to publish letters, diaries and other accounts of historical interest. It would be sheer luck if someone called you the next day and told you that they had a collection of superb letters on hand for you to look at, although stranger things have happened. What is more likely is that at some future date a person who has read the newsletter will find some papers which he believes to be of interest, remember your announcement and call you.

- *Browse through bibliographies.* Check especially the bibliographies in histories or biographies that deal with people or periods that you especially like. Are manuscript collections cited there? Is reference made to unpublished letters or diaries? If so, track them down. They are all grist for your writing-publishing mill.

- *Contact professional historians.* Get in touch with historians who are specialists in fields in which you are interested. Every university faculty has those historians on its staff who have spent their lives finding out everything there is to know about the documents, published and unpublished, that are important to your area. Ask if they know of historical accounts, letters, or diaries deserving of publication but still unpublished. Let it be known that you are interested in seeing that the materials are published. This may generate some suggestions. You may find it useful to suggest that the person to whom you are writing contribute an introduction to the materials. You can do this to make sure you have the wholehearted cooperation you need, but don't give so much that the work of the specialist detracts from your own efforts. After all, your goal is to publish a book under your own name as editor or author.

- *Contact librarians.* Most large libraries have specialized staff dealing with various areas. Get the name of the person in your area of interest. Ask if there are any unpublished or out-of-print items that are in demand and that you might successfully publish. You may unearth leads this way and without encountering quite so strong a spirit of competition as is possible when you consult professional historians. Do not neglect the specialized libraries. The Georgia Historical Society, for instance, has a library of its own that is a gold mine for researchers. The Department of Archives and History of the state of North Carolina has an extensive collection. Check for such sources in your own part of the country.

- *Visit manuscript collections yourself.* Manuscripts in libraries are meticulously catalogued. Look through these catalogues and see what you can discover that is of interest to you. Check even those items that do not seem particularly promising. You never know what you will turn up. If you can get into the stacks, do so and browse along the shelves. Many very important writings have been discovered almost by accident lying forgotten and under generations of dust on little-frequented library shelves. Once you have discovered the material you wish to publish, read it carefully. Read it both with an historian's eye and with the eyes of the bookseller. Is it important? Fine. But will it sell? Can you find an angle to make it marketable? If the answer to these questions is positive, then go ahead with your project. You can even go ahead if you come up with a "yes" answer to the last two questions alone.

If the material is dramatic enough and of broad enough scope to interest a reasonable number of readers, all you have to do is write an introduction, prepare any transitional material needed to bind the text together, prepare an index (which always makes your book more valuable to those who use such publications), and provide some art and illustrations.

Book Idea Number Four:
The Strange, the Uncanny and the Supernatural

Are there strange beings in outer space? Yes, indeed. Very strange beings. Who are they? These strange beings are…us! Our world, perched on the edge of a minor galaxy in the infinite blackness of space, is as mysterious and inexplicable as any world could possibly be. Readers are convinced of that and love books that secretly feed this belief. They may not admit it. A kind of simple-minded materialism has been pounded into most of us so thoroughly that we often don't even admit to ourselves that we really would like to believe in ghosts. But let two or three people get together on a front porch at twilight or around a campfire and the stories begin.

The Supernatural Sells!

Good books that plug into this love—even thirst—for the supernatural sell year after year. The only requirements are that the material be fresh, dramatically presented, and, for the entrepreneurial publisher, have a niche. That's what happened to Dr. Raymond Moody, a philosopher by trade, when he wrote his incredibly successful book *Life after Life*. This little book, easily researched and even more easily written, broke no new ground. Yet it sold hundreds of thousands of copies and made this former college professor a wealthy man.

You can slant such a book toward the local and regional market and count on steady but less than dramatic sales. Or you can slant it toward a wider market and sell off mass market rights once you have a book of proven appeal and strong local sales.

A Supernatural Guide Book

If you live in an area with a strong tourist trade, an interesting supernatural niche may be open to you. When I was living in France a few years ago I traveled extensively around the country and read a lot of guidebooks (the French are masters of the art of guidebook writing and publishing).

I was interested to find, alongside the standard guides, a parallel series which overlooked the usual monuments and museums in favor of the dark side of life. Called *Mysterious Normandy*, or *Mysterious Paris*, or mysterious whatever-part-of-the-country-I-happened-to-be-visiting-in, these little books were fascinating, and I always bought one. In them I found the story of every strange, uncanny, bizarre, or supernatural event that had ever happened or been rumored to have happened in that locality, along with directions on how to get to the site of the occurrence and descriptions of what I would find when I got there.

I thought it a good idea then, and I still do now. In fact, I feel so positive about it that I'm tempted to file this chapter on a remote and private sector of my hard drive and save the idea for myself. But I won't, because I think that the book that I am now writing is a great idea, too. What I suggest to you is a book that you might call *Mysterious North Dakota* or *The Dark Side of Tampa: The Ghosts Among Us*. Or, to take a different direction, a book on Savannah, Charleston, Mobile, or New Orleans that might be called *Murder Among the Magnolias*. Experiment and find the format and presentation that works best. You can publish the same book with two different titles or two different covers to see which one sells best.

Could Be a Series

By now you have discovered my liking for projects that can be profitably repeated. That is certainly the case with your book on strange and violent happenings. If your version works in Savannah, do another in Charleston, Wilmington, Norfolk, Washington or any other city of your choice. At the very least, there would be a lot of tax deductible travel to fascinating places.

Where Do You Find Your Material?

- *Send out news releases.* Send a news release to the local newspaper announcing that you are doing a book on the supernatural, uncanny and mysteries in your town. Let people know what kinds of topics you will cover: ghosts, unsolved murders, UFO's, mysterious occurrences, etc. Invite those with stories to call or write. You may or may not get some useful calls, but the article in the newspaper will let everyone know what you are doing. There will scarcely be a social gathering of any kind at which some friend or acquaintance will not come up to you in private to tell you of a story that he or she knows about and that you might be interested in.

- *Utilize book sources.* Research previously published and out-of-print books. You will be looking for records or stories of happenings that you can then research yourself and perhaps put a new twist on. Reading such books will sometimes generate new, but related, ideas. Take care to note every one of them down as they occur to you. The pocket notebook that you will carry around with you for this purpose is your best friend. Despite your best intentions, if you do not make note of these flashes of inspiration you will not remember them later no matter how unforgettable they seemed at the time.

- *Research old newspaper files.* Most of these will be on microfilm, and many of them will have been indexed for you. You can find the microfilm at most municipal libraries or at the newspaper office itself. Go back to the very earliest days. Read every article that looks at all interesting.

- *Create in yourself the frame of mind that you need.* Cultivate the mental attitude of expectation. *Expect* to find the supernatural. Let yourself feel it all around you. Read some of the classics of psychical research to find out just what is possible, what has happened before and can be expected to happen again. Read books like F.W.H. Meyer's *Human Personality and Its Survival of Bodily Death*, Rosalind Heywood's *Beyond the Reach of Sense* and Robert Thouless' fine book, *Experimental Psychical Research*. Read the memoirs of Eileen Garrett and Stewart Edward White's classic *The Betty Book*. Consult Nandor Fordor's *Encyclopedia of Psychic Science*.

Great Free Publicity

One good thing about a book in this field is that you, as author and expert, can easily arrange to appear on television and radio talk shows. Just let them know that you are available. They'll call, and you will get the guest slot you need to sell books. Remember to make sure that books are available in book-stores when you do get on the air, and always be sure to let viewers or listeners know where to go to buy them.

Your book of ghosts and mysteries is great for the tourist trade and will sell steadily, over a long period of time, in locations with high tourist traffic. The hundreds and thousands of onetime visitors who come to see the sights and to spend money on souvenirs constitute a continually renewed group of fresh customers. Your book will also work in cities or even states and regions. There the potential readership is very large to start with. It will not do so well in smaller towns, especially when the stories it tells are of fairly local interest. Once every interested person in a small town has bought a copy (or checked one out from the library) you will have pretty much saturated the market and sales will quickly taper off. In metropolitan areas and in strong tourist areas your book can sell year after year.

Book Idea Number Five:
New Editions of Out-of-Print Books

One of the quickest ways to break into print is to bring out a new edition of some previously published work for which there is a demand, but which is no longer available. Such books are said to be out-of-print. You can't choose just any book, of course. You must find one that is in the "public domain." This is a book which was never copyrighted or whose copyright protection has expired. Such a book may be used by anyone, at any time, for any purpose, including publication as a new edition.

The Public Domain

Here are the rules of the game. Before January 1st, 1978, when the current version of the U.S. copyright law went into effect, the maximum copyright protection for a book published in the United States was 56 years. But there are some fine points:

- Under the old law, this maximum protection was obtainable only if one renewed the copyright after the initial 28 years. Otherwise the work it had protected would fall into the public domain at the end of that time. The larger publishing houses routinely renewed their copyrights, al-though you may find some surprising lapses. But the smaller publishers often overlooked renewal or simply went out of business before renewal time came around.
- Some books carry a notice of copyright but were never formally regis-tered. Under the old law such books are in the public domain.
- While the new law was being researched and written, some protection

was given to books whose copyrights might otherwise have expired during the 1960's and 70's. As a general rule, any book published before 1902 is in the public domain, since its full measure of protection would have expired before 1960. Many books published later—such as those whose copyrights were not renewed in timely fashion—may or may not be in the public domain. If there is a more recent book that you wish to republish, you should write to the Register of Copyrights, Library of Congress, Washington, DC and ask for a copyright search. This will turn up any protection that still exists for the work in question. The staff at the Library of Congress, especially in the copyright office, is shorthanded, so allow six to eight weeks for the search to be completed.

What to Look For

What kind of book makes a successful reprint publication, one that you can not only republish but profitably sell? Here are some guidelines:

- Look for a title that, in your opinion, would be in demand if it were made available to the public. There are fashions and fads in publishing as in other fields. Some books (an out-of-print history of your area that has no competition and that is constantly being checked out of the library) is a good bet at any time.
- Look for a title that has no competition from more recent titles. There is not likely to be a widespread market for a picture history of a town when the same photographs and a great many more appear in a later book that is on the market and easily available.
- Look for a title that is out of print and scarce. It is not enough that a book be in the public domain. If old copies are easily available in used book stores then there is no market for your new edition. The book that you choose to reprint must be both *in demand* and *scarce*.
- Look for a title for which there is sufficiently strong, on-going demand. The best reprint titles are not one shot deals where you saturate a limited market and then have no one else to sell to.
- Look for a title that you can sell as a limited, numbered edition. Such editions cost very little more to produce but sell for as much as twice the retail rate of normal editions.
- Look for a book that has the possibility of intensive sales within a limited geographical area or to a highly-targeted readership.

A Personal Illustration

When I first began to do research on my picture history of Greenville, I had to consult a book called *Sketches of Pitt County*. This book had been out of print since 1911, and it was in the public domain. It was the only county history available. Libraries where I worked treated their copies of the *Sketches* as a rare and valuable book. I often had to get special permission to use the book, even in the library's own reading room. Those families that possessed a copy, I discovered, considered it almost an heirloom. When a copy of *Sketches of Pitt County* found its way onto the market, it always brought a very high price. This book was a natural for the reprint market. I wrote a new introduction and provided an exhaustive index—a feature that the earlier edition had lacked. My name as editor and introducer was prominently displayed on the title page, just below that of the original author, Henry T. King.

Your Contribution to the Project

You, as writer, do contribute to the project. The introduction can be as brief or as substantial as you wish to make it. You can add editor's notes, or even a section to bring the book up to date. The choice is yours alone. The introduction that I wrote to King's *Sketches* won me a very unexpected medal from the local chapter of the DAR....which sold a lot of books for me.

Small Cost, Big Return

The nice thing about reprints is that they are often quite economical to produce. The cost of typesetting is entirely eliminated, except for the new portions you write yourself. The printer will make negatives and burn plates from the original edition.

I produced 500 numbered copies of King's *Sketches* and was able to sell them at twelve times production cost. If you take care to make your book a handsome one and if you have followed the reprint selection rules outlined earlier you will have a virtually certain success on your hands, although you can never eliminate risk altogether. You will, in addition, have performed a significant community service in getting a good book back into print and available again. From a strictly business point of view, you will be marketing a book that people want to buy, that they will pay a substantial price for, and that you were able to produce economically.

Book Idea Number Six:
Biographies of Notable Citizens

Here's an idea that can be a real winner for you, especially if you are a writer as well as an entrepreneurial publisher. It can bring you heightened, valuable visibility in your community, up-front profit and the possibility of repeating the project again and again in new towns or for other individuals. These are not difficult books to write. You are not researching the biography of some historical giant. You are doing a book on assignment for the person who is the subject of your research or for this person's family.

Writing a Biography the Easy Way

I won't say that writing well is easily done at any time. It is not. But undertaking a biographical book need not strike fear into your heart nor take more than its share of your time. The goal, remember, is to make the personality, accomplishments and values of your subject come through. You want to present and project the flesh and blood reality of your subject, not every hidden or forgotten detail of time, place, and date. To prepare for your task, gather the following information and documents from your subject:

- Previously published news stories, booklets, clippings of all kinds.
- Scrapbooks and memorabilia.
- Photographs. These are especially valuable. As in the other book projects I have discussed, their importance can scarcely be exaggerated.
- Letters to and from your subject.
- Articles, books, booklets, manuals or other publications that your subject may have written.
- Awards, certificates, diplomas, transcripts, etc.
- Extensive interviews both with the subject of your book, if that person is still living, and with family, friends, business associates, and other acquaintances of your subject.

With these materials in hand—many of which can be gathered by the subject or the family of the subject—your book should practically write itself. I believe you could reasonably expect to have a first draft ready for editing two or three months after beginning work.

An Illustrated Narrative

Your book can be a kind of illustrated narrative. You write a biographical thread, which you then flesh out with reproductions of documents, letters, photographs, news stories, diplomas, etc., each of which carries a very fully written cutline. Your subject is likely to be very pleased with this approach, and it is good for you, too. It transfers some of the burden of the continuity of your text to the commentary that accompanies the illustrations, simplifying your work by breaking it up into more easily handled segments.

What Kind of Money Can You Make?

The question you will be asking yourself, of course, is "Can I make any money on this deal?" You know you can write the book, but you are uncertain about the profit potential. After all, if you are going to spend a block of several months digging into someone else's life you don't want to do it for nothing.

The answer to your question is that you can indeed make money, even a great deal of it. And these funds will come in to you far more quickly than they would from royalties or the sales of other, more traditional, books that you might write. The compensation to you as writer comes through a contractual agreement that you will negotiate with your subject himself or herself. You will receive a fee for services. Like those fat advances that some writers get from publishers, your money will come in to you in advance, in large, lump sums and so will be far more usable than even the same amount spread out over a long period of time. Your profit is guaranteed.

How It Worked for Me

I discovered the possibilities and profitability of this kind of book almost by accident. A friend of mine, the book editor of a large metropolitan daily, was the featured speaker at a weekly Rotary Club luncheon in her town. After her talk, a distinguished gentleman approached her. He had collected his papers, he said, and was looking for a writer to help put together his autobiography. Could she help? My friend called me, and I contacted the man who had made the inquiry. We met, and just a week or two later I had a book contract in hand. I would write his biography, utilizing materials that he would furnish to me and interviews that I would conduct. I asked for and got a fee in the five digit range. Since I was involved in a number of other projects at the time, I could only work at the biography on a time available basis. A year later I had completed the assignment. A few months later the book appeared to strong reviews in the local and regional press. I could have done the book, I estimate, in three months if I had concentrated at least half my time on it.

The late Legette Blythe, a fellow writer and, in his day, a well-known novelist and biographer, was kind enough to teach me the ropes. He had done several such assignments. He was far better known than I was, so his fee was steeper—upwards of $40,000 (in 1960's money) for such a project.

A Rich Vein

This is a very rich vein for writers who are willing to do the groundwork and promotion that will enable them to tap into it. There are people out there who want such books written but haven't the foggiest idea how to go about finding someone reliable to work with them on it. My own client, a very successful and savvy man, was in the dark when it came to finding and dealing with writers. He had to ask a stranger, a speaker at a civic club luncheon, for a lead. My writer-friend's clients, too, had simply gone to the only writer they knew to cut a deal.

I wrote and published *We Choose America* for the chancellor of a well-known state university. The book was illustrated with cartoons by Pulitzer Prize-winning editorial cartoonist, Eugene Payne. It was later republished by a national publisher. Such projects have a quick turn-around, financially speaking. You are paid up-front, on the signing of the contract.

The moral here is that you do not wait for clients to come to you; you seek them out. If you do the necessary promotion and personal networking, you will eventually hit pay dirt. You will make a nifty sum and get your name on the title page of a published book at the same time. Perhaps a classified advertisement in the pages of the *Wall Street Journal*, the *Rotarian* magazine, *Modern Maturity* and other publications routinely read by affluent and older people will be all you need. When someone inquires, you can answer with a personal letter and request a meeting.

How Much Do You Charge?

Let me begin this all-important section with a story. I once bought a virtually bankrupt weekly newspaper. Since I had absolutely no experience in the newspaper business and I had to bring out an edition the following week, I hired every consultant I could find to come in and tell me how to do it.

One of the key things, of course, was selling the advertising that would pay the newspaper's expenses. I am happy to say that one of the best people who came in to consult with me was superb in the field of advertising sales. I particularly remember one piece of advice he gave me that has been invaluable to me ever since in and out of the newspaper business. I had been a teacher, a college professor, and was now a small town newspaper publisher. My consultant took one look at me, another at the furnishings in my newspaper office, and said: *"Remember, Tom, never judge anybody else's pocketbook by your own."*

And I realized suddenly that I had always done just that. I had chosen to spend my life in the kinds of work that I loved but that were not the most lucrative in the world. I lived well, but I seldom had more than a few thousand dollars in the bank at any given time. For some reason it just never dawned on me that others *did* have more than a few thousand, a great deal more.

I am not talking about the Sam Moore Waltons, the Rockefellers, or the J. Paul Gettys of this world. I am talking about the guy down the street. Far more people have far more money to spend than you ever dreamed. Not that they give it away. But when such people decide that they want something they don't quibble about reasonable costs.

I am not suggesting that you do any profiteering. Just ask a fair price for the work that you do. Think of it on the basis of the time you will spend on it, in the same way that a lawyer or a accountant would. If you think that the project will take six months, and if, as a professional writer, you expect to earn $80,000 a year from your writing, then ask $40,000, plus expenses incurred to carry the project out. Remember that such a project is going to take a good deal of your attention for a substantial length of time. Charge what your time is worth.

Once your first contract is signed you have established your fee for future assignments that will come to you, based on the quality of the work you turned out the first time around.

Who's the Author?

You want your name on the title page, of course. But your client may want his or hers there, too. It can even be a selling point to suggest that the client appear as author or coauthor. So how do you handle this problem? There are several options:

- Have your client's name appear as author and yours as coauthor. *The Life and Loves of John Doe*, by John Doe and Robert Roe (you) would be an example.
- I prefer a second solution: *The Life and Loves of John Doe*, by John Doe with Robert Roe. This wording has become transparent to most readers these days. They easily understand that though Doe did the talking, Roe did the writing. I like this approach because others who might like a similar book done will know at once which of you to call. Your phone will ring, not Doe's.
- Of course, the name of the client alone can appear. You are thus a ghostwriter, and the book appears as an out-and-out autobiography. Since you are a well-paid ghost writer, the solution should be acceptable to you. This was the arrangement my own client suggested. I did not object because I wanted the fee and because I had already published enough books so that having my name on the title page did not mean all that much to me. It was only later that I realized that by not having my name on the title page, I was eliminating the business that might have been generated by others who wanted a similar book done and who would then have known who I was and where to find me.
- Your name alone can appear. Some clients may think it prestigious to have it appear that someone else has simply decided to write a book about them.

Your Author's Agreement

It is important in an arrangement like this to have an agreement drawn up and signed by both you and the client. You will want it written in plain English, and you will want to keep it very simple.

Have your attorney draw up a fill-in-the-blanks generic contract that you can use over and over again. Go to the attorney with the agreement written up in your own words and let him rework it for you. The agreement you use will, among other things, deal with the following points:

- *What you will do for the client.* Specify that you will, for instance, write two drafts of a manuscript on his life, based on materials he will furnish you, plus interviews with himself or herself and others (and specify their names, too, if you can). Specify that the manuscript will consist of no fewer than a certain number of typewritten pages and no more than another number. The idea here is to avoid an open-ended commitment.
- *Who will own the copyright.* This kind of project is essentially what the copyright law refers to as a "work made for hire," and is an exception to the general rule that the writer owns the copyright unless otherwise specified in a contractual agreement. It is usual, but not mandatory, for the client to own the copyright.
- *If you are going to design and print the book for the client* after it is completed this is a separate matter. You should state clearly that the fee for typography, design, and printing will be negotiated at a later date. It would be impossible to do so now, because you do not even know how long the book will be, nor the graphic materials it will contain.
- *How the names of the author or authors will appear on the title page* (see the earlier discussion of this point).
- *The fee that the client will pay you in return for your work* and when he will pay you. I usually specify one-third of the total fee on the signing of the contract, one third on the completion of a first draft, and one-third on completion of the final draft. These percentages can be altered to fit the circumstances, but you should always require a substantial portion of your fee on signing and get an additional substantial sum as the work progresses. Your client wants this book. You need to be paid before you put a completed manuscript in his hands. Once you hand it over without having been paid you have little leverage in any dispute.

Book Idea Number Seven:
How to Buy It Cheap, and Where

Most of us want more things than we can afford to buy. A book that can tell us how to get hold of these things at a price we can afford is a natural for the self-publisher. The fact that there are a good many of them around only proves that there is a ready market for them. Such books tell how to buy expensive things cheaply and cheap things even more cheaply.

A Success Story

A few years ago a saddle-stitched (stapled along the spine) book of a few dozen pages appeared on the counter of my favorite bookstore. It was rather ordinary looking, obviously the effort of an enthusiastic but inexperienced writer-publisher. It was really rather unambitious in content as well as format. It just listed the factory outlet stores in the area where clothing and other items could be bought at below wholesale prices. But it did give the basic information necessary:

- It told the name of each outlet,
- It told where the outlet was and gave detailed instruction for getting there,
- And it told what you would find when you arrived.

This little book was a great success. It went quickly into an expanded and revised edition. It began to cover a wider and wider area. It also began to sell advertising, which quickly became more lucrative than the money generated by the sale of the booklet itself.

Value Added

It's the value-added, the color and personality that you can add as a writer that will set you apart from the competition. It can't help but be successful if you write and market it with imagination. What does imagination have to do with it? Well, you write about each of the places you suggest for shopping. Ask yourself the following questions:

- What does it look like?
- What is the atmosphere? Down-home or Madison Avenue?
- Can you bargain to get the price down even further?
- Are the salespeople knowledgeable about their products?
- What are the best buys?
- What do you avoid?
- How do you identify seconds?

Travel Tips, Too

In addition, your book can be a bit of a travelogue. In my part of the country we often have to drive fifty or a hundred miles to reach some really great outlet. Is there a restaurant in the vicinity? Are there enough outlet stores nearby to warrant an overnight excursion?

- What about the motels?
- How much do they cost?
- Which offer the best value?
- Are there other fun things to see and do nearby?
- What about discount services as well as merchandise?
- Are they available? Where? For how much?
- Are there other things to do in the area? Is there anything to interest children?

The focus, of course, remains squarely on the outlets and other bargain-basement storefronts. But the patter, the value-added through your vivid writing, the first-person, insider tone that you derive from first hand experience—all this adds flavor and enhances the readability of your book many times over. Your book clearly stands out from the pack.

A Targeted Market

You can't be everywhere at the same time, of course. Your book will have to deal with an area with definite boundaries of some kind. If you live in a major metropolitan area such as Atlanta, Washington, Baltimore, L.A., or Miami then there is plenty to see, sample, and write about in that area alone.

Another approach is to do a major highway guide, producing a book, for instance, that you might call "The Great I-95 Outlet Guide". You could hit the road and do a month's leisurely travel from New England down to Miami—every last bit of it fully tax deductible. You can sell advertising at the same time that you visit stores and interview owners for the text portions of your book.

Your book can be sold at bookstores, to libraries, at point of purchase racks in restaurants, hotels, motels, and other traveler's stops along the interstate. If you sell enough advertising, you may ultimately opt for free circulation and an inexpensive newsprint format. In that case contact the official welcome stations at the borders of each state for possible distribution.

RECOMMENDED RESOURCE!

There are several books out there on entrepreneurial book publishing. I have read them all, and I can tell you that Dan Poynter's *The Self-Publishing Manual* is by far the best of the lot. If you are thinking about going beyond the specialty markets that I discuss in this chapter and marketing your book nationwide, get a copy of Poynter's book.

Other Projects

Your imagination will suggest many other such projects, suitable to the area where you live. How about a directory of country auction houses, where the buys are often phenomenal? Or, where I used to live, there are the furniture outlet houses. An *Insiders' Guide to Furniture Outlets* would sell very well indeed in the hotels and motels of Piedmont North Carolina.

- What do you have to know to get the really good buys?
- What do you avoid?
- Which "outlets" are not really outlets at all?
- Are any salespeople in individual shops better than others?
- How do you know the true retail selling price?
- How do you decide just how much of a bargain you are getting?
- How do you get the furniture back home?
- Who includes shipping and who does not?

Who knows, you might need a new edition each year, with new books to sell and new advertising to fatten your bank account. Your where-and-how-to-buy-it-cheap guide could form the bedrock of quite a publishing empire.

Book Idea Number Eight:
Your Local Color Novel or Poetry

Many people will tell you it can't be done, but I am convinced that it is possible to find the right novel or even collection of poetry that an entrepreneurial publisher can write and publish with reasonable expectation of success. Just this morning I read a report in *Publisher's Weekly* (the trade magazine of the publishing business) on a high-level conference about the present state and future opportunities in publishing. Almost without exception these top publishing executives cited the niche publishing done by small, independent publishers as the one area of the business that had the strongest potential for growth and profit.

Is there a niche market for novels and poetry? Yes, if you understand that word in the right way. The one niche for fiction that I have identified and that I am prepared to recommend to you is the one with strong local color elements. I use the term "local color" in a very definite and precise way.

Two Kinds of Local Color

For our purposes we will define local color in two distinct ways:

- A novel set in a recognizable, very popular locale which builds the people, places, and history of that locale into its plot structure.

- A novel set in the context of a well-defined milieu or activity that piques the reader's curiosity.

A Novel Set in a Recognizable and Highly Frequented Locale

Eugenia Price's very popular novel *Savannah* will illustrate this kind of local color. This book is a combination historical novel and romance. It is a good, light read, and in its pages old Savannah, its people, places, and history come alive. Why is such a novel a good bet for you? Because if you can't find a major publishing house to bring it out you can easily publish it yourself. You can do this because the book passes the essential marketing test: it has the possibility of intensive sales in a limited geographical area.

A modest first edition can be sold in the city itself and surrounding areas. Had Price self-published she could easily have gotten her book in bookstores, tourist gift shops and specialty stores, hotel and motel paperback racks, and point of purchase sales spots in restaurants. She could have done this in Savannah and also, to some degree, in Atlanta and other Georgia cities and towns. There would have been only a limited amount of travel involved, and she could have managed with ease. Further, in a tourist hot-spot like Savannah, there would be an ever-renewable group of new book buyers to keep sales going month after month. After the first edition was selling well, the author of such a book as Price's would have had three interesting options:

- Use the funds to sell the book to a wider market herself. This is the least attractive alternative because it takes a sizable, experienced marketing apparatus and enormous amounts of time and energy to sell a book nationwide. A good novelist might do better to spend his or her time writing a new book and leaving the wide selling of the old one to others who are skilled in the activity.
- Send the book directly to major publishers, along with sales records and reviews, offering reprint rights.
- Send the book, sales records, reviews, etc., to a good agent, who can not only negotiate reprint rights on more favorable terms for you but also market other subsidiary rights, such as television and movie rights as well as foreign translation rights. The same agent who simply could not afford to invest his time in the work of an unknown first novelist will look with real interest on a book such as this, one which has proven to have strong sales potential.

The old port city of Wilmington, NC, in Cape Fear country, has just the kind of colorful past that would lend itself to such a book. Although it does not have as strong a tourist trade of towns like Savannah or Charleston, it is none-

The Future is Here: Print-on-Demand Book Production

A new technology is making life a great deal easier for specialty book publishers. By virtue of the Print-on-Demand (POD) process, publishers can now order as few as twenty-five copies of a new title with the assurance that quality will be wholly satisfactory for all but the most photograph-laden coffee-table books. Books are perfect bound or casebound and covers are in full color (at no extra charge). Prices are modest. At present, a 6 by 9 book will cost .015 a page per copy, plus .90 for a laminated, perfect-bound cover or $4.95 for hard cover.

Two major companies supplying the trade are Lightning Source (a subsidiary of Ingram Book Group) and Deharts Printing Sevices Corp.

Contact these book manufacturers and ask for a current price list and description of the services they provide. You can reach Lightning Source at 1136 Heil Quaker Blvd., La Vergne, TN, 37086. You can go to their web site at www.lightningsource.com.

DeHarts can be reached at DeHart's Printing Services Corp., 3265 Scott Blvd., Santa Clara, CA 95054. (888) 982-4763. www.deharts.com.

Lightning Source deals only with publishers, while DeHarts deals both with publishers and individuals.

theless a good candidate for such a book. There are doubtless many such towns in your area.

A Variation on This Theme

There are variations on this theme. One of these has been very successful for my friend Carole Marsh, president of Gallopade Books and the author of many titles for young people. Carole has written several books for teens and preteens set in major theme parks and other tourist sites. Any location with a heavy traffic of young people with a few dollars of souvenir money in their pockets or the pockets of their parents is a good candidate.

A large theme park in this part of the county is Carowinds, on the border between the two Carolinas just south of the city of Charlotte. So Carole wrote a book that she called *The Carowinds Mystery*. There is a strong, continuing sale of this and similar books that Carole Marsh has written, books that are linked to a highly frequented, colorful location.

Poetry, Too

A collection of poetry that has a strong appeal to the residents of a densely populated area or, better, both to residents and to tourists passing through, can be successfully marketed in this way.

My publishing company recently brought out a fine collection of poetry called *Anson County*. It was very good poetry, but, as we all know, this is not enough to insure sales. What made this volume do well in the marketplace was its local color hook. One hundred copies were sold off the bat to the county development office at a price that almost paid for the entire first printing. Then most state libraries bought copies, the poet gave terrific readings at which more copies were sold, and the book was off and running.

How about *Poems of the Outer Banks*, *Atlanta*, *Cape Fear Country*, *Frontier Poems* (Alaska), *Gold Coast Blues* or any one of the dozens of others you can think of yourself. Drawings, photographs and any other illustrations will make such a book sell even better. Remember, it is being bought both as a book of verse and as a souvenir. I am currently thinking of bringing out a book of poems called *Key West Cats*. With millions of tourists passing through every year, this book cannot help but sell well.

A Novel Set in a Colorful Milieu

The second kind of local color is not geographically centered. Instead it conveys the sight, smell, personality, and feel of a particular institution, activity, or profession. Readers love intimate, inside glimpses into kinds of activity that they would not otherwise know about or which, for one reason or another, fascinates them. This is one of the great secrets of success in novel writing. The interesting conflict or crime is not enough. The setting within which the action takes place is often even more important.

You don't have to write as well as Tom Clancy to understand one of the most important facets of his success: the fascination for his readers of the technological, military, gadget-infested environment in which he sets his action.

An Inside Look

Part of the fun of the activity-centered local color novel is the pleasure the reader derives from getting an inside and detailed look at an environment that he or she is glad to know more about. What makes Margaret Truman's crime novels salable is her trick of putting each into a context that intrigues the reader. *Murder in the Supreme Court,* one of the recent titles, is a good example. The intrigue itself may not be as strong as those to be found in the books of some other writers and the characterizations not as richly detailed. But the ambiance of the Supreme Court does come alive for us and is enough to sell books..

The late Harry Kemelman's mysteries about the crime-solving talents of his Rabbi Small take us right into the life of the Temple the Rabbi serves. We see a human reality and experience a cultural context that most of us who are not Jewish know nothing about. It is not so much the prospect of reading about a murder and its ultimate solution that makes us pick up books like these but rather the promise of living for a few hours in the physical, colorful ambiance that the title offers to us.

I remember a book from a few years ago called *The Dewey Decimal Murders.* When I saw it, I bought it. I love books, libraries, and people associated with these activities, and the lure of spending some time among them while having a good time following the plot through its complications and resolutions was very appealing to me. And think of the natural sales appeal to librarians—one of your major customers. The secret is, or course, that you've got to know what you are talking about. No one not brought up in the Jewish community could have written the Rabbi Small books. A writer unfamiliar with the technology of nuclear submarines could not have written *The Hunt for Red October*.

Take Inventory

Take inventory of your own store of knowledge and experience. What do you know about that others would want to know about? I was once editor and publisher of a weekly newspaper. Weeklies are a world unto themselves, not only a job but a way of life. Thus a weekly newspaper office, with its characters and comings and goings, could be a fruitful setting for conflicts and a fine, salable novel.

For three centuries tobacco culture—for all its recent fall from grace—was a way of life in rural areas along the east coast. I wrote this highly targeted book for that market and sold the entire first edition to the PR firm that handled the R. J. Reynolds account. It was used as an executive Christmas gift by the president of the company.

This kind of book will be more difficult to market on your own than the one that can be sold—at least to start with—within a fifty mile radius of your home. In the latter case, you can call on all the outlets personally and see to it that your book gets on the shelves.

When dealing with institutional local color you will have to send out review copies to generate some kind words in the press. Hopefully your chosen environment will be one that is easy for a reviewer to like. If I wrote my weekly newspaper novel, getting reviews would be a cinch. I'd send a review copy and a packet containing a ready-made short review, a long review and a feature story in it, along with a photograph of the book itself and another of the author in action—at the typewriter or in the weekly office, etc.

Your book will also be mailed out for review to other sources. Since you know which group your book will appeal to, you know which magazines are good bets to review it. You then cull the good reviews as they appear and make up a one-page flyer. Cite what the critics have had to say and send it off to libraries. When you begin to generate some favorable press and make some sales, you can go to an agent or directly to reprint publishers as with your city-focused novel.

16

How to Publish
Association and Membership Directories

You are up and running. Your basic equipment is in place. You have started one or two successful publications. You have a number of good salespeople to assign to any project that comes along. You know which free-lance writers and designers can do the job for you. You are market-sensitive. You begin to recognize other opportunities for profitable publications that you would not have noticed before. One of these is the association directory.

From time to time friends and associates, knowing that you are in the publishing business, will come to you with ideas. When that happens to me, I am always willing to spend a little time looking at the suggested project. Not all of these projects will be feasible; far from it. Sometimes there will be a readership, but no true market for advertising; sometimes there will be a readership and a market for advertising, but you can't reach the advertising base readily enough or cheaply enough. Or perhaps the natural advertising base will be made up of individuals and firms unlikely to have advertising budgets that can support the cost of placing an ad. Occasionally, though, it will all fall into place. You look the project over. You realize that you have a highly-targeted pool of advertisers who are likely to have more than adequate budgets to purchase your space with. Moreover, you know that you can readily contact any one of them in the course of a normal business day.

An Association Directory

Such was the case when an old friend came to see me one day with the idea of doing a membership directory for a growing statewide world trade association. The association had been formed not too many years earlier. Its members included every major bank in the state, as well as manufacturers, shippers, attorneys, and all the other businesses that serviced international trade.

My friend was a member of the association. He showed me a mimeographed, stapled list of names and addresses. This, he said, was the association's current membership directory. He also told me that the organization wished to develop a high-profile, powerful image that would enable it to wield some influence in molding state policy toward international trade as well as give it clout in actually building international markets for the state's exports.

One place to start in building this desired image, my friend suggested, would be with a first-class, professional-looking membership directory. The directory he envisioned would be in a magazine format, with a full color cover. On the inside it would contain advertising from the prestigious corporate and financial members of the organization along with the normal listings of the names, addresses, and specialties of the members of the association.

A Natural for the Home-based, Entrepreneurial Publisher

I saw at once that the idea was a natural for any entrepreneurial publisher capable of bringing out quality publications. Since I had, by that time, designed and published successful city and regional magazines—as well as several books—I was sure that I qualified on that score. And being small was actually a great advantage in this case. Here's the way I saw it:

- I did not carry the financial baggage of excessive overhead that other, larger, periodical publishers would have to factor into their profit and loss analysis. I could therefore be very competitive at no loss in quality or profit.
- The ads could be sold by telephone, for the most part, to members of the association itself. There would be no need for any hard sell.
- There would be triple motivation for these members to buy:

    1. First of all, they could afford it. Most advertising prospects had budgets more than adequate to handle the cost of advertising. Since it was an annual publication, the cost would occur only once each year. Availability of funds would be no problem.
    2. Furthermore, they would be likely to buy ads, at least in the first issue or two, purely out of loyalty to the organization.
    3. Finally, the directory would offer a strong, targeted advertising opportunity. There was no other place where these advertisers could so easily reach their most sought-after potential customers: those involved in the import-export trade and international distribution of manufactured goods.

Structuring the Deal

The publication of an association directory is always structured as a win-win deal. When you make your presentation to the association director (or president) you can be quite effective when you make the following five points:

- The association will never again pay out a cent for the creation of a membership directory. Even the little mimeographed booklet that the World Trade Association was using did cost them something. The big, new full-color one would be delivered to them free of charge and in an agreed-upon quantity.
- No volunteer member or overworked staff member will ever again have to spend a minute of his or her time trying to do something that he does not really know how to do: publish a membership directory.
- The publisher (you) will attend to every detail, while carefully working within association policies and guidelines.
- The publisher will sell the advertising.
- The association not only gets these expensive, color membership directories free of charge, but it earns money on them as well. The publisher will pay an agreed upon percentage of his gross revenues to the association, usually about 10%. This amount usually satisfies the association, since the association is also getting thousands of dollars worth of directories. And, in every case that I am aware of, this percentage still offers a solid profit for the publisher.

This is an almost irresistible sales pitch, especially for an association which has never had a membership directory or which has been limping along with an inadequate one. Still, some associations may want too much of the take, and you'll need the determination to just walk away from projects where this is the case. I recently had an association director ask me to sell all the ads, guarantee a certain dollar amount return to the association, regardless of what ad sales were, and pay for all ad design and color separations for advertisers who were members of the association. In addition I was to have all advertising checks paid directly to the association, which would hold them in escrow until the completion of the project.

When I learned all these details, I declined to submit a proposal. Another publisher decided to take on the project of publishing the directory and, in due time, it did indeed come out. As I looked through it, counted the pages of advertising and calculated maximum possible profits after subtracting the very high costs of the project, I saw that I had been wise. The publisher had made very little on the project and will not undertake it again. I could easily see the ways in which the publisher, faced with the possibility of taking a loss, had cut corners in producing the directory. It was not the piece of work it could—and should—have been. Nobody was happy. This scenario is not the rule, but neither is it as rare as you might think. There are many people in the world who think they know your trade, but they are almost always badly mistaken. When they get their way they make trouble for everyone concerned.

Designing the Product

Take pains to be sure that your clients understand precisely what the publication you are going to produce for them will look like. The vocabulary of publishing and publication design is confusing to many people. Worse, they will assume that they know what you are talking about when they really do not. It is important that communication be clear and accurate. After you have sold the job, write a letter to the client describing the publication exactly as it will appear: page size, stock, color, type style, name and specialty listing, etc. Then go a step further; show the client a sample of another publication that exemplifies the features you are describing. Almost every technical word in an agreement between a layman and specialist is a misunderstanding just waiting to happen. If you say that your directory will be "saddle-stitched" and, in answer to a question as to what this term means, you answer "stapled," you may be shooting yourself in the foot. The client will tend to think of the office stapler (the only kind he is familiar with) and the wire staple in the upper left-hand corner holding a sheaf of papers together. This, of course, is not at all what you have in mind. At the very least, tell your client that the directory will be "magazine stapled" like the finer magazines he may see on the newsstands. But the best policy is to say the directory will be "saddle-stitched" and then hold up a copy of *Smithsonian* or another equally fine magazine and add, "Like this." Other terms that frequently cause problems are "self-covered", "page" (one side of the leaf or both sides, your client will wonder), halftone, color separation, article and many others. The best policy is one of "show and tell."

Things to Keep in Mind

When designing an association directory, here are some things to keep in mind:

- *The design should be planned to convey distinction and prestige upon the association.* I once got a thank-you note from the president of an association whose directory I had designed and published. "Your directory exceeded my fondest expectations," he wrote. "You have raised our organization to a new level of professionalism." Which is precisely what I had attempted to do. I created a prestigious product, and the president of the organization recognized that fact. When the directory looked very good, it made him look very good. Never forget that the reputations of the association officers with whom you are working rise or fall with the product you produce. "Rising" is the preferred direction.

- *Design for ease of use.* A membership directory should be as easy to use as possible. It should lie flat, or nearly flat, on the table when it is being consulted. It should fit neatly on a bookshelf or in a briefcase. A reader must be able to find the names he needs with ease.

 To the left is the cover of the directory of the NC World Trade Association, designed and published by my company some years ago for the association. We kept this project for three years, during which time it was quite profitable. We lost the project when the association decided to take it in-house. I discuss this particular hazard to the directory-publishing business elsewhere in this chapter.

- *Employ the three-shot listing.* If the number of members is not too great and space is available, list each of them three times: alphabetically by name; alphabetically by business specialty; and, if appropriate, list them alphabetically by the local chapter of the organization to which they belong. All people like to see their names in print; business people like to see their names in print and get business at the same time. The three-shot listing will convince them that anyone who is looking for them or for someone who specializes in the goods or services that they offer can find them with minimum effort.

- *Stick with standard page sizes.* The standard page sizes (8.5 by 11 inches; 6 by 9; 5.5 by 8.5) represent the most efficient use of sheets of paper. Any deviation from standard will cost you money. Worse, it will cost some of your major advertisers money. When they listen to your sales pitch and mentally add up the costs of placing an ad with you, they will have more in mind than the simple cost of the space they are buying. They have to take into account the cost of preparing the ad itself. A major bank, for instance, will have an ad agency to create its advertisements. The creative cost is usually greater than the cost of the space. They will probably want to stick with something they already have on hand, or, if they do have the agency create a new ad, they want it to be usable elsewhere. All of these ads will have been designed for one of the standard page sizes. When you stick to the standard you make it easier and less expensive for big companies to advertise with you. Even with the standard sizes you still have a decision to make. Which one will you choose? My recommendation? Other things being equal, the standard magazine format (8.5 by 11) has more clout. The ads are bigger, the cover more impressive. There is more space on each page, so type can be a point larger than in small-format publications. Further, you can charge more for ads placed by your more affluent clients in the larger publication, especially for the so-called premium positions: back page, inside front cover, inside back cover, center-spread, opposite the table of contents, opposite any lead article or section opening. The smaller page sizes may be used when there are fewer members and you want to create a thick-looking publication, when your client requests it, or when a smaller size would, for some other reason, create greater use or be more practical.

- *The binding is important.* Review the section on bindings in the chapter on printing. Of the bindings discussed there, perfect binding may not be suitable for association membership directories because publications bound this way do not lie flat easily. They can be forced flat, but at the cost of breaking the hold of the glued spine. If the directory is not likely to be used often, a perfect binding becomes more feasible, and many people are impressed by them. For you, of course, perfect binding has the disadvantage of requiring a separate cover, which, in turn, requires a separate print run and increases your costs. Saddle-stitching is the binding of choice whenever it fits the project at hand. This technique works very well for directories of up to 96 pages (depending on the stock on which they are printed). Stitched directories will lie relatively flat. They also have the advantage of utilizing low-cost, self-covered formats. For thicker directories, you can utilize a plastic ring (comb) binding, as do many cookbooks, for instance. These will lie absolutely flat. They have the disadvantage of being the most expensive of the three bindings listed here. You will have to print a separate cover, then you will have to pay the cost of the greater binding time and the cost of the plastic combs, as they are called, as well. These publications, while quite usable, are somewhat less prestigious in appearance. My recommendation: always stick with the saddle-stitched binding unless circumstances force you to do otherwise.

- *The membership listings.* Typeset the membership listing with hanging indents. The main name should be set in bold with the details in lightface. If any further emphasis is required, lightface italics can be used. A listing of this type is shown below:

Venture Press, Publishers. 1317 Pine Ridge Drive, Savannah, Georgia. Publishers of books, magazines, association directories and other specialized periodicals. Tom Williams, Ph.D., President. Telephone, 912.352.0404. Publish@gate.net.

Selling the Ads

If your project is one which has never been published before, or never in a high quality format such as you plan, you will need a media kit (see the earlier discussion of marketing), sample cover, sample pages, etc., to demonstrate to advertisers that the product you are selling is a truly fine one. It is show and tell time again.

You notify the membership of your planned publication in two steps.

1. The president of the organization will send out a letter (written by you) over his own signature and on association letterhead, announcing the project and asking for participation. There will be a business reply card, postpaid, to send in for further information.
2. You will follow this up by contacting potential advertisers directly with your own, more detailed, materials. You may find it more effective to send along your media kit after you have made contact by telephone. In selling advertising for the state world trade association, I was able to do all of the selling by telephone. I had to do it this way because I had no statewide sales force out to call on customers individually. In-person calls on larger firms in two or three major cities may have shaken out a few more advertising dollars, but I doubt that it would have paid for having salespeople on the road.

The largest ads will be the easiest ones to sell. But, as always, the smaller ads will be even more lucrative in terms of dollars per inch of space. Be sure to design smaller ads to make it possible for virtually anyone to buy something. Try not to let anyone off the hook until they commit to at least a business card-sized ad. The larger of these ads will be placed in strategic positions throughout the text, with every effort made to satisfy clients' requests for special position. Ads of one-twelfth page can be run in with the column listings in the business specialty section or perhaps placed in the back of the book in a special advertising section with its own heading, such as "World Trade Directory of Goods and Services."

Use a modular rate for the small ads, two-thirds page ads, one-third page, one-half page, one-sixth page, and one-twelfth page. Each of these will be more expensive than the next larger one on the basis of space occupied. The page rates for the large ads should be as expensive as any in your city magazines, chamber of commerce magazine, or tourism guides. Remember that your readership is *highly targeted* and that exposure to such a readership always comes to advertisers at a premium.

Going the Extra Mile

Continued success may be in the little things you do, the extra touches, the additional services, the extra miles you travel. You will find many a way to do these things if you keep your eyes and ears open. Here are some things that have worked for me:

- Always take your camera to meetings of the association. Take as many snapshots as possible. Retain the rights to these photographs but allow the association director and other officers to make use of them if they desire to do so. Present snapshots, enlarged and mounted, to the association officers and to advertisers.

- Write association news releases and other marketing copy.

- Suggest other marketing opportunities that come to your attention or that your own analysis and imagination suggest to you. Remember that you, and not they, are the expert in the area of print media marketing. It would be great if they came to depend upon you.

- Suggest ways that the directory can be upgraded. In the case of the world trade association I suggested that articles on the year's work, forecasts for the future, personality profiles, market analyses and general articles be published, (magazine-style and supported by photographs), in the front of the directory. This idea was immediately accepted. It was more work for me, but it made the directory interesting to look at, to hold, and to read. It struck a responsive chord with the membership that was responsible for the continued success of the project.

- Always take a booth at association trade shows. Offer to give talks as needed on advertising and marketing. Host "hospitality tables" at association conventions.

Remember that you are not the only publisher in the world. As soon as the others catch the smell of success wafting over from your preserve, they will make a try to poach a little of the business themselves. You must become as nearly indispensable as possible. You must create reasons for the association to keep you around.

Keeping the Business

Once you've got the business you want to keep it. If you perform well it will be easier and easier to sell your ads year after year. The second time around, many sales will be repeat business, closed with a telephone call. The directory will have become established and will have been included in advertising budgets. Moreover, the formatting and design work will all have been done and the associated costs eliminated.

Hanging on to your directory assignment, though, can be harder than it seems. There is a hurdle to overcome. You have one chief competitor, and it is not the hungry, competing publisher that I mentioned above. This competitor is the association itself. Once you create the publication and sell the ads, someone back at headquarters will sooner or later begin to make some calculations and send a memo or two out to the leadership. These people will study the memos, look at the profit possibilities, and decide to do the directory in-house and keep all the money for themselves. It all looks so easy. Why do they need their original publisher year after year?

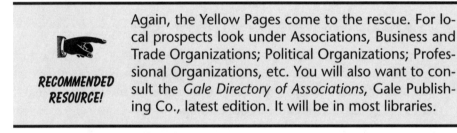

Again, the Yellow Pages come to the rescue. For local prospects look under Associations, Business and Trade Organizations; Political Organizations; Professional Organizations, etc. You will also want to consult the *Gale Directory of Associations*, Gale Publishing Co., latest edition. It will be in most libraries.

RECOMMENDED RESOURCE!

Such a decision is almost always a mistake for the association. They will have to hire salespeople; they will have to find a volunteer to manage the project; they will have to find writers and graphic artists; they will have to pay retail costs to some local printer and pay out an arm and a leg for printing.

Nevertheless, this is a decision that is often made. I kept the world trade directory business for three years, after which the association decided to do it themselves. It was a lucrative piece of business, and I hated to lose it. Had I known then what was likely to happen I would have started much earlier to protect myself against it. The customer service activities outlined in the section on going the extra mile, if put into effect earlier and with more determination, might have kept this project alive for me a bit longer.

In addition, I would have carefully cultivated the friendship of both the paid employees and the elected officers of the association (past, present, and future) with personal letters, favors, photos, etc.

Many associations have only one paid staff member, an "executive secretary" or "executive director." This individual is typically overworked and underpaid. He or she is blamed for all glitches but not particularly recognized when things go right.

Your job is to get to know this person. Establish a liaison. Find a way to help the executive director share in the wealth, possibly by paying for articles, typesetting, and other information that he or she furnishes you for the directory. Use the Executive Director in projects distinct from the association and its work to avoid conflicts of interest. Do everything possible to make it more pleasant, happy, and downright profitable for the Executive Director to continue to work with you than to take a blind chance with in-house production. Let this person know, too (in ways both subtle and obvious), that if the association should take over the publication of its own directory, this enormous work load, totally outside his field of experience or expertise, would fall to him to handle, on top of everything else he has to do.

The paid help is your natural ally, and, in the long run, can be one of the keys to your long-term survival as the association's publisher.

Prospecting for Business

While association directory opportunities are fairly rare, you can prospect for them within the limits of the time available. You never can tell when something interesting will turn up. Consult the Gale Publishing Company's *Directory of Associations* in your library. Look through the Yellow Pages of telephone books from major cities in your area, especially state capitals. Many associations locate their headquarters near concentrations of financial or political power.

Prepare a list of associations that seem to fit the profit profile that has emerged in this chapter. Prepare a marketing letter on your computer and circulate it from time to time. When you least expect it your phone will ring, and you will be off and running again.

17

How to Make Money from Secondary Profit Centers

My wife Christina once owned a ballet school. Her principal source of income came from the monthly tuition fees that her students paid for their instruction. This tuition income was sufficient to pay all her expenses and generate a comfortable income. But from time to time she developed other sources of income. At recital time, for instance, she photographed each student in costume and sold these photos to the parents. The sale of these photos was a nice secondary profit center. It was not her main job. Teaching ballet was. But it was available to her because she was in the ballet business. The opportunity to sell the photographs simply came her way, and she took advantage of it.

The Pleasures of "Chunk Money"

Secondary profit centers will come your way, too, once you become known as a publisher. These can be very important to you as you work to build income from your publications. Later on you will want to leave by the wayside some of the more marginally profitable of your sidelines. But you will surely want to keep others. While I was publishing regional magazines, I was asked to develop a sixteen page image-enhancing publication for a five-county consortium in my part of the state. This consortium came to me because they had seen and liked my magazine, *NCEast*. The contract brought in about $5000 in profit. I did the project with the same facilities and free-lancers I used in my other work. There were no ads to sell, no risks to take. The client was simply paying me for my expertise. The money, needless to say, was a very welcome addition to my bank account, the kind of usable lump sum cash that James R. Cook, in his book *Start-up Entrepreneur*, calls "chunk money."

There was not enough of this kind of work available for me to do it full time. For me the custom design of publications for others is a very profitable secondary profit center that I will continue to take advantage of as long as I am in business. You will discover secondary profit centers available to you because of your particular combination of talents and publishing activities. Here are some that have been important to me.

You Can Broker Printing

In the chapter on buying printing, you learned that small local print shops do not have the equipment to handle most publication work economically. From time to time you will get a call from someone who wants you to print a publication for them. Often this is a paperbound or hardcover book.

Because you know where to get the best prices you can often get such a favorable price from your printer that you can mark the job up 30 to 40%, quote this to the customer, and still come in under the price that the local printer has quoted. Sometimes the customer will not even have gone to the trouble of getting another quote. You can also handle any design or typography work that needs to be done.

Get It in Writing

You should take care to undertake such projects only when you have a signed agreement in hand and when you have taken the trouble to determine that your client is creditworthy. One reason this person may be coming to you is that no other print shop will give him credit. I never take on such an assignment without a credit check and a substantial advance payment of no less than a third. Half is better.

I also insist that the final payment—I make exceptions for large companies of impeccable credentials—be made prior to shipping the completed print job, and often prior even to printing it. I have never lost money on such a job but I certainly could, if I did not take the necessary precautions. Often there is a fairly large sum of money involved, so that a single sour deal would be a damaging blow for you. Handled carefully, though, print brokering can be a nifty secondary profit center.

Utilize "Printers to the Trade"

A customer goes into the neighborhood print shop and orders 1,000 business cards. A week later he returns, picks up his cards, and pays his bill. He assumes that his cards were printed locally. He would be surprised to learn that they were actually printed 2000 miles away in Mankato, Minnesota, headquarters of the Carlson Craft company. There are many other such companies, some of which may be in your own backyard.

The same company can provide local printers with letterheads, envelopes, business forms, and many other products—all at wholesale prices. It also specializes in the printing of wedding invitations.

The truth is that many routine printing jobs are done by "printers to the trade," highly specialized print shops that do work sent in by small printers who pay for them at discounts of 40% and more.

You can use the services of these wholesale houses, too. While you may or may not want to bother with single business card orders, where the typical profit ranges from $10 to $30, orders that include business cards, letterheads and envelopes, statements and invoices, and perhaps a logo design can certainly be worthwhile.

Since you will have a great deal of contact with many businesses, large and small, while selling advertising and doing feature articles, you will be in a position to pick up such orders. You can get other leads by reading the newspaper carefully for stories about business start-ups and looking over the new business license applications at the local register of deeds office.

You can check the back pages of trade magazines like *Printing Impressions* and *American Printer* where the printers to the trade advertise. You will find everything available there from the paper products mentioned above to embossed foil labels and four color presentation folders.

Capabilities Brochures

With the capabilities brochure we get into the higher levels of income potential from secondary profit centers. Such a project gives you the opportunity to make money in several ways. You can profit from writing, from design, and from brokering the printing of the job.

A capabilities brochure is a company's chief sales piece, and it must be very well done. Elsewhere in this book I emphasized the necessity of an impressive capabilities brochure for your own company.

The customer is usually willing to pay whatever it takes to get the job done right. He is not, however, interested in wasting money. The advertising agencies that will compete for such jobs are likely to be much more expensive than you are. You can do a 100% markup and still be competitive. Agencies typically have a much higher overhead than you will have, and they will be staffed with highly-paid graphic artists. You will be using free-lancers for the most part, and you do not have to maintain the expensive image in your offices that the ad agency does. For the agency, remember, such brochures represent primary rather than secondary profit centers.

They have much less room to play around with pricing, since they have to factor a major portion of their overhead into their quotes on such work. Your own overhead is covered by your publishing business. I am talking about full-fledged, multi-page capabilities brochures. The small, three-panel jobs will not be profitable for you, and your prices will not be competitive. Any print shop can, and will, throw one of these together at rock-bottom prices, often including the (admittedly unimaginative) design work into the bargain at no charge. Stay away from these. They bring too much grief for too little money.

Once you have assembled the necessary talent—whether free-lance or in-house—you can begin to keep an eye out for work designing and producing product catalogs for your clients. Product catalogs are photography and design intensive, and the printing is likely to be expensive. You will be dealing with a considerable sum of money, so no matter what your percentage of markup you are likely to make a good profit on the job. Another nice thing about such jobs is that they tend to be repeated. If you do a good job at a competitive price this year, the client will come to you again next year for an update. Sometimes you will get requests to reprint the very same catalog.

Annual Reports

Corporations that are publicly traded must prepare annual reports for their shareholders. These reports are typically showpieces of design and printing. If the shareholders knew how much the report actually cost them, they might decide to instruct management to send out photocopied sheets with the same information on them. But, happily for you, they do not do this, and the fancy, expensive annual report has become a fixture in American business. Your clients will be those corporations that are large enough to require such an annual report but small enough that they do not have an ad agency or a public relations firm on retainer.

There are many such firms. Local and regional banks and savings and loan institutions are excellent prospects. Your proposal will have to be made to the corporate headquarters. If you live on the east coast and discover that the corporate headquarters of the business in question is in Los Angeles, then you cannot service that prospect. In the area where I ran one of my former companies, the giant, multinational drug manufacturing firm Glaxo has its American headquarters nearby. But it was too large a company for my small firm to approach successfully. On the other hand, a new regional chain of banks had just begun to do business. This was a prime candidate for my company. So is the small plastics manufacturing firm that has set up shop in the industrial park nearby, and there are many others.

How much time do you spend prospecting such potential customers? I find that a phone call or two, each day, to purchasing agents or others in charge of getting the reports, catalogs, and capabilities brochures done, will land an opportunity to make a proposal and generate as much of this kind of work as I can handle. If you find that you are really good at getting this kind of business and producing documents that please your clients, you can profitably spend more and more time doing it. It could in time move up from secondary to primary profit center or become the nucleus of a separate business.

Operations Manuals

There are many business documents that owners and managers require but which they cannot themselves generate. Usually a limited number of copies is needed, so printing is not an important factor in the cost. It is the writing and desktop design services that you will provide.

A short time ago, a young entrepreneur came to my office. He had developed an idea for a chain of fast food restaurants in shopping malls throughout the region. In order to franchise his idea he had to develop a complete operations manual. He asked if we could help, and we immediately said that we could.

The entrepreneur, whom I will call Stan, was not a writer. It is doubtful if he had ever even written a long letter. But he was a man of action and knew the fast food business from top to bottom. Since Stan could not generate even a rough draft of his ideas for me to revise, I took another approach. I interviewed him and got everything down on tape. Some sections he dictated into my recorder while driving from one of his business locations to another. I transcribed all of this material and edited it.

I designed and printed this catalog for a customer who originally came to us as an advertiser in one of my magazines. We made several thousand dollars profit at no increase in overhead. We already had the know-how and certainly had the time. It was a nice secondary profit center for us.

This constituted the first rough draft. I then gave it to Stan for revision. He dictated new passages, filled in the blanks, and we followed the same process through again. After we had a second draft, I asked him to have his operations manager, his attorney, and his accountant read through the manual and add their own notes. Their additions were duly incorporated. I then generated a final proof copy. After correcting the typos and making a few minor textual changes, this became the final version. Stan signed the authorization to print form that I always use, and I printed the operations manual and had it bound in looseleaf form so that later additions and changes could be made easily. There were just fifty copies. Since I am a writer and had time to take it on, I did the manual myself. Had I not been a writer, I could easily have assigned it to a freelancer. My profit on this job, after all expenses, was several thousand dollars. In a major metropolitan area I would have made much more than that, but of course my overhead would have been much greater and my chances of getting the job reduced because of the more competitive environment.

Business Plans

The business plan is a key document for any business, especially any new business. The care and professionalism with which it is written and designed will favorably influence the decisions of bankers and others important to the financial success of the enterprise.

The business plan is also important to the entrepreneur himself, since it is his personal map of the commercial terrain he intends to conquer and his guidebook to the way he intends to do business. I have developed many business plans over the years for my own businesses, so I have learned what the elements of a good one are. When developing a business plan for a client I often use the same interview method that I used with Stan and his fast food franchise. I simply ask the appropriate questions and help the client work through his ideas to develop good answers. I am not a lawyer, so I steer clear of giving hard legal advice. But I do get the facts down in such a way that they become clear to any interested reader. From time to time I insert house ads in one of my own magazines offering a business plan service. Each time I place the ad I draw a couple of responses from entrepreneurs who become paying clients. Many of these people are under-financed, so you cannot always get top dollar for your work. Nevertheless, it is a profitable sideline, a financial gap-filler.

Work with Accountants

Another approach is to work with accountants. You call on them, make them aware of your capabilities, and ask for the opportunity to do the business plans (and annual reports) of their clients for them. Often they will be very happy to farm their work out, and they pay well for it. The accountant deals with the customer, you deal only with the accountant. As a result, you know from the very beginning precisely what is to be included in the plan, and you are furnished with raw copy that is usually in pretty fair form. You simply take and edit this material, design the financial tables, graphs, spreadsheets, etc., and provide the accountant with the necessary number of copies.

Employee Manuals

There comes a time when every growing business needs an employee and operations manual. For larger enterprises these are separate documents, but for smaller businesses they are easily combined. My own company uses the combined version. In the first months we simply communicated our company policies, procedures, and benefits to each new person individually. Soon, however, this was no longer sufficient. We were still a very small firm by any standard. I did not always see everyone every day. I needed a written statement of what I offered my employees and what I expected from them.

An employee manual is very simple to do. You can prepare a questionnaire for your client and put together the manual by collating and rewriting his answers to your questions. There are many good books on this subject that will provide an outline for you. The Small Business Administration offers a free one.

Seminars

If you have a flair for speaking and think well on your feet, you can put together a menu of two or three-hour seminars that you can present on your own or under the auspices of your Chamber of Commerce, Community College, or the SBA.

The seminars you give will grow out of your background and abilities. They are generally directed toward small business people. Sample topics might be such subjects as "How to Advertise for Success"; "How to Market Professional Services"; "How to Prepare a Business Plan"; "How to Write an Employee Manual"; "How to Position Your Product or Service in the Marketplace"; "How to Design and Publish a Company Newsletter or Magazine"; and many others in the same vein.

You can profit from these seminars in two ways. First of all, you get paid the usual fee as seminar presenter. In addition to this, you make contact with business people who are impressed by your knowledge of the subject, unsure of their own, and who will contract with you to prepare the materials that they need. Since I spent some years in the classroom before becoming a publisher, seminars are right down my line. I enjoy doing them and find the fees I earn to be quite pleasant additions to my bank account. I have prepared a separate brochure for my seminars under a company name.

Editing and Ghost Writing

This kind of work just appears on your doorstep from time to time. There is usually not much you can do to attract it. I have done this work profitably, although it was often more time consuming than I anticipated. You have to be careful to deal only with those who can afford your services. I ghosted an "autobiography" for which I had a wonderful collection of memoirs, diaries, and letters to draw upon. My subject was a good natural writer, and this helped. I set the fee at $10,000. Based on the time it took, I should have asked $20,000 or more.

On shorter jobs I generally will work for $75 an hour. The client usually wants a firm price, so I estimate how long it will take and multiply that figure by my hourly rate. Ghost writing requires concentrated effort and attention. To try to do it at a fire-sale rate is neither possible nor profitable.

I occasionally send a mailing piece to CEOs and purchasing agents in my area advertising my services as a publications consultant. I also find it worthwhile to advertise these services in the pages of my. As a consultant, I help business, government, and industrial clients develop publications that accomplish the goals that they set for them. I develop editorial formats and physical formats. I show them how to write, edit, lay out, and print their publications. I help them set up schedules and procedures that assure a timely, quality product. All of these services are very valuable, and I find that whenever a client who does need my services comes my way he is generally willing to pay a reasonable price for them.

Financial understandings with your secondary profit center activities should be made quite clear, otherwise you risk trouble. Verbal agreements are easily misinterpreted. Ambiguity has no place in a financial transaction. You need a written agreement, signed by both you and by your client, specifying precisely what goods and services you agree to deliver, the sum of money your client agrees to pay for them, and how and when payment is due.

18

How to Hire the People You Need
(at a Price You Can Afford to Pay)

In the beginning you can do everything yourself. Very soon, however, you are likely to find that you really do need some help. There will simply not be enough time to get everything done. If you focus on the job at hand, you neglect prospecting for more work. If you spend your time looking for more work, you neglect existing sales. Meanwhile, who is back in the office designing all those ads and writing and editing all those articles you will need?

The need for help is especially acute in the case of advertising-intensive publications—the ones that are likely to produce the most immediate, profitable return. It takes time and effort to sell all those ads, and time can be difficult to come by, especially if you are moonlighting. Even in book publishing, you will find that, in the long run, you just can't do it all. If you center your effort on book development, editing, design, and production, you neglect the after-production task of marketing. The problem becomes much more serious if you actually write your own books, as many small publishers do. You can't stay on the phone with wholesalers and retailers selling last year's books if, at the same time, you are trying to write next year's.

How Do You Pay for Help?

So you have a need for help. But where do you get it and how do you pay for it? As a start-up publisher you don't have the money to meet a hefty weekly or monthly payroll. The limited supply of cash in your bank account is important to you. You can't afford to pay others for their work until they bring in the money that enables you to do so. You have to find ways of getting very good people to join your enterprise on a work now, pay later basis. I have done this very thing many times, and I expect that I will continue to do so until the day comes when I turn off my Macintosh for the last time.

The Perfect Employee Profile

So where do you find these wonderful people who will agree to work for you on a deferred payment basis? Where do you find people who can afford to wait for a check until they earn for the company the money that you will pay them with?

A profile of the perfect writer or salesperson for your start-up publishing firm would look something like this:

- The people you are looking for want to be paid well for the work they are doing, but do not need to be paid immediately. An immediate check is not necessary to pay the rent, get Junior's tonsils removed or to put dinner on the table every day. These people will have a financial cushion or income of some kind that will enable them to wait a reasonable time to be paid. Such people will be willing to do so as long as they understand how and when the payment will be made and how much it will be.
- The people you are looking for will be self-starters who actually enjoy writing their own financial ticket by linking their income to their production.
- The people you are looking for are intelligent, well-organized, and mature enough to work independently once you have given them the basic orientation that they need.
- The people you are looking for will be interested in the work itself. There is a certain romance in the minds of many about the world of publishing. The truth of this proposition is born out by the large numbers of our brightest and most talented young people who earn college degrees in journalism—one of the least lucrative professions (for salaried people) known to man.

Are there such people out there? You bet there are, and here's how to find many of them. Let's take sales first.

Your Sales Staff

When I start a new publication I generally place an ad in the paper and have all the respondents come in at the same time. I hold a meeting at which I describe the product we're going to be selling, talk about sales in general, give a good, generalized pep-talk, and describe clearly the method of compensation. This information will eliminate those who need a job at all costs and can't afford to work on a delayed-pay basis. It is not possible to begin generating commission income in the first few days, or even the first week or two. If you inadvertently hire such dire-straits salespeople you cannot help but make them unhappy. And you will be unhappy, too, since your heart and your pocketbook will often be at odds.

Of those who continue to show interest in the job, sort out those who are not presentable as well as those who, for any number of other reasons, you would not want out on the street representing you. Then, give all of those who pass the first two tests a chance to show what they can do.

The Proof Is in the Pudding

In sales, the proof is in the pudding. You never know who is going to bring in the orders. Give a list of, say, five prospects to each salesperson.

- Some will call on only a few of their prospects.
- Others will make the calls but not be able to close the sale.
- Finally, there will be one or two who make the calls and also make sales.

These last two you keep on and the others you let go. Then advertise and go through the same procedure with the new batch. At the end of a week or two you should be fairly well set. But even if you can't be sure of good performance before sending your salesperson out to make a call, you can improve the odds of finding a good one by looking for a person who:

- is attractive, outgoing and literate
- knows the trade area well
- is active in many groups
- can meet the most ego-driven executive on a one-on-one basis without feeling second best

Nevertheless, bear in mind that you can't always judge the potential for outward success by personal appearance. Sometimes the strangest, most unlikely and least charismatic rep can go out and bring in a bumper harvest of orders day after day. So always be alert for those special salespeople who don't fit your fancy profile but sell ads like mad in spite of themselves.

Salespeople who come to work for you should know the trade area well and have some personal contacts to prime the sales pump. This is the girl-scout cookie principle of sales. Twenty-five little girls who can sell several dozen cookies each to Mom and Dad, Grandma and Grandpa and ten nearby, neighborhood families don't have to be polished salespeople to move a lot of girl-scout cookies. When you put on ten people, each of whom can sell an ad to five friends, you've suddenly sold 50 ads. It can add up quickly.

Bright, Talented (but Under-Employed) Women

There are two existing pools for sales reps that will fit your profile of talented people who can wait to be paid. The first of these is that vast number of energetic and ambitious young women who can sandwich only a few hours of selling time into their heavy schedules of child care.

Raising children and keeping house is great, and many bright women rightly make this a priority in their lives. But housework and mothering—as fulfilling as they may be—are clearly not all of life. Many young mothers are looking for something to do during the hours when the children are in school—and the more interesting and challenging the opportunity, the better. They get enough of routine at home. Many of them will be overjoyed to work for—and be involved in—the work of a publishing company like yours. Specify in your ads that you will be happy to talk to women who can work only while the children are in school.

Retired Persons

Men and women retire today earlier than ever before. When IBM or some similar corporation offers early retirement to 40,000 of its employees, these people, often in their late fifties, become candidates for your sales force. The same is true for military men and women who are retiring after twenty or thirty years of service. All of these people are accustomed to success. They can meet with anyone on a basis of equality. They know many members of the community, and they have standing in it. They desire to supplement their retirement income, but they are not in immediate need of grocery money. Health benefits and other perks are usually part of their retirement package, so they have no need of fringe benefits. Such people can and will work on a deferred payment basis. In the long run, they can earn considerably more on a commission basis than they could on an hourly rate. The clincher is that even when their retirement income is sufficient to meet their needs they can't stand the boredom of doing nothing and will welcome the opportunity to be associated with a business as inherently interesting as a publishing company.

Compensating Salespeople

Pay your salespeople on a straight commission basis, with no advance against commissions and no weekly or monthly draw against commissions. (Draws and advances can be costly and nonproductive. You can string along an ineffectual salesperson, hoping for better, for several weeks or months. If this person is drawing $150 a week against commissions—a modest enough figure— you will still be out a thousand or more dollars before the relationship ends. I have always been able to find very good people without having to pay a draw.) I generally set the sales commission at 20% of the gross sale amount for new business, with a lesser percentage for renewal of old business, say 15%. I set the commission level high enough so that I do not have to pay expenses, except for out-of-town travel that I have pre-approved. This relatively liberal commission rate also helps compensate the salesperson for the delayed pay arrangement. The sales commission is *always* paid only when the money actually comes in.

Freelance Writers and Artists

If you are neither writer nor a graphic artist you will have to get someone to do the work of writing and design for you. Most assignments can easily be handled by any one or two of the dozens of free-lancers who are constantly looking for work in most towns and cities. A brief classified ad in the newspaper, coupled with a news release to the book and arts editor of your local paper, will bring in many inquiries. The ad will simply read: "Freelance writers, artists and photographers wanted for assignments by local publisher. Send resume, clips, reviews to (address)." Carefully review your replies, reading the work sent in by writers very carefully and asking the artists who reply to bring a portfolio for you to look at.

By using free-lancers you will have a great variety of talents to draw from. You can more easily find precisely the right person for the job at hand. And you will never have a payroll. Freelance writers and artists essentially do piece work. With a writer, for instance, you commission an article of 1,500-2,500 words at so much per word. Payment will be on publication. By this time you will have collected sufficient advertising revenues to cover the free-lancer's fee. In the early stages of their careers free-lancers must get the publication credits that they need to build their portfolios. Thus they are often willing to work inexpensively in return for publication of their work. Your end of this bargain is to deal with the free-lancers on the highest professional level. Make payment as soon as it is feasible to do so and showcase their work in your publication as much as possible.

Get Others to Pay

Occasionally you can do both yourself and your free-lancers a favor by getting your client to pay them directly. If one of your advertisers needs considerable artwork for an ad or for an advertorial, put him in touch with one of your faithful free-lancers. Often a much higher price can be negotiated by the writer/artist with your client than you would be able to pay.

Moonlighters

If typesetting, layout, or other chores are a problem, you can utilize a stable of moonlighters very effectively. Those who work for printers, newspapers, and other publishers in the production process—typography, layout, etc.—can be recruited to work for you in the evening on an as-needed basis. Advertise for the people you need, specifying evening work. Develop relationships with the people who serve you at the newspaper and the local print shops.

Get in touch with them after hours and tell them what you need. Some of them will be glad to come in and work for you to help get your publications out.

Individuals who work for you irregularly may be considered "casual labor" for tax purposes. This means that you will not have to withhold taxes from their checks. Rules on casual labor change from year to year, so ask your accountant for current guidelines.

Internships

Many educational institutions recommend or even require internships (actual, "real world" work experience) for students in journalism, art, and other communications programs. A student-intern typically is sent out to work in an actual communications company for a period of three to six months, doing a variety of jobs. Many such internships are unpaid. Indeed, for a variety of reasons, educational institutions often *require* that interns be unpaid. The student will come into your company and work for you for a period of time, receiving academic credit for his or her effort but no hourly wage. Your job is to assist the student in learning as much as possible about the overall structure of the business, as well as to teach him how to perform the routine daily tasks expected of him.

To find out about internship programs, call the heads of appropriate departments at the community colleges and universities near you.

Bridging the Gap: On-the-Job Training

It may become necessary for you to hire at least one full-time employee sooner than you think. The person you need will probably specialize in one or another of the functions of your business—sales, editorial, production, management—but will also fill in elsewhere as needed.

The federal government has programs that help the small business owner and the employee at the same time. These programs, usually administered through state employment security agencies, subsidize employment of workers through a period of apprenticeship and training. The state employment agency will have a list of the various occupations and the number of weeks or months that it considers a reasonable training period for each of them. These time estimates are usually very liberal. A few years ago, when I last used the program, the training period for a typographer was almost a year and that of a graphic artist very nearly the same.

The program works this way. You interview and hire a person for the job you have available. You will have been careful to write a job description that fits the government's own criteria. When you interview a candidate who has the talent you need and meets the income and other eligibility requirements of the OJT program, you inform the employment security agency, which checks the candidate out. If the candidate qualifies, you put him to work. You pay him as you would any employee, except that, at the end of each month, the government will refund up to half of the salary that you have paid out.

19

How to Save Money on Printing

One of the keys to profitability in the publishing business is to get quality printing done as cheaply as possible. For the independent publisher who is buying printing for the first time this can be a problem. Often he will pay far too much money to get the job done. Sadly, unnecessarily high printing costs have jeopardized the profitability of many an otherwise viable project. Cash is one of any publisher's most precious assets. The time that you put into writing or editing books and magazine articles and the care with which you design your publications are valuable items as well. But at least they do not pull money directly out of your pocket. They are the sweat equity elements that all successful entrepreneurs invest in their enterprises during the early days.

A Cash Transaction

Printing, on the other hand, is a cash transaction. It drains the bank account as well as the sweat glands, and it can do so very rapidly. For new accounts, especially for new accounts that are also new businesses, the printer will usually ask for at least 50% up front and the balance before shipping. The best terms I ever had as a new customer were one-third on the signing of the printing contact, one-third on the approval of blue-line proofs, and one-third thirty days after shipping. And these are very generous terms. Most printers require full payment before the presses ever start rolling.

So what do you do? How do you make sure that you are getting the best possible price? Read the following pages thoroughly. Utilize the techniques they present to you. When you do, you increase your profit margin dramatically, protect your cash flow, and wind up with a better product.

How to Do It Wrong

I got into publishing when I decided to bring out a picture history of the city of Greenville, North Carolina. I was a quick study on research, wrote easily and clearly, and even had a pretty good idea of what I wanted my finished book (*A Greenville Album*) to look like. But when it came time to get the book printed and bound, I was in the dark. I knew virtually nothing about the whole production process. I naively believed that a printer was a printer. I thought that they were all pretty much alike. I was ignorant, but I did not know it. As a result, hard experience was about to teach me a very costly—but ultimately very valuable—lesson.

A Friend in the Business

It happened like this. I had a friend who owned a small print shop. I knew he was a good printer. How did I know? Well, he had printed my business cards and stationery, hadn't he? And for years he had had the contract for producing the football programs for the university where I then taught, hadn't he? Very thin qualifications indeed, but at that time they seemed adequate to me.

We'll call my friend Jimmy. Jimmy's small company was staffed by his wife as business manager and general assistant, a receptionist-typographer, and Jimmy himself as master of the press room. He had two small presses, a Multilith 1250 and an A. B. Dick 360. In one corner stood a folder and across from it a paper cutter. A closet served as darkroom. This machinery was perfectly adequate for the bulk of Jimmy's work, which consisted mainly of letterheads and envelopes, undemanding three-panel brochures, a lot of broadside flyers and, of course, all those football programs. This work, incidentally, is typical of most small print shops that ply their trade in every town and city in the country.

RECOMMENDED RESOURCE!

When new publishers start dealing with typefaces and specifications, they are most often entering a new and strange domain. Most publications that look poorly designed do so because of the unwitting misuse of type. The best reference book and type guide that I have found is *Practical Typography from A to Z* by Frank Romano. It was published by the Printing Industries of America, through the National Composition Association. If it is out of print it is definitely worth getting through a used book dealer or interlibrary loan.

Besides, Jimmy was a nice guy and easy to work with. I liked him. So, I took him my book. "Can you print it for me," I asked. He smiled and said yes, he was just right for the job. And he gave me a price. He would take care of everything for just $10,000. I had nothing whatsoever to compare Jimmy's price with. I figured I could pay him and still make a profit, so I agreed to his terms. I assumed that the calculating of printing quotes was an exact science and that, no matter where I went, others would apply the same formula and come up with the same price—or very close to it.

Today I know that printing quotes can vary wildly, and that I could have done the same job, far better, for less than $5,000. The extra five I paid Jimmy came right off the top. By making a deal with him before I knew the rules of the game, I had cut my profit margin in half. Now here's the real point. My friend Jimmy was not ripping me off. He just did not have the equipment to do the job in the most economical way. Printing a 120 page, large-format (8 1/2 by 11) book on his small presses was a little like cutting down an oak tree with a pen knife. And he had to send the job out to do the case binding, a sure way to run the costs up. The fact was that it took Jimmy a long time to turn the job out. He had to work day and night. And, as is the case in any business, Jimmy had to charge me for his time. For Jimmy, $10,000 was a fair price, but it was a price that I did not really have to pay.

All Printers Are Not Created Equal

Printing, I would soon learn, is a highly specialized business. What I needed would have been well beyond the (affordable) capabilities of any small print shop. In a world of specialists, the local guy is likely to be a generalist. He has a few small pieces of equipment that can do a little of this and a little of that but that are wholly incapable of meeting the needs of even the most modest publisher. Books and magazines require million-dollar presses and sophisticated bindery equipment that works twenty-four hours a day, seven days a week. Because this equipment is built to do a certain kind of printing job—and to do it quickly, well and affordably—you will pay considerably less for the finished product when you go to the right place for the job. The hourly rate may be far higher than that of a lesser printer, but they do the job so quickly that the total cost is still much lower. So much lower, in fact, that when you begin to get really competitive printing quotes you may find them hard to believe.

The First Step: Define the Specs

So you have a publishing project in hand and you want to buy printing. How do you proceed? The first step is to define the specifications of your publication. There is a standard language that you will need to know so that you can describe your book, booklet, or catalog to a printer in words he will understand. If you are new to the business it may be a bit tricky coming up with specifications in the language of the printer, but there is no substitute for doing it, one way or the other. In the pages that follow we will go through a sample set of specifications (specs). After we have done so, you should be able to define your project fairly well.

The Request for Quote (RFQ) Form

The Request for Quote form that I use for detailing the specifications of any project that I am currently working on is reproduced in the back of this book. Once I have decided on each item on this list, I can call a number of printers, go down my list, and get a quote. In the beginning I contacted two dozen or more printers. I called other publishers and asked them who they used. I sent RFQ forms to printers who advertised in the newsletters of professional associations I belonged to. Now that I know my way around, I have decreased this number to three or four. But I would never have found the final four if I had not surveyed the field. Since I use the same specs with each of them, I am sure that they were all quoting on the same job.

The following sections give a point-by-point rundown of the things that you will need to know to spec your work for a printer.

Quantity

You will have to tell the printer how many books you want to print. Here are some things you should consider.

1. *Books.* The per unit cost on relatively short press runs grows smaller as the print run grows longer. Thus, a book which costs $2 per unit on a press run of 500 may cost only $1.50 on a press run of 2,000. At some point you will reach a stage (say, 5000 or more copies) where a longer run will not produce appreciable per unit reductions. To find this point, you can specify your quantity in multiple choices. You ask, for instance, for a price on quantities of 1,000, 3,000 and additional thousands (or whatever quantities are appropriate for your project). When you study the actual quotes included at the end of this report you will see that this is precisely what I have done. Much money is wasted when you buy more books than you need. If your book sells better than expected you can always go back to press for more copies. While this technique may cost you a bit more in the long run, it is certainly a wise business decision. And by the time you reorder books you will have a far better idea of the long range profitability of the project. Not to mention the fact that in a second printing you can correct whatever errors readers will have found in the first printing.

A good rule of thumb, and one recommended by some of the most respected consultants in the business, is that you should never print more books that you expect to sell over a twelve month period. Even if you think you have a good book that will continue to sell small quantities over a long period, it may not be wise to print them all at one time. Cases of books on your storeroom shelves represent an enormous drain on your working capital. It may not leave you with enough money on hand for necessary promotion. The cash flow from even a steady dribble of sales will not be sufficient to get your bank account back up to usable levels. Publishers who are new to the business often overestimate the number of books they should print. The fact is, that though you may love to buy books and read them, only a small percentage of the population shares your enthusiasm.

When I published my picture history of Greenville and had to specify the quantity of books I wanted to print, I proceeded as follows. The population of Greenville, I knew, was 50,000. I felt that my book, coupled as it was with a local bicentennial celebration, would have strong sales. Yet I was realistic. There were 50,000 individuals in the town, but there were only 12,000 households. Of these households, I estimated, only half ever read anything at all, leaving 6,000. Of this six thousand, half read only the newspaper, leaving 3,000. Of this three thousand, half might want to buy a book, but not have the money to do so, leaving 1,500. Of this 1,500, many would want to buy the book, have the money to buy it, and plan to buy it. But at least a third simply wouldn't get around to it, leaving a core of 1,000 potential customers. Some of these, say 250, simply would not like the book when they saw it. Thus my base of good prospects for this book was 750. I decided to print 1,000 copies, which would serve the local market, give me some to sell to libraries and a few to keep on sale over the long haul. (These "long haul books" I was able to sell a few years later as collector's items, at three times the original price.)

2. *Magazines and periodicals.* Magazines and periodicals will be printed in much higher quantities (see the appropriate chapters for calculating a print run). To make your periodical successful over the long run, you must get results for your advertisers. Advertisers like to see high numbers—say one publication per household in the trade area—whenever possible.

Magazine and periodical printers are not likely to be the same ones that handle books. This is a specialty, and you'll have to find a list of printers who do it regularly. Each of these printers will specialize further in certain print runs and certain trim sizes. Be sure to get ten or twenty quotes on your first go round to make sure that you get the best price.

Runs of ten to fifteen thousand magazines will probably be printed on a sheet-fed press. Longer runs will require a web press.

Trim Size

The term "trim size" describes the dimensions of the finished page. How wide is it and how deep (high)? When specifying the trim size, always let the first number represent the width of the page and the second number the height. "Nine by six", for instance, means nine inches wide and six inches high. "Six by nine," on the other hand, means six inches wide and nine inches high.

Unless there is a very good reason to do otherwise, stick to the standard trim sizes. These standard sizes are determined by the presses in use in a given print shop. The standard sizes are five-and-a-half by eight-and-a-half (often referred to in magazine publishing as "digest size"); six by nine; and eight-and-a-half by eleven. Sometimes there is a slight variation, say five-and-three-eighths by eight.

Nonstandard page sizes can be accommodated, of course, but they often result in an uneconomical use of paper and extra trim work—both of which run up your costs. Even if you specify, say, a six by nine page you should ask the estimator at the printing firm whose quote you are soliciting a simple question: "What is the most economical trim size for this publication?" Because of some feature of his equipment, he may be able to suggest a slight trim size variation that will be just as acceptable to you as the one you specified, yet save you a significant amount of money.

Unders and Overs

Bear in mind that the "customs of the printing trade" allow a printer to deliver as many as ten percent fewer books than you ordered or ten percent more, with an appropriate price adjustment. If you wish to be sure that you receive at least the quantity ordered, you must specify "no unders." Though this will usually result in your paying for extra copies, it is worth it when exact quantities are important to you.

The Number of Pages

The printer will want to know how many pages there are in your book or periodical. While this may seem to be a simple question, there are some things that you must be aware of.

The first of these is the question of "signatures" and how many of them your book will contain. What is a signature? When a sheet of paper with a portion of your book printed on it comes off the press (or rolls off, in the case of a web press job) it does so flat and unfolded. The overall size of this sheet depends on the size of the press on which it was printed. If your publication has a trim size of six-by-nine, it is likely that each sheet that comes off the press will have at least 16 and probably 32 pages printed on it. When it is folded down to page size it is called a "signature." Signatures are then stitched or glued together to form a complete publication.

You will have to ask your printer how many pages will be included in each signature. This is because the most economical way to print your publication is in a number of pages that jibes with the number included in full signatures. Thirty-two page signatures, for instance, fall naturally into publications of 64, 96, 128, 160 and 192 pages....and so on. If you send a publication to press that contains 154 pages, you are likely to pay more than you would for the even signature 160 page version. For this reason, some books have unnecessary half-title pages in addition to the title page and why they may also have a blank page or two at the end.

You can fairly easily add pages to reach the even signature number or edit your material so as to delete an extra page or two beyond the even signature

RECOMMENDED RESOURCE!

A valuable, easy-to-use reference book that explains all mysteries of printing terms and techniques is *Pocket Pal: A Graphic Arts Production Handbook.* Published by the International Paper Company, it is a standard in the field. If you can't find a copy in your bookstore, write directly to International Paper at 77 W. 45th St., NY, NY 10036.

level. Adding or subtracting graphic materials may be another way to attain this goal, as well as adjusting the typeface size or the space between the lines of type (leading).

If you find that it is simply not possible to design your publication on the basis of even signatures, then do so on the basis of a given number of even signatures and one half-signature. But even signatures is the way to go if at all possible. Almost without exception, half signatures have cost me more than the higher number of pages that even signatures would have required. This is because the signature adjustment involves special cutting and folding setup and time for which you will be charged.

Text Stock

The term "stock" refers simply to the paper on which a publication is printed. Text stock has four main characteristics: weight, color, bulk, and surface qualities. You are already aware that the paper used in printing most bibles, for instance, is not as heavy as that used in printing most books. This difference in the heft of a sheet of paper is measured in terms of weight. Bible paper may be thirty-five pound stock or even lighter. The average casebound book is printed on sixty pound stock. Mass market paperbacks are printed on lighter stock of much lesser quality. Quality magazines will be printed on stock at least 60 pounds in weight and often heavier. Sixty pound stock for printing of books and magazines is so common that you will always be safe in your specifications if you say that this is what you want. You can go to seventy pound, or perhaps even eighty, if you have a publication of exceptional quality, perhaps filled with photographs, etc., that you expect to sell for a premium price, and therefore want to set apart from the ordinary, run-of-the-mill variety. However, heavier stock can add considerably to the cost of your printing job and must be justified by marketing considerations.

Specify House Stocks Whenever Possible

You will want, whenever possible, to utilize the "house stock" that large printers have available in their warehouses. Since they buy these papers in enormous quantities, they can charge you less for them. Printers can buy any paper that you need and are willing to pay for. But their house stocks almost always represent the best buy you are likely to get, and I recommend using them almost without exception. In fact, I can't think of a time in recent years when I haven't done so. The house stock is also a reliable guide to what most publishers are using and what is most nearly standard in the publishing trade.

As a publisher, you will need a library of samples of available paper stocks so that you can begin to choose more precisely the one that you want for your project. You can do this in two ways. When you deal for the first time with a printer, always ask to be sent a sample booklet of the house stocks which they routinely have on hand.

You can also look through the yellow pages for the name of a wholesale paper distributor. Call this company and ask to speak to a sales representative. Tell this person that you are a publisher and desire to have a sample pack of his standard text and cover stock. Paper wholesalers will normally be happy to furnish you with a sample pack in the hope that, when you ask for a book quote, you will specify their paper. I have two complete sets of samples on hand at this moment, one from Unijax, Inc. and one from the Henly Paper Company. There will be other such wholesalers in your part of the country. It is important to remember, when specifying paper for your book, that deviation from the standard will be expensive, and that you should not indulge in this luxury without very sound economic justification.

Printing stock also has color. Some text paper is so highly bleached and white that it becomes difficult to read. At least I find it so. I use it only when I need it as a neutral medium on which to print photographs. Unbleached or "natural" stocks have an off-white and sometimes even an eggshell appearance. I find these easier to read and more restful to the eyes. Both the natural and the white stocks are available in the house stocks of most large printers. Ask for samples of the stock if the precise tone of the natural color is important to you. Bleached stock is generally cheaper than natural.

Printing stocks also have varying surface qualities. Some may be richly textured, but these are used mostly for brochures and other specialty products. In book and magazine publishing, the main difference is between enameled (slick or coated) paper and plain (uncoated) paper.

Most books are printed on uncoated stock, although some art books may be printed on high-quality, slick paper. Magazines are usually printed on enameled stock, but with exceptions. *Mother Earth News* and *Writer's Digest* are two examples of magazines very successfully printed on uncoated stock. In fact, the cheap paper becomes an intrinsic part of the magazine's design.

Again, large printers will have house brands of enameled stock that will be much more affordable than custom-ordered papers.

The "Bulk" of Your Paper

Printing stock also has "bulk." This word refers to the thickness of the page. For example, 160 pages of a high-bulk paper will produce a thicker book than the same number of pages of an average or low-bulk paper. If you have a short book that you want to look thicker, go for the high bulk. Surprisingly, a high bulk paper can come in all weights and can sometimes be less expensive and lighter in weight than a low-bulk paper. I recently specified that a book be printed on a 55 lb, high-bulk stock. This paper was cheaper that the 60 lb stock that was not high bulk, and it produced a thicker looking book. Bulk is measured in PPI, or pages per inch.

Not long ago I had a problem with a book of poetry. I wanted to perfect bind it, but at 48 pages I was having some difficulty. It was too thin for the binding method I had ordered. My printer suggested another paper of the same weight but with a bulk rating that gave me more pages per inch. This solution worked perfectly.

The Cover Stock

If your book is to be paperbound you will have to choose a cover stock. Cover stocks are measured in "points," with 8 pt. and 10 pt. being the most common. There will be a wide variety of cover stocks available for inspection in your sample kit.

If your publication is going to be sold in bookstores, take care that your cover looks and feels as good as those surrounding it on the shelves—and better, if possible. You will want to have it laminated (or some equivalent process) to get that extra-shiny appearance that is so popular today. This process is inexpensive, yet it does much to make your book look like a premium product.

One way to save on your cover is by the imaginative use of color. If you use a full-color photograph or drawing you will have to buy a costly color separation and pay extra for increased prep time and press time. This may be unavoidable in some cases, but often a good artist can design a cover that uses fewer colors. I have designed handsome covers in black only, and I have another at the press now in just two colors.

Self-Covered Publications

For periodicals, it is not necessary to print your cover on a separate stock. If you are printing a magazine, for instance, you will choose to have it "self-covered." This option is much more economical that a separately printed, heavier cover, and it is utilized by most saddle-stitched magazines today.

Self-covered magazines have covers that are simply a part of the outside signature itself and consequently of the same stock as the rest of the publication. If you want a separate cover you will specify, for instance, "64 pages plus cover." If you want your magazine self-covered you will specify "64 pages self-covered." The self-covered magazines look every bit as good as the others and are always much less expensive.

Specifying the Binding

A publication can be bound in several ways:

- Most magazines are saddle-stitched, that is, stapled along the spine. Most books of 48 or fewer pages are saddle-stitched as well, because their bulk is too slight to support other binding methods.
- A publication can also be perfect bound. Perfect bound books and magazines are squared off along the spine, and their pages are normally glued into the cover. *Playboy* magazine, once saddle stitched, is now perfect bound, as are some other premium magazines. Almost every paperback book you will find in a bookstore is perfect bound. Perfect bound books are generally considered more prestigious and better looking than saddle-stitched books. There was a time when perfect bound books sold for much lower prices than hard cover books, and in the case of mass market paperbacks, this is still true. But times are changing. One of my own perfect bound books is retailing at $19.95, another at $18.95. I just bought one perfect bound reference book for $25.95 and another for $34.95. These books and others like them are referred to as "trade paperbacks," as distinguished from their mass-market cousins.
- Casebound books are covered with the cloth which you have chosen and embossed with the name of the book, the author, the publisher, etc. The signatures of the printed text are then sewn or glued together and inserted into the case. Not too many years ago, sewn ("smythe-sewn" is the trade term given to this process) books were clearly superior, but new glues have now been developed that are quite satisfactory for many uses. Most readers will not even notice the difference. Specify that your pages be glued and you will save some money. An added expense in case binding will be the cost of designing a handsome dust jacket. To get this done economically you can, in this case, try a local printer. The book manufacturers will be happy to do it for you, and their work is quite good. But their forte is the printing of the books themselves. When it comes to the dust covers they are not as competitive. On a book I am currently doing, my printer gave me a cost of $825 to print 1000 four-color dust jackets. My local printer quoted me $550. Hardcover binding may add $1.50 or more to the cost of your books. The other side of this coin, however, is that some casebound books, which cost only a dollar or two more to produce, can sell for twice as much money at retail and

sometimes more. This is especially true for limited or special interest editions that people want to purchase and save. Whether or not to go to the extra expense of publishing a casebound edition is really a marketing decision. A solution may be to do a "split run." In a split run you instruct your printer to deliver, say, 2,000 books to you of which 500 will be casebound and 1,500 paper bound.

This is quite a lot to decide. Here are my rules of thumb on bindings:

- If you are producing a book that will be bought as a collector's item—a city or county history, for instance—have it casebound and sell it for a premium price. It is not unusual to price such books at $40 a copy and more.
- If you are producing almost any other kind of book, have it perfect bound with an attractive cover. There is a growing acceptance today of the quality paperback as an acceptable substitute for the casebound book, even among librarians, who traditionally have opted for hard cover editions. Times are changing.
- For a periodical, go for the self-covered, saddle-stitched version.

The Blueline

The blueline is a cheaply produced checking copy of your book or magazine. It is made from the same film that will be used to make the offset printing plates that, in turn, will be used to print the book itself. The blueline will be identical to the finished product insofar as page sequence, design, graphics, etc., are concerned. The printer will ask you whether or not you want to see "blues," and you will answer that you do. There is a small additional charge for this service and it extends production time a bit, but the blues are an essential last check. In theory every typographical error will have been caught and corrected by the time you reach the blueline stage. You may not want to make a change this far along in the production process for a single, late-discovered typo. But if you have misspelled the business name of your largest advertiser or if the printer has inexplicably gotten your book's pages out of order, this is your last chance to do something about it. I have caught many potentially ruinous errors in bluelines and remedied them. Whenever I have let a pressing deadline tempt me into skipping the blueline stage, I have lived to regret it. The charge for the blueline proofs is money well spent.

Color

Your printer will want to know whether you are going to use color in your book or magazine, and, if so, how much and where. The truth is that you simply can't afford to use color in most books. It runs up the cost like a sky-rocket. Just tell him that you are using "black ink throughout." If you are printing a magazine and have some full-color ads to print, ask your printer where it is most economical to position them. You cannot scatter them at random through your publication. You must position your color ads and photos on pages that are printed on the same side of the sheet as it goes through the press (on the same form, the printer will say). This is an element of what is called "page imposition," and asking your printer to go over it with you with reference to the best way to position your color will save you big bucks over what you would pay if you positioned color at random or to suit some whim.

Bleeds

When ink is applied up to the very edge of the page on which it appears, it is said to "bleed." Bleeds can occur on one edge only or on two or more edges of a page. There is an additional charge for bleeds, so use them judiciously. Bleeds occur mostly with photographs and background color screens. They are far more common in magazines but do occur from time to time in books. A full page photograph may bleed, for instance. The dust cover almost certainly will.

Halftones

A halftone is a black and white photograph that has been processed for printing. The printer will want to know how many of these you will need. If you don't know or aren't certain, simply ask for a "price per halftone."

Freight

You will want a quote on freight charges from the print shop to the place where you want your books delivered. A lower quote from a distant printer can sometimes be more than balanced by greater freight costs. When you order several thousand books or magazines, freight becomes a significant cost factor. Ask your printer include the cost of freight in his quote.

Always Get Multiple Quotes

Do not give your book or magazine to any printer before you have received and compared several quotes from shops whose work you respect or which come highly recommended to you. Even among the good, professional shops that specialize in book and magazine production quotes can vary widely, often by as much as 20, 30, or even 50 percent.

Why this variation? Price differences are usually a function of work load and equipment. Sometimes a shop will need work, and the price quoted will be a little lower than usual. Sometimes the shop will be flooded with work and quote high. One company may have just the right equipment to fit the job you are getting the quote on. Another with almost right equipment will have to quote higher because the job will take longer and be more difficult to do. One company may be able to handle the entire job in-house, whereas another may have to job out the binding or some other aspect of production. This almost always results in an unacceptable increase in cost. Only when you get and compare a number of quotes, all based on the same objective specifications, can you be satisfied that you are getting the best job at the best possible price. Examples of varying quotes? Here's a recent one. A short while ago I asked for a quote on a newcomer's guide my company was printing. It was a digest-sized magazine, saddle stitched, self-covered and printed on 60 lb. coated stock. I was ordering 50,000 copies, each containing 112 pages in full color. The pre-press work was all done by us, in house. All the printer had to do was make the plates and turn on the presses. Yet one quote from a large printer in Tennessee came in at $42,000. A competing quote from a printer in North Carolina set the price at $25,500 on the very same job. Quite a saving. Was it worthwhile to compare multiple quotes? You bet it was.

Get a Quote, Not an Estimate

Please note that I have been using the word "quote." I do not say "estimate." An estimate, which is just somebody's best guess at what a job will cost, is useless for your purposes and is not binding on the person who gives it. The final price may well—and probably will—be quite different from that which was estimated. I have never known a final price to be lower than an estimate. Somehow it is always higher. A quote, on the other hand, is a firm price, a commitment to produce the work as described in your specifications for a definite and agreed upon sum of money. If the specifications for the job do not change, the price quoted will not change, either. A quote is furnished to you in written form and is usually valid for a specified period of time. The printer signs the quote, as do you when you accept it. This then forms a binding legal agreement.

You can simplify your work by filling out your "request for quote" form (sample provided elsewhere in this book) and faxing it to printers from whom you desire to get quotes. This way the facts are all before the estimator, and he can get to work on it immediately. There is no two or three day delay (or more) as the U.S. Mail travels its leisurely way across the country. It's all there, in black and white: paper, quantity, binding. . . everything. You should fill out this form even if you are going to use the telephone to solicit your quotes. That way you are sure to omit nothing and make no mistakes. I have had good luck with telephone quotes. This kind of direct conversation was particularly helpful in the early days when I had so many questions to ask and needed so much guidance. I just picked up the phone and talked directly to my customer service rep. I read my specs and asked them to get back to me as quickly as possible, both with a price and a turnaround time. I asked that the quote be telephoned or faxed to me as soon as it was ready, then followed up in standard written form through the mail.

Stay on Schedule

At any print shop, and especially at the larger ones, schedules are important. Press time for every job is scheduled well in advance. If you promise that your camera-ready copy will arrive on a certain day, do everything in your power to see that it does so. If you are going to be delayed, and you know this in advance, call the printer at once and reschedule.

If your work does not arrive on time, it can create major problems. At the very least you risk being bumped from your spot on the printing schedule. Another job will be moved up to fill the gap, and it may be days or weeks before your turn comes around again. Like other business people, printers have long memories. They have their own businesses to protect. Habitual failure to meet your agreed-upon delivery schedules in getting materials to the printer can have important consequences, some of them economic. If you develop a reputation for being late, the printer will not be as likely to do rush production for you when you truly need it. He is also likely to raise his prices somewhat the next time to cover the loss of time and the general production headaches that he suffers because of last minute press changes.

The opposite is also true. Develop a reputation for coming in on time and you will regularly get the best prices the printer has to offer.

Furnish Camera-Ready Copy

Camera-ready copy is a paste-up or printout that is ready to be used to make negatives and plates. It is typeset and laid out on the page. It is much to your advantage to do this part of the job in your own shop, and, now that we all have desktop hardware and software available, it is also easy to do so. Printers can do the typesetting and page layout for you, but that is not cost effective for either party, publisher or printer. The printer's business is printing. Everything else is done simply for the convenience of his clients. You will find that you save great sums of money when you furnish camera-ready copy to your printer. You become just the kind of customer he prefers to do business with. If you do not have the necessary computer and software for typesetting and layout, you should consider investing in it.

Color Separations

If you are going to be printing in color you will need color separations. If you order them from your printer, he will often have to send out for them and your costs will be greater than they need be. Instead, look for local, regional or national sources that specialize in low prices and quick turnaround.

Solicit quotes from these color houses just as you do on the printing. Again, equipment is a key factor in costs, and you can find specialists with the latest equipment who can give you color separations at a far lower cost than some other companies in the same business. You then send these separations to your printer along with the camera ready copy.

When pages have extensive use of color—a background color, reversed type, two or more separations, etc.—ask your color house to give you a price on a "composite" for that page. A composite consists of four pieces of film sufficient to produce all the color that appears on a given page. Your print shop, if it wants to bother with these composites at all, will often have to send the work out and charge more for the job.

Like printing, color separations vary widely in cost for pretty much the same thing. There is a scale of quality in separations. If you were doing an art book of the work of master painters, you would want separations of the highest fidelity. But for most magazine work and book work (dust covers, etc.) a lesser quality is quite acceptable. This everyday quality, in the trade, is known as "pleasing color," and you should always specify it unless you have very good reason for doing otherwise.

Too Expensive? Reevaluate the Format

One of the most important ways in which you can save large sums of money printing your publications is to reevaluate the format that you have chosen, or at least alter it somewhat. Here are some techniques that I have found very useful and cost effective.

I have said that paper is to be specified in terms of its weight. You should be aware that heavier paper costs more than lighter weight paper. Although I have said that 60 lb. paper is pretty much the standard for most purposes, you may well be able to get by with 55 lb. or even 50 lb. stock. Most readers, especially of publications like tourism guides and various handbooks and directories, simply do not care whether the paper on which the information they need is printed on 50, 55 or 60 lb. paper. They want the information itself.

One warning. If your magazine or booklet contains few pages—say, a one-signature publication of 32 pages—then you may opt for the heavier stock as a simple marketing decision. Perhaps you have competition, and you want your own publication to seem and "feel" more substantial in the hands of the prospective advertiser.

A very useful technique is to specify the use of mixed weight signatures. I once published a full-color apartment guide for a major city. My competition was well established, and, consequently, their publication had more pages than mine. I wanted mine, nevertheless, to feel substantial in the hands of advertising buyers.This guide was 128 pages long and was printed on fairly expensive coated stock. Printing costs were by far the largest cost I had in this business, and I kept looking for ways to control and, if possible, reduce them.

A printer with whom I was doing a good bit of business suggested a strategy that has worked like a charm ever since. My 128 page publication was made up of four 32 page signatures. "Why not print the outer signature on 60 lb. stock and the inside ones on 50 lb.?" the printer asked. He went on to say that many publishers did this and that often the readers and even the advertisers were unaware of it. He explained that the weight and quality of the paper were almost universally judged by the outer signature, and that readers seemed not to notice the change to lower cost, lighter stock in the inside signatures. I accepted his suggestion and found that everything he had said was true. No one noticed the difference in my magazine, yet I was able to save thousands of dollars on printing costs over a year's time.

The Tabloid Alternative

When you become accustomed to the prices you will pay for quality printing on book and magazine presses, you will be astonished at the values you can get by using the services of a newspaper printer. The presses used to print newspapers are very efficient and very expensive pieces of equipment. Since most small town newspapers must be printed in just a few hours a day—or a few hours a week, in the case of weeklies—the management of such papers regularly seek "outside work" to keep their presses busy and help defray the enormous cost of owning them.You can benefit from this search for outside work. Many of your publications may be suitable for publication in a format that will roll right off a newspaper press. Most of these presses produce publications in the following sizes:

1. *Broadsheet*. This is the standard, full-size newspaper. It will probably not be appropriate for most of your projects.
2. *Tabloid*. Fold a broadsheet in half and you have a tabloid. The *Christian Science Monitor*, for instance, is published as a tabloid.This is a useful format for a variety of publications. Many real estate and advertising publications come out in tabloid format. A city magazine-type publication can also be printed in a tabloid format where the budget requires it. I once published such a magazine in a very sparsely populated area of North Carolina. In my first issues I did a regular magazine—slick paper and all. Profitability was marginal. But I converted this to a well-designed tabloid format and found that it was just as acceptable. In fact, it was more widely read than before and got better results for my advertisers. And it cost only a fraction of what I had been paying for printing.

The Single Most Important Question

When you have done everything else you can do, when you have adjusted the print run to the most economical level, chosen the paper with an eye toward cost, typeset and laid out your own publication, contacted several printers, and secured multiple quotes, there is still one more absolutely essential step.

Give your printer a call with his quote in hand. Tell him that you are just about ready to make a commitment, but that his price, though good, is just a bit beyond your budget. "Can you," you ask him, "see any way that I can get this down just a bit?" Specify here just how much of a reduction you're looking for. Maybe he can help you and maybe he can't. But in a surprising number of cases the printer will come up with some money-saving ideas. He will do this because he wants and needs your business. He may do this for any one of a variety of reasons:

- His shop is empty, a big customer has just delayed a job and he has pressmen standing around without anything much to do.
- He quoted you a bit high in the first place just to see what the traffic would bear. Now he knows, and he will come down a bit to please you.
- He really does know a way to get the price down a bit, one that will lower his costs in a way that he can pass on to you.

So always ask this "single most important question." It does not always work, but the money you save when it does is pure gravy.

3. *Mini-tab*. The mini-tab can be quite useful. It is half the size of a tabloid, which is simply folded again to make the mini-tab. The resultant page is roughly eight by ten and a half inches in size—very close to that of a standard magazine. The mini-tab is saddle-stitched or glued, depending on the capabilities of the press you are working with, and it can be quite useful for informal magazines, tourism guides, and other publications.

The newspaper printer who takes in outside work will have a number of different paper stocks available to him, in varying weights and degrees of whiteness. Ask to see his samples before you make a decision. He will not normally be able to order special paper for you unless you have an enormous press run, since he buys paper in giant rolls that contain enough surface for many jobs the size of yours. Drawbacks to the tabloid alternative include a lesser quality in halftone (photograph) reproduction and limited color capabilities. A bonus of the tabloid alternative, on the other hand, is the ability to greatly increase your total circulation. The name of the game is getting your advertiser's message into as many hands as possible. Though some advertisers may initially be inclined to place their ads in fancier publications, they quickly change their minds when your ads start bringing in far more business as a direct result of greater market saturation. You've simply got more sales messengers—copies of your publication—out there in the marketplace doing a job for them. In the long run this pays off. Tabs are also more recession proof. If your publication offers more circulation and equal or better results for the same price or a lower price, advertisers will naturally stick with you during the hard times. You will be the most cost effective avenue for getting their message out.

20

Cashing In: How to Sell Your Publication

One of the benefits of being a periodical publisher is that when your magazine or weekly newspaper is successful it becomes a valuable property in the publishing marketplace. You can expect that from time to time, especially after you have come out for two or three years and established a track record of profitability, you will have an occasional nibble from some individual or company who wants to buy you out.

I was in the third year as publisher of my weekly newspaper when one of the large chains began to buy up newspapers in my part of the state. Eventually their interest turned to my newspaper, and I had a brief telephone call from the president of the chain. Would I be interested in selling? he wanted to know. Since I had already considered putting the newspaper on the market, I replied that I was. He asked me what my circulation base was. I told him. He asked if all those readers were actually paid subscribers. I said yes, they were. He asked me how much I wanted. I replied that my previous year's gross was a certain amount of dollars and that I would take that amount for my paper. He replied that it sounded okay to him and, in fact, six weeks later I was sitting in the conference room of my bank filling out and signing an impressive stack of papers and getting, in return, a check for a very substantial sum of money.

Preparation Begins Early

Selling out is something you can either just let happen, as I did in this case, or make happen. Either way somebody, someday is going to offer to buy one of your publications. When that happens you want to be ready. Some of the most important things you can do with an eye to profiting from the sale of your publication are done in the very beginning, as you organize your business.

Here is a prime example. Under U.S. tax laws, the money that is made from the sale of a corporate asset is taxed as a capital gain of the corporation, not as ordinary income to you. You will still have to get the money out of the corporate account and into yours before you can spend any of it.

There have been times when tax rates on capital gains were very much lower than any other rate. When I sold my newspaper, treatment of capital gains income was very favorable to me. Later, those benefits largely disappeared. Your accountant needs to be aware that you want to be set up to take maximum advantage of any possible sale. He will study your financial situation and make recommendations. One thing that he will probably recommend is that you organize as an "S" corporation rather than as a regular "C" corporation. That way you can avoid double taxation.

What is double taxation? Well, if you are set up as a regular corporation and sell off an asset such as a magazine, it is the corporation that makes the money from the sale, not you. This is true even if you own every single one of the outstanding shares. So the corporation pays whatever taxes are due on the profits from the sale. When the money passes from the corporation to you, it does so as ordinary income, and you pay income taxes on it all over again. So if you are organized as a regular "C" corporation and sell an asset for, say, $500,000, the corporation would first pay approximately 30% in capital gains taxes, and you would pay an additional 30% or so as your personal taxes on whatever was left and came through to you. On top of that there are the state income taxes to pay. All in all, you could pay out as much as $300,000 of your $500,000 profit in taxes. Quite a bite.

On the other hand, if you organize as an "S" corporation you avoid the double tax burden. Since you cannot change from "C" status to "S" status at the last minute, you should select the status that is best for you from the beginning. I emphasize that this is all amateur accounting on my part, although it grows out of considerable personal experience. *You must consult your own accountant and do what is best for you.*

I should add here that most accountants are not experienced in the sale of publications, which are valued differently from most other businesses. You might give him or her this chapter to read and evaluate.

What Is Your Publication Worth?

Publications are not valued like other businesses (where asking price is most often related to net income). In the world of periodical publishing, price is more likely to be related to gross income. If you have a solidly established weekly newspaper or magazine, but one which has not been published over a long period of time, a fair asking price might be the equivalent of the previous year's gross income. That's the price I got for my weekly, in spite of the fact that just three years before, when I bought it, it was on the brink of bankruptcy and was still not showing much of a profit on the corporate level when I sold it, although it was generating a decent income for me in my role as editor and publisher. And it was beset on all sides by competitors, ranging from big city dailies to free-circulation shoppers. If you are showing a good profit, if you are in a growth market, if you are the only such publication in town (a monopoly), or if you have a long track record of successful publication, then the percentage goes up from one times gross to one and a half, to two, three, or even more in exceptional cases.

Never forget that you are selling, in essence, the goose that lays the golden egg. Say you are taking a modest $30,000 a year from this particular publication. What is $30,000 a year worth to you? What will you trade a $30,000 a year income for? How much money would you have to have in the bank to generate that in interest?

When put in that perspective, you can see how important it is for you to get top dollar for something that you have worked so hard to build.

What You Are Selling

To begin with, understand clearly what you are selling. It is more than first meets the eye.

- You are selling not only all the profit that you are currently making but all that you will make in the future.
- You are selling the entire future potential of the publication.
- You are selling hard-won market position.
- You are selling name recognition and good will.
- If you have paid subscribers, you are selling access to a faithful, signed-up group of readers. Your subscriber list is an extremely valuable item. You built this list of subscribers slowly, over time. It would cost tens of thousands of dollars to come in and attempt to duplicate your list. They would still have no guarantee of success.

So if a buyer wants to get into your market in a hurry, and has the money to pay, it makes sense for him to pay you a substantial price for the successful publication you have already built. It would cost even more to try to duplicate the work you have already done. Big buy-out corporations do not operate on the kind of sweat-equity you invested to get your magazine up and going. They have to pay for everything with real dollars—lots of them.

The Selling Package

When you set your company up and were trying to impress the bankers and others with your prospects, you prepared a business plan with great care. Now you should prepare another report with the same care, this time with a view toward furnishing a prospective buyer with the information he believes he needs and the information that you want him to have.

This report will share many of the same features as the business plan. Your own credentials may be important if, as part of the deal, you are to stay on to run things. You will characterize your publication, explain its editorial policy, and show how it has developed over the years in response to market needs and challenges.

- Summarize the financial history of your publication and project its growth curve four or five years into the future. A graph showing an income line rising continually can be quite effective.
- Describe your circulation methods, and if you have paid subscribers, tell how you got them and how you keep them. Tell why your publication worked and became a strong presence in the market. If you have a success story to tell, tell it well.
- Discuss competing publications and tell how you have positioned your magazine to overcome the challenge offered by the competition.
- Be certain to include a discussion of growth patterns in your trade area that will increase the profitability of your publication.
- Put as much of this information in graphic form as possible. Everyone will study the diagrams. Fewer will read the entire report.

Be absolutely certain that all the information you put into your report is accurate. In the financial summary, particularly, you must be scrupulously correct. The facts are what they are. You can state them in such a way as to make their strong points apparent and easy to grasp, but state them you must. Any deviation from this path will surely come back to haunt you.

Structuring the Deal

When you agree on a purchase price, the real negotiations begin. The way the deal is structured is all-important. An example: The buyer will want to pay you part of your compensation in the form of a non-compete agreement. He does this for at least two reasons. First, he really does need a formal agreement that you will not simply move across the street, start another paper or magazine, and take all your customers with you. Second, the money paid by way of a non-compete agreement is wholly tax deductible to the buyer as an expense of doing business.

The buyer will want to assign other values to parts of his purchase: so much for the subscription base, so much for good will, so much for your fixed assets and equipment, etc. All of these decisions can have tax consequences. You will want to have a very sharp accountant on your side throughout this process. The way the deal is structured can have a major impact on how much of the money actually sticks in your pocket.

The buyer may also want to stretch payment out over three, four, or even five years. As tax laws now stand there is no benefit to you in this; only risk. Work to get your money in as short a period of time as possible. If you do go for a long period, be sure that the purchaser is entirely creditworthy before you enter into an agreement. Be sure that he pays the highest going rate of interest on any unpaid balance deferred to future years. In addition, try to be sure that he pays a higher overall price for your business if he wishes to make payments year by year.

If you do accept a note as partial payment, be sure that the note obligates the parent corporation and not merely some new subsidiary set up only to run your magazine, with few assets to back up its promise to pay. Otherwise, through mismanagement or other errors, the publication and its new corporation might fail, and your balance due would go down the tubes with it. Do not sign anything at all that is not carefully reviewed by your attorney and, especially, by your accountant.

Can Business Brokers Help?

In every profession some practitioners do better work than others. Unfortunately, when most of them get into water that is too deep for them or unfamiliar to them, they prefer not to let you know about it. They just go home, do what reading up they can do, and handle the matter as best they can.

Because the sale of a publication is not an everyday event, you may find that your accountant and attorney are not adequate when it comes to negotiating the particular structure the deal takes. They may simply not be aware of all the alternatives.

There are business brokers who specialize in publication sales. They can be most helpful to you in seeking out potential buyers, since they will know the players in the publications game. They will know who is looking for what, who will pay top dollar, and all the ins and outs of structuring a deal. (Conversely, business brokers who are not experienced in publication sales, no matter how impressive their credentials in other areas, are not likely to be of any help to you and can actually get in the way.)

The typical broker wants 5 to 7% of the gross sales price, though this can be negotiated. The 7% covers the tab when they actually do a national search for prospects. If you already have an interested buyer and wish to retain a broker to handle the deal, you may negotiate 5% or less. Not every broker of reputation will be interested in handling the smaller deals. For some, any transaction under $1,000,000 is small potatoes. For others, such a deal is right up their alley. Find out about a broker before you retain him. Ask for references. What successful transactions has he concluded in the last one to three years? How does he think he can find a buyer for you?

Whether the sale of your company or one of its publications is an immediate goal or not, it is comforting to know that when retirement time comes, or when you wish to change career directions for some reason or other, the publication that you have put so much of yourself into—heart, soul, sweat, and pocketbook—has a real value that you can turn into cash.

Appendix One
A Simple Sales Manual
That Works

A Simple Manual for Your Salespeople

*O*ne sure fact of life in the independent publishing business is that you will be hiring salespersons more frequently than you might wish to. You can count on yourself and on one or two other persons—probably part-time and for one reason or another less mobile than the others—to hang around and continue working. But most of your salespeople will come and go.

Some will join your staff, fail to sell enough to meet their financial needs or expectations, and wander off to other, in their eyes less chancy, jobs. Others will do very well indeed with you, but then be attracted to much higher paying sales jobs with larger companies that have generous expense accounts and loads of benefits and perks—companies that you cannot compete with. An unfortunate few will sit at their desks, stare at the telephone, and never summon the courage to call a prospect at all.

So, for whatever reason, you will be constantly hiring and training salespeople. Although you will train these people personally to the degree that time allows, there will be a need for a simple sales manual that you will put into their hands. You will want this manual to do a number of jobs.

- *You will want it to give the salesperson some information about the background of the company.*
- *You will want it to give the salesperson clear instructions on procedures and policies, though not repeating the detail of the operations manual.*
- *You will want it to summarize the tried and true sales techniques that you know will work, if intelligently and assiduously applied.*
- *You will want it to tell the salesperson in clear, unequivocal terms just how you expect the work to be done.*

Just remember that you are not writing a treatise on the art of selling. Your sales manual should be brief and to the point.

The following is a brief, concise sales manual I developed for one of my earliest magazines, Historic Washington and Beaufort County Magazine (and which I used continually, for publications large and small, thereafter). With this little manual in hand to reinforce a day-long sales training session that I had given them, an enthusiastic crew of five part-time and totally inexperienced salespeople went out into a town of 14,000 inhabitants to establish a city magazine. They succeeded, and the magazine was published regularly until I sold the business five years later.

Will this kind of manual work for you? I believe that it will. Details will vary, of course, as the particular publishing project at hand varies. But the heart of the message will remain unchanged. I have used this manual again and again over the years, with just slight variations. I will use it again when I begin to market my next publication here in South Florida.

Manual For Advertising Salespersons

ENTREPRENEURIAL PUBLISHER (your company) is a company that publishes newspapers and shoppers of the highest possible quality, containing the most effective advertising and offering the greatest possible circulation for our readers and clients. To do this we must all bring into play our creative energies and imaginations. Although some of us will be more heavily involved in some areas of activity than others—ad sales, circulation, management—we work as a team, and the input of each of us is very important.

Middle City News and our shopper *Bucksworth* will be the first of many that we will publish. As such, we will take great pains to make them publications of real excellence. No effort will be spared, and you can rightfully take pride in the product you are selling.

Product Knowledge

Few things are more necessary for successful sales presentations than product knowledge. As a newcomer to the publishing business, you will not know everything you need to know when you start out. But as you make your presentations, answer customer queries, and become better informed by asking your own questions of the editor-in-chief, you will soon begin to acquire and master product-knowledge information.

Here are some of the basic facts you will need to develop your sales presentation:

1. *Historic Washington Magazine* will be published in a standard magazine format. [Remember, I wrote this manual before the first issue had appeared.] The trim size is eight and a half by eleven inches. The page format is a typical one of three columns. This format has proved to be more dynamic in appearance than other formats, creating higher reader interest and more powerful results for advertisers.

Our magazine will be printed on slick paper, have a full-color cover and back cover, and many full color pages inside. If you want to show your prospects just what the magazine is going to look like, pick up a copy of *Mid-Atlantic Monthly* or a similar full-color, slick paper magazine from the newsstand.

2. There is no other town of our size anywhere in the country that will have a magazine of this quality. In fact, few towns and cities of any size will be able to match it.

3. The magazine is a local product, designed, written, and distributed by a local company. This fact will be important to your prospects because the publishing business, unfortunately, is a favorite of fly-by-night operators, the kind that take your money and disappear.

4. No money need be paid until after publication, although discounts and other incentives will be offered for payment in advance.

5. The editorial content will be designed to create the highest and most favorable reader response, thus creating a positive response to the advertisements of our customers. The magazine will contain:

- Feature and profiles of leading personalities, creative talents, and people who get things done—in every walk of life.
- Success stories from the business community. How an entrepreneur gets an idea, makes a plan and builds a business. . . .at the same time as he is helping to build his community.
- Articles on local history, richly illustrated with drawings and old photographs.
- Articles on future possibilities. What does the future hold? How do we get there from here?
- Homes and gardens.
- Fun and recreation.
- Things to do and places to go.
- Drawings, maps and dozens of great photographs.

6. *Historic Washington* magazine will be circulated to every household in the city where any discretionary income is likely to exist.

It will be mailed to political and governmental leaders statewide.

It will be sold in stores and on newsstands both locally and regionally.

7. *Historic Washington* magazine will be edited and designed to become a collector's item. The newspaper is here today and gone tomorrow. An ad in *Historic Washington* will stay alive and continue to sell indefinitely.

Planning Time and Selling Time

Salespeople are expected to prepare lists of clients on whom they will call. Their initial list will be of persons with whom they may have some special relationship or "in." Whenever possible, salespeople will be assigned those prospects that appear on their list.

After these initial sales calls, salespersons will call on other prospects on a daily basis.

No salesperson should begin a day's work without a definite list of prospects to call on.

Prepare your prospect lists and sales schedule in the evening or during other non-prime sales hours. Do not let planning time run over into prime selling time. The best sales hours (nine to four-thirty, daily) are for calling on prospects, not for making lists.

Dress Code

You have a quality product and you work for a quality company. The way you dress should reflect these facts. Women will wear businesslike dresses or blouse-skirt combinations. Men will wear coats and ties. Suits and sport coat-slack combinations are acceptable.

Dress should be on the conservative side and in good taste. Don't neglect the details of good grooming, shined shoes, etc.

Sales Tips and Guidelines

The following tips and guidelines are distilled from many years of experience in advertising space sales. They will put money in your pocket when you follow them.

1. The key to making more sales is to see more people and to make a well-prepared presentation to those whom you do see.

2. The good salesperson constantly researches sources for leads: Yellow Pages, newspapers, personal contacts, friends in business, referrals, cold calls, etc.

3. Prepare lists of prospects to be seen each day. This is one of the great keys to success. Your prospect list will include name, address, telephone number and the specific benefits that each prospect will enjoy if he makes a decision to advertise in *Historic Washington*.

4. Always sell benefits; features are secondary. You can tell the prospect what a fine magazine the county will have, but *sell him on the ways it will increase business activity and profits for him or her, personally.*

5. Qualification: Make sales presentations *only to those who can buy*. To talk to anyone else can actually kill a possible sale.

6. Presentation:

- Individualize your presentation.
- Rehearse your presentation in your mind.
- Have something to show every time you make a call. Showing customers spec or sample ads can increase your closing rate by as much as 33%. We will be happy in the office to help you create spec ads.

7. Product Knowledge: You must know your product inside and out. How many readers? Circulation? Features? Ask questions, think, imagine. For instance: slick paper, full color; many photos; modeled after the best and most successful; saturation circulation, Reader Service, qualified leads, preferred customer cards, etc.

8. Understand the three most important buying motives for a magazine such as ours: profit, ego satisfaction, and community support.

9. Prepared presentation: There is real power in a prepared presentation. Before you call on a client ask and answer the following questions:

- What is the client's chief product or service? What benefits are relevant to this product or service?
- What is the client's chief motivation in buying? Prospects buy from a variety of motivations, not the least of which is ego. Sometimes the suggestion of a photograph of the client in his place of business will help make the sale.
- How can our magazine help him achieve his goals?
- How can I show him that I have his interests at heart, that I understand his business and his needs in the area of advertising and promotion, that I have given real thought to helping him meet those needs?
- The essential part of a prepared presentation is the physical object, an ad culled for a magazine, newspaper or the Yellow Pages, a sketch, a border, a spec ad, etc.

Daily Call Report

We are publishing our magazine in a small trade area with a limited number of clients. We must be sure to call on all possible prospects. You never know who will buy. To keep track of our calls, salespeople will fill out a dally call report and turn it in as directed.

Insertion Orders

When a sale is made, the sales rep will prepare an insertion order. The insertion order must be completely filled out, including full billing address, telephone number, etc., of the firm purchasing the advertisement.

Each insertion order must be signed by the person who places the ad and who has authority to purchase advertising space. Be sure to print the name clearly if the signature is not legible. When your insertion orders are turned in, they must be accompanied by all necessary materials, instructions, and information needed to design an advertisement to the customer's satisfaction. No sale will be credited to a salesperson's account until all of this information is in.

Compensation:

Salespeople will be paid a commission of ___ percent on the gross cost of ads sold. Commission checks will be issued on the first and fifteenth of each month, as monies are received from advertisers by the magazine. When salespeople collect a percentage of the cost of the ad in advance, commissions will be paid out of this advance payment.

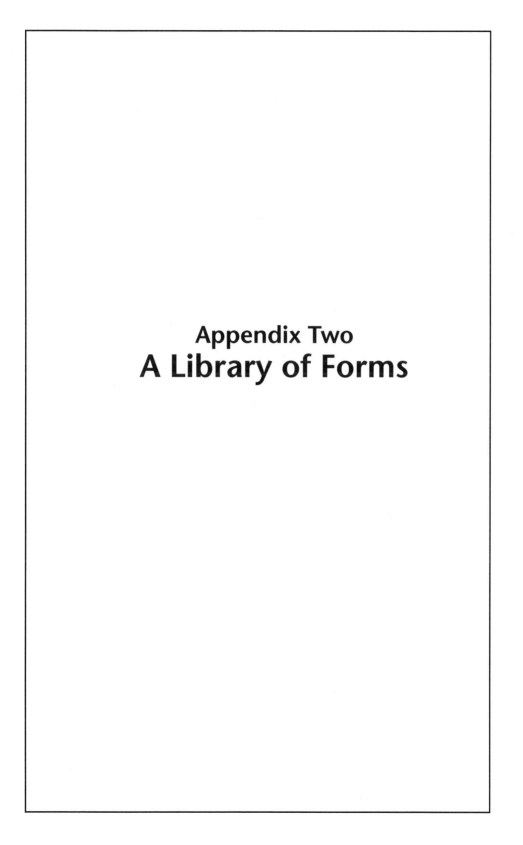

Appendix Two
A Library of Forms

Advertising Sales Report

Salesperson _____ **Start Date** _____ **End Date** _____

Advertiser	Amount of Sale	Commission Due	Amount Paid

Note to salespersons: This report constitutes your record of sales on which commissions are due. Commissions will be paid as revenues are received. Please note that no commissions will be paid until all the elements and information needed to produce the advertisement that you have sold have been received. Please file this report in the main office on Thursday afternoon.

ADVERTISING INSERTION ORDER

I. I authorize (publication name) to insert an ad in in the issue of _____,
closing date _____, as follows:

1. Size of ad:_____
2. Color:
   - ❏ Black & White
   - ❏ 2 color
   - ❏ 3 color
   - ❏ Process color

3. Provided:
   - ❏ Camera ready
   - ❏ We design for advertiser
   - ❏ Film composites
4. Position
   - ❏ ROP

II. Conditions and terms of this insertion order:
1. Cost of space _____
2. Production cost: _____
   - ❏ Halftones
   - ❏ Color separations
   - ❏ Design

- ❏ Typography
- ❏ Bill separately when known
3. Total due: _____
4. Less discounts _____
5. Paid with this contract: _____
6. Balance due: _____

III. Additional terms. Ads paid for within 15 days of the signing of this contract may be discounted at the rate of 3% of the total space charge. Where no credit terms exist, ads must be paid in full prior to publication. All balances are due 15 days after publication, where credit terms are granted. Balances unpaid after 15 days will incur a service charge of 1.5% per month. Advertiser agrees that if ad materials which it has agreed to furnish do not arrive prior to the closing date, then [publisher] may insert appropriate copy of its choosing into the space reserved for the advertiser. Such insertion by [Publisher] will constitute fulfillment of this contract. [Publisher] is not responsible for errors and/or omissions which may be present in advertising copy once the advertiser has signed the advertising approval form.

IV. The advertiser's billing address is:

V. Make all checks payable to [Publisher] and mail them to [Publisher], 000 Main Street, Anywhere, USA.

Notes:_____
_____
_____

Signed:

_____   Date: _____
For the Advertiser

Your advertising insertion order is one of your most important forms. The one shown here has served me well over the years. I modify it from time to time as needed for projects with special requirements, as I advise you to do. You should also obtain and review the insertion order forms for all competing publications, including your local newspaper(s), shoppers, etc. When you finalize your form, have your attorney review it.

Contact Name	Company Name	Telephone
Address		

Package Contains:	Date Package Sent

Notes and Information: Date, Person Spoken To, Results.

CONTACT SUMMARY

This **contact summary form** can be very valuable to you, even essential. If a salesperson resigns or falls ill, or if you simply want to divide the work between two salespersons, there must be a careful record of contacts and the results of those contacts to facilitate the work of the new representative making the call. Otherwise much important work will be lost. Many salespeople do not like to take the time to fill out these forms, but you should encourage them to do so each week.

Salesperson's Call Report

Salesperson _____ **Start Date** _____ **End Date** _____

Person Contacted	Date	Business Name	Results

Note to salespersons: Please fill out this report at the end of each day's work and turn it in to the office of [your company] on the next working day. It is very important that a complete and up-to-date record of your calls be maintained. In the event of your absence due to illness, vacation or any other reason, your sales call record is your only way of reconstructing your work and knowing what must be done to service your accounts.

PROOF APPROVAL FORM

JOB NAME:_____

_____

☐ THIS IS PROOF NO. _____

☐ THIS IS YOUR FINAL PROOF BEFORE
PRINTING
PLEASE RETURN BY_____

_____
For the Advertiser

☐ OK TO PRINT
☐ OK TO PRINT WITH ALTERATIONS
☐ PLEASE SEND NEW PROOF

_____
For publisher

☐ OK TO PRINT
☐ OK TO PRINT WITH ALTERATIONS
☐ PLEASE SEND NEW PROOF

Please read carefully: Attached is a proof copy of your ad as it will appear in [publication name and date]. Please review it carefully. Check it for spelling, typographical errors, addresses and telephone numbers. Colors will be indicated by PMS numbers. These should be carefully checked as well. (Your company) takes great care to produce ads that are typographically correct in every respect; however, the final approval to print is the responsibility of the advertiser. Your signature on this form constitutes your approval of the advertisement as it appears on the furnished proof and your authorization to print it as is.

Your Company Name
Street, City, Phone

The **proof approval form** can be quite a boon. From time to time an advertiser may be dissatisfied with an ad you have designed, or perhaps there is some small error in one part of it or another. When this occurs, payment is often withheld. Your proof approval form, signed and in your files, permits you to say, "The ad is just as you approved it."

Advertising Manifest

Advertiser Name	Issue Date	Ad Size	Date All Info In	Date Proof Mailed	Date Ad Approved	Notes, Special Instructions, etc.

Your **Advertising Manifest Form** is an important record-keeping tool. As hard as it may be to believe, in the rush of making a deadline a key advertiser's ad may be inadvertently omitted, unless your manifest is carefully kept and is up to date. In addition, you may be working on more than one issue at a time, or an advertiser may place one order for space in several issues. When this happens, enter the ad on the manifest for all the issues included in the insertion order. The manifest also enables you to calculate at a glance the amount of advertising sold and plan the number of pages that a particular issue will include.

Article Manifest

Article Name	Writer	Estimated Length	1st Draft Received	Editing Done	Typeset Done	Notes

As an editor, you will often be working on several issues of your publication at the same time. You may be lining up next week's issue of your weekly newspaper, for instance, while simultaneously preparing the March Bridal Supplement or the May Home and Garden section. Your **Article Manifest** will enable you to keep track of all the editorial work that is going on. Trying to wing it without such a form is a recipe for disaster.

This Week's Projected Sales Call Activity

Salesperson _____ **Start Date** _____ **End Date** _____

Name of Advertiser	Individual to Contact	Address	Telephone #

The Projected Sales Call Activity form has several uses. First, when you have several salespeople out making calls, you don't want more than one salesperson to call on any single prospect. Second, you need to know who individual salespeople are calling on so that you can plan the work of others. Third, a successful salesperson prepares his or her calls ahead of time. Without advance planning, salespeople will waste valuable selling time sitting in their offices trying to decide what to do next. Lack of advance planning is a major reason for failure in selling.

Your Company
Your Address
Your Telephone Number

(Your company) commissions _____ to write an article entitled

_____

as follows:

Length (in words): _____

Photos, if any: _____

Deadline: _____

Special requirements and/or conditions:

_____

_____

_____

Payment shall be as follows:

1. On speculation. Payment is subject to editorial approval of finished product. If approved, article will be paid at the rate of _____ per word. If rejected, no payment will be due.

2. Assigned article. Payment for approved article will be at the rate of $_____ per word, or $_____ for the entire article. In the event that an assigned article is deemed by (your company) to be unacceptable for publication or does not, for any other reason, meet the needs or standards of (your company), the writer will receive a kill fee of $ _____. When a kill fee is paid, (your company) relinquishes all rights and interests in the article and returns them in their entirety to the writer.

3. Fee per photo: _____

Rights purchased: _____

_____

_____
Publisher

_____
Writer

_____
Date

> *Note: The use of simple, clear agreements like this one will help the* (your company) *avoid misunderstandings with freelance writers with whom he enters into agreements. The wording of the form may be easily altered to cover agreements with freelance artists, photographers, etc.*

A Freelance Agreement Form

Name of publication:

Quantity:

Trim Size:

Number of Pages:

Text Stock:

Halftones:

Binding:

     ❏ Casebound and glued

     ❏ Casebound and sewn

     ❏ Self-covered

     ❏ Cover additional, saddle-stitched

     ❏ Cover additional, perfect bound

Embossing: ❏ Stamped spine   ❏ Stamped front and spine

Cover Stock or Cloth:

Color:

     ❏ Spot color. Where?

     ❏ Process color. Where?

     ❏ Separations furnished?

Bluelines: ❏ Yes ❏ No

Estimated turnaround time:

Estimated freight charges:

Job to be delivered to:

_____

_____

_____

Please return your quote on the above job ASAP to [your address]

Appendix Three
Contacts and Sources

I
Books

The books listed below are few in number but very solid in content. Each of them has been a valuable source of information and inspiration for me in setting up and managing my publishing businesses. Each contains concrete, usable information and techniques that can make you money. I highly recommend them to you. Since many of these books exist in a variety of editions, some expensive and some much less expensive, I suggest that you consult *Books in Print* and *Paperback Books in Print* at your library or bookstore to find the one that best fits your needs and pocketbook.

AP Style Manual. Almost everything you need to know about newspaper style is contained in this book. It can become a valuable manual for setting specific style standards for all your publications. It is inexpensive and can be furnished to everyone in your editorial department.

Balkin, Richard. *A Writer's Guide to Book Publishing.* Written from the writer's perspective, Balkin's book is a primer on the business side of publishing. There is a useful and thorough discussion of book publishing contracts, though the agreements that Balkan discusses are far more complicated than those that will be needed to carry out most of the projects outlined in this book.

Bodian, Nat. *The Publisher's Direct Mail Handbook.* One of the classics in direct mail marketing for publishers.

Brabec, Barbara. *Homemade Money.* (3rd Edition). Betterway Publications. Barbara Brabec's book is a gentle but very useful introduction to running a small, sideline enterprise from your own home. *Homemade Money* will reassure nervous publishers that "doing business" is not really so scary as it sounds and can even be a lot of fun.

Cook, James R. *The Start-up Entrepreneur.* E. P. Dutton. This is a solid, common sense look at the pleasures and perils of going into business for yourself. It will be very useful for any of you who are considering going into publishing in a serious way, publishing your own poetry series and maybe even a literary magazine or two.

Fletcher, Tana, and Julia Rockler. *Getting Publicity: A Do-it-Yourself Guide for Small Business and Non-Profit Groups.* Self-Counsel Press. Good tips for those in literary publishing and the arts.

Haldeman-Julius, Emmanuel. *The First Hundred Million.* In *The First Hundred Million*, newspaperman-publisher Haldeman-Julius tells the fascinating story of the creation of his "Little Blue Book" series. The Blue Books were simple, saddle-stitched pamphlets containing reprints of the classics as well as practical information on such then-taboo topics as sex education for women. Everyone interested in the publishing and book world should treat themselves to a read of this book. There is a great chapter on Haldeman-Julius's "Book Hospital," to which he relegated booklets that weren't selling well, tinkered with the title and transformed them into profitable publications. If you don't think the choice of a title is important, this chapter will change your mind.

Glenn, Peggy. *Publicity for Books and Authors: A Do-It-Yourself Handbook for Small Publishing Firms and Enterprising Authors.* Aames-Allen Publishing Co. I found Peggy Glenn especially helpful in her chapters on dealing with radio and TV public relations and promotion.

Henderson, Bill. *The Publish-It-Yourself Handbook.* Harper & Row. Henderson's book presents a dozen or more essays by literary writers and poets telling how they took charge of their own careers, published their own work and, often, the works of others as well. Inspiring and reassuring. You really ought to read it.

Kamaroff, Bernard. *Small-Time Operator: How to Start Your Own Small Business, Keep Your Books, Pay Your Taxes, & Stay Out of Trouble!* Bell Springs Publishing. If you are a writer sending work out to magazines and book publishers, or if you are publishing your own work, you are in business. Kamaroff tells you how to keep the records that you need to keep. Very clear, and written for the accounting-impaired—that is, for people like me. This book is one of the great self-publishing success stories, by the way. Published by Kamaroff himself, it has been on bookstore shelves for years and through many editions.

Kremer, John. *1001 Ways to Market Your Books.* Open Horizons. Kremer's book is a great idea generator. When sales on one of my books are languishing, I browse through Kremer. Almost always, I will discover an avenue I haven't explored, or something Kremer says will bring another, related idea to mind. An excellent resource for anyone selling books.

A Manual of Style for Authors, Editors and Copywriters (Chicago Style Book) University of Chicago Press. This utterly complete handbook is as close an industry standard as any. It should be on every writer's bookshelf. Academic (scholarly) writers may prefer the *Modern Language Association Stylebook*, and social scientists sometimes prefer the *American Psy-*

chological Association Stylebook. The *Chicago Manual* is the big one, and the most generally accepted.

Lant, Jeffrey. *How to Make a Whole Lot More Than $1,000,000 Selling How-To Information.* More ideas on niche market publishing than you will digest in a year.

Moyer, Page Emory. *The ABC's of a Really Good Speech.* Circle Press. While a poetry reading or seminar is not really a "speech," you can learn a great deal from Moyer's book about connecting with the audience in an effective way, something many writers who give presentations need to work on.

Poynter, Dan. *The Self Publishing Manual.* Para Publishing. A thorough introduction to the self-publication and marketing of adult non-fiction. Much of the information is also of use to literary publishers.

Simon, Julian. *How to Start and Operate a Mail Order Business.* There is an immense amount of savvy information on ad copywriting and customer response in this book.

A Writer's Guide to Copyright. Poets & Writers, Inc. It may be hard to believe, but few writers are really familiar with copyright law. This book will tell you what you want (and need) to know.

Internet Books

There are hundreds of books out there on building web sites and on marketing your publications and services on the internet. I'm going to save you some time and money. All the good stuff is in these three:

Kent, Peter. *Poor Richard's Web Site.* Peter Kent has written a no-nonsense guide to the creation of a website. Everything is here, directly and clearly written. I highly recommend this book (although I think the author goes a bit overboard in his praise of the Frontpage HTML editing program). Check out Kent's site at www.poorrichard.com.

Kent, Peter. *Internet Marketing and Promotion.* In this book Peter Kent takes up where he left off in *Poor Richard*, telling you how to get people to come to your web site once you have it up and running.

O'Keefe, Steve. *Publicity on the Internet.* Steve O'Keefe has written a fine book, full of how-to information on the distribution of public relations, advertising and promotional material via the internet.

II

Design and Production

Arnold, Edmond C. *Designing the Total Newspaper.* A thorough treatment of all aspects of newspaper design, rich in illustrations. Glossary.

Book, Albert and Dennis Schick. *Fundamentals of Copy and Layout.* More recent than Arnold and very useful for those learning the ropes of publication layout and design.

Hurlburt, Alan. *The Grid.* National Composition Association. Hurlburt explains the grid system of design and layout. It works like magic for brochures, catalogs, magazines and other publications. I found it very valuable, as it allowed me, in the days before I had any track record in design, to do reasonably good-looking work.

Parker, Roger C. *Looking Good in Print: A Guide to Basic Design for Desktop Publishing.* Ventana Press. Through each of its three editions, Parker's book has become a standard resource for publication designers. Great for your media kit and promotional material design.

Rice, Stanley. *Book Design* (2 vols.). R.R. Bowker. These two slim volumes are the only source of complete book design that I have been able to find. Very usable and easy to understand. A thorough discussion of the rules of the game.

Romano, Frank. *Practical Typography from A to Z.* National Composition Association. Made up of easy-to-use alphabetical entries, this small book contains almost everything you need to know about type specifications. One entry, for instance, deals very clearly with the relationship between type size, leading, and line length. Misunderstanding these factors can lead to the creation of unnecessarily hard to read pages.

White, Jan V. *Editing by Design.* A classic in publication design, it is especially good in its discussion of the relationship between text and graphics, particularly photographs. No magazine or newspaper publisher should be without this one on his or her shelf.

III

Principles of Advertising Design

Caples, John. *Tested Advertising Methods.* If you want to know what makes advertising work, read John Caples's book. It is a classic in the field. Caples learned the art of selling through his work in the mail order business. He learned what worked and what didn't by a simple means: if he wrote a bad ad there were no orders. A good ad brought in profitable replies. His analysis of hundreds of such ads give us all valuable insights into writing effective promotional material and advertisements.

Ogilvy, David. *Ogilvy on Advertising.* An invaluable manual of creating advertising that works, by one of the great men in contemporary advertising and founder of the firm of Ogilvy and Mather. As gracefully written as it is brilliant.

IV
Periodicals

The following periodicals are useful in keeping you up with current trends and opportunities. They are especially valuable as a source of information about vendors and suppliers to the trade.

Folio. Folio is the trade magazine of the magazine publishing industry. As such, its focus is on the big business of magazines, but it is interesting reading and quite useful for the small fry as well.

Publishers Weekly. Publishers Weekly is the trade magazine of the book publishing industry, and it is a must read if you are going heavily into book publishing.

Foreword Magazine. This new magazine is a trade publication for the smaller, "independent" book publisher.

Editor and Publisher. Editor and Publisher is the trade magazine of the newspaper industry. Use for keeping up with trends, statistics, vendors and suppliers.

Free Paper Publisher. The trade magazine for publishers of free circulation weeklies and niche market newspapers, tabloids and mini-tabs. Rich in networking opportunities, supplier leads, etc. Highly recommended for those who go into this branch of the business.

V
Syndicates

Los Angeles Times-Washington Post News Service. 1150 15 St. NW, Washington, DC 20071-0070. Tel: 202-334-6173 Fax: 202-334-5096 Email: latwp@newsservice.com

AP Newsfeatures. 450 W. 33rd St., New York, NY 10001. Tel: 212-621-1720 Fax: 212-506-6210. Columns on word humor, health, education & careers; book reviews.

Black Press Service. 166 Madison Ave, New York, NY 10016. Tel: 212-686-6850 Fax: 212-686-7308

Cartoonists & Writers Syndicate. 67 Riverside Dr., Suite 1-D, New York, NY 10024. Tel: 212-362-9256, 212-CARTOON Fax: 212- 595-4218. Daily, weekly & monthly selections of cartoons & graphics (political, humor, caricature, illustration) from 50 countries. "Views of the World" (political). Caricatures of the World (monthly portfolios). "Symbolics" (sociopolitical graphics), "Wit of the World" (humor: daily panel &/or Sunday color). "BizWit" (humorous business cartoons). "KAL" (political cartoons from Baltimore Sun), "SIGNE" (political cartoons from Philadelphia Daily News). "WitWomen" (humor cartoons about women), "Ecotoon" (ecological cartoons by world's top artists), "SportsWorld" (humor panels about sports). Over 1,000 subscribers.

College Press Service, a division of Tribune Media Services. 435 N. Michigan Ave, Suite 1500, Chicago, IL 60611. Tel: 312-222-4444, 800-245-6536 Fax: 312-222-2581. National news & graphics syndicate to college newspapers & high schools; youth market features to non-college media. Six hundred college, 400 high school newspapers. Submissions accepted for freelance articles, editorial & humor cartoons which appeal to a college-age audience; news relating to college issues; feature & pop culture pieces.

Community Press Service. 117 W. 2nd St., Frankfort, KY 40601. Tel: 502-223-1736 Fax: 502-223-2679. Newspaper syndicate for weekly, small daily & shopper publications throughout the USA with various features & advertising services; seasonal ads such as graduation, Christmas, New Years..

Copley News Service, Division of Copley Newspapers. Box 120190, San Diego, CA 92112. Tel: 619-293-1818. Features on photography, cars, books, music, films, fashion, sports, gardening & other special interests.

King Features Syndicate. 300 W. 57th St., New York, NY 10019. Tel: 212-455-4000, 800-526-5464 Fax: 212-983-6099. Daily or weekly political, medical, consumer, business, entertainment, family, puzzles, sports, financial, humor.

Los Angeles Times Syndicate. 218 S. Spring St., Los Angeles, CA 90012. Tel: 213-237-7987 Fax: 213-237-3698. Commentary, humor, business, real estate, sports, health & fitness, entertainment, environmental, advice, astrology, genealogy, bridge, food, lifestyle, comics, editorial cartoons & editorial art & other features.

MCT Direct. 700 12th St., NW, Suite 1000, Washington, DC 20005. Tel: 866-280-5210, 200-383-6080 Fax: 202-383-6181 Email: news@mctinfoservices.com. News stories, photos, news and feature graphics, illustrations, caricatures, paginated news and features.

New York Times Syndicate. 609 Greenwich St., 6th floor, New York, NY 10014. Tel: 212-499-3300 Fax: 212-499-3382 Email: nytsf@nytimes.com. Syndicator of NY Times News Service, NY Times graphics & photos as well as features columns, packages & news services from sources around the world.

Appendix 4
A Glossary of Publishing Terms

A Glossary
of Publishing Terms

agate line

A line set in 5.5 point type, typical of classified pages.

agency ad

An ad that comes into the office from an advertising agency, ready for reproduction.

alley

The white space between the columns on a page.

alignment

Orientation of type with regard to edges of the column or paper, such as aligned right (flush right), aligned left (flush left), and aligned on center (centered).

author's alterations (AA)

Discretionary changes made by the author after initial typesetting.

back matter

Appendices, index, author bio, order form and other materials which may or may not be included in the back of a book.

bar code

Usually printed on the back cover of a book or the front of a newspaper which is sold (not free circulation). Includes publisher ID, International Standard Book Number and sometimes price. Most bookstores require bar codes. Cashiers scan them for price and inventory control.

bleed

When printing (or background color) extends to the very edge of the page it is said to "bleed." Such printing is referred to as "a bleed."

blueline

Photographic proof made from negatives which will be used to etch printing plates. Also referred to as "blues." This is the publisher's last chance to check for errors, although by this late stage of production it is hoped that all corrections will have been made.

blurb

Among other uses, a quote of praise or endorsement usually appearing on the back cover of a book.

boldface

Type that appears darker than the next type of the same typeface. The main word entries in this glossary are set in boldface type.

broadsheet

Also referred to as "text stock." Category of paper suitable for publication printing.

brightness

Characteristic of paper or ink, referring to how much light it reflects.

bullet

Bold dot placed before an item, usually in a list, to emphasize it.

C1S

Coated on one side. Cover stock that is coated (has a gloss) on one side only.

cataloging in publication data

Library of Congress cataloging data, usually printed on the copyright page to assist librarians in cataloging a book. Not necessary in books of poetry.

camera-ready copy

Pages of a book or other publication that are ready for the printer to use to make negatives and plates.

center spread

An advertisement or feature that spans the two pages that open in the middle of a publication.

change order

A change in the original specifications for a book or other publication. Change orders should always be in writing.

character

Any letter, numeral, punctuation mark or other alphanumeric symbol.

clip art

Drawings available for purchase for unlimited reproduction. Clip art is in the public domain. Clip art collections may be purchased in printed form or on computer disks.

color separation

Film negative for printing color. One film negative is needed for each color. To print a "full color" photograph, four pieces of film are necessary, one for each primary color: cyan, magenta, yellow and black.

column inch

A space measure that consists of one inch of space one column wide.

continuous-tone copy

All photographs and those illustrations having a range of shades. Contrasted with "line art," which is pure black and white.

copy

>   For an editor or typesetter, all written material.

copy editor

>   Person who checks and corrects a manuscript for spelling, grammar, punctuation, inconsistencies, inaccuracies, and conformity to style requirements. Also called line editor.

credit line

>   The line beneath a photograph or other art which identifies the person who created it or, in some cases, the publication which gave permission for its use.

cutline

>   The editorial matter placed beside or beneath a photograph which describes the image depicted.

dash

>   Typographic mark that indicates a break between thoughts. An em dash (—) is longer than an en dash (–) and much longer than a hyphen(-).

desktop publishing

>   Term invented by Apple Computer in the mid-1980's to describe the revolutionary typesetting and graphic arts capabilities of its new Macintosh computer and laser printer. Now extended to all such devices.

dingbat

>   Typographic symbol, such as a bullet (*), used for emphasis or decoration.

display type

>   Type used for headlines, advertising and signs.

double truck

>   A two-page advertising spread, often in the middle of a publication or section of a newspaper.

dropped cap

>   Large capital letter that extends down into the first two or more lines. Used as a design element.

dummy

>   A rough approximation of a finished publication, made by drawing it or by actually pasting up finished elements.

ears

>   Small blocks of editorial matter on either side of the flag of a newspaper.

editorial matter

>   All of the textual matter (exclusive of advertising) in a publication.

fair use

>   Provision of the copyright law allowing short quotations to be used without permission of the copyright holder.

feature article

> Newspaper article that reads more like a magazine article, as distinguished from a news article.

filler

> Short items used to fill small blank spaces in a layout. Short, humorous verse can be used as filler.

fixed costs

> Costs incurred before the press starts running, which remain the same no matter how many or how few copies of your book are printed. Typesetting and proofreading are examples of fixed costs.

flag

> The banner usually at the top of a publication (though it is sometimes elsewhere) proclaiming its name, i.e. *Washington Post* or *Atlanta Constitution*.

flush left

> Type aligned along the left edge only. Also called left justified and ragged right. See below:

> > What is mysticism? Everyone knows and no one knows. According to the widest range of historical testimony, the mystical experience is ineffable. One hears, one sees, one knows, but one cannot tell.

flush right

> Type aligned the right side of the column. Also called right justified and ragged left. See below:

> > What is mysticism? Everyone knows and no one knows. According to the widest range of historical testimony, the mystical experience is ineffable. One hears, one sees, one knows, but one cannot tell.

folio

> Term used to designate the page number.

font

> A typeface family and all its characters and symbols.

footer

> Information, such as page number or chapter title, that appears regularly at the bottom of every page; running foot.

format

> Trim size or chosen page design of a book.

front matter

> Title page, copyright, dedication, etc. All pages in a book before the actual text begins.

frontispiece

Illustration or photograph appearing on the page opposite the title page.

galley (galleys)

Preliminary proofs of actual pages. "Bound galleys" are often sent out for review before the actual print run of finished copies.

gutter

The white space between two facing pages. See "jump the gutter."

halftone

A black and white photograph, as it appears in a printed book.

headline schedule

A listing of the type faces, styles and sizes to be used for various headline situations in a publication: one column, two column, banner, etc.

imprint

In book publishing, the name of the publisher as it appears on the title page. Some publishing companies have multiple imprints.

ISBN

International Standard Book Number, abbreviated as ISBN. Every book published needs one of these, obtained from the R. R. Bowker Company. When you have an ISBN you will be listed in *Books In Print*, the chief national database of published works.

italic type

Type slanted to the right to resemble handwriting, as compared to Roman type. *This sentence is set in Italic type.*

jumpline

A line beneath a column indicating that the story "jumps" to another page.

jump the gutter

Said of art elements or copy which crosses over the white space between two facing pages.

justified type

Type set flush right and left. See the example below:

> What is mysticism? Everyone knows and no one knows. According to the widest range of historical testimony, the mystical experience is ineffable. One hears, one sees, one knows, but one cannot tell.

kern

To reduce space between characters so those characters appear better fitted together.

kicker

Short phrase, usually placed at the top left of a headline, designed to attract the interest of the reader.

leading

The distance between the baseline of two succeeding lines of type.

line art

Drawings or other art that has no grays or continuous tones.

mark up

Instructions written on a manuscript to let the typographer know the font, size, leading, etc. to use.

markup

The difference between the wholesale price and the retail price.

masthead

Block of information in a publication that lists publishing, production and editorial staffs and gives addresses and telephone numbers for key departments.

newsprint

Inexpensive paper on which newspapers are printed.

op-ed

The page opposite the editorial page in a newspaper, usually containing commentary and opinion.

overrun

Number of books printed in excess of the quantity ordered. Overruns and underruns occur because it is impossible for the printer to know how many books will be spoiled in the printing and binding process.

page

One side of each leaf in a book.

page proof

Proof of type and graphics as they will look on the finished page, complete with elements such as headings and rules.

perfect bind

Binding method where pages are glued into a cover, which is squared off at the spine.

pica

A horizontal unit of measurement used in publishing. Column width, for instance, is usually described in picas. There are approximately six picas in an inch.

PMS

PANTONE Matching System, used to specify color.

point

The unit of measure used to express the size (height) of type and leading.

point of purchase display (POP)

Rack which contains books for display near the cash register. Especially effective for chapbooks and thin books of poetry.

ppi

Pages per inch. All text stock has a ppi rating. This rating allows the designer to calculate the thickness of the finished book.

print run

The number of books to be printed in a single printing.

prepress

All of the work performed to ready a book for publication.

process color

Also known as "full color." The creation of continuous tone color by combining the primary colors of magenta, yellow and cyan through the use of color separations.

proofread

To read a manuscript to detect errors in typesetting. Proofreading is a skill that many writers, though thoroughly familiar with the rules of grammar and orthography, do not possess.

proofreader marks

Standard symbols and abbreviations used to correct manuscripts and proofs.

publisher

CEO or owner of a publishing company. If you self-publish, you become the CEO of your own publishing company.

pulled quote

Colorful quote from a story set in larger type and placed between rules or emphasized in some other way to attract reader interest.

quotation

Also known as a "quote." This is a firm price, in writing, for the production of a book based on your specifications.

reverse

Type reproduced by printing ink around its outline, leaving the color of the paper beneath to form the letters.

RFQ

A request for quote. An RFQ form is reproduced earlier in this book.

saddle stitch

A binding method whereby pages are stapled together on the spine.

sans-serif type

Type without serifs. Also called Gothic type.

About the Author

Thomas A. Williams, Ph.D., has written for magazines ranging from *Esquire* to *Writer's Digest*. The author of fourteen books, Williams is comfortable on both sides of the editorial desk. In addition to his free-lance writing, Tom Williams has started, edited, and published city and regional magazines and is currently Editor-in-Chief of Venture Press, book publishers.

In 1979, Williams bought *The Mecklenburg Gazette*, a weekly newspaper in North Carolina. In three years, he increased circulation 400 percent and revenues by 1,000 percent, and sold out to a newspaper chain for twent;y times the purchase price.

Subsequently, Williams founded Venture Press, a home-based book publishing company. The Venture Press list includes how-to books and eBooks for writers and publishers, historical reprints, civic histories, folklore, oral history and poetry.

He has started and published many magazines, including *Tar Heel: The Magazine of North Carolina* (a state-wide magazine), *The New East*, *NC East*, and other regional, consumer magazines. He published association directories, chamber of commerce "quality of life" magazines, newcomer guides, and tourism guides.

Williams is a student of hard knocks. He learned how to position his publications for success on his own and shares his knowledge with us in his books. You can contact Tom Williams through his web site at www.PubMart.Com.

Get More Writing and Publishing Advice from Tom Williams!

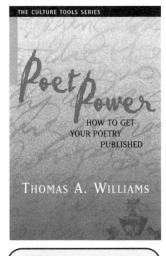

Sentient Publications, LLC, publishes books on cultural creativity, experimental education, transformative spirituality, holistic health, new science, ecology, and other topics, approached from an integral viewpoint.

Our authors are intensely interested in exploring the nature of life from fresh perspectives, addressing life's great questions, and fostering the full expression of the human potential. Sentient Publications' books arise from the spirit of inquiry and the richness of the inherent dialogue between writer and reader.

Our Culture Tools series is designed to give social catalyzers and cultural entrepreneurs the essential information, technology, and inspiration to forge a sustainable, creative, and compassionate world.

We are very interested in hearing from our readers. To direct suggestions or comments to us, or to be added to our mailing list, please contact:

SENTIENT PUBLICATIONS, LLC

1113 Spruce Street
Boulder, CO 80302
303-443-2188
contact@sentientpublications.com
www.sentientpublications.com